Cities

Bibliographic Guides for Contemporary Collections
Series Editor, Peter Doiron

Cities

by Dwight W. Hoover

R. R. Bowker Company
A Xerox Education Company
New York & London, 1976

Published by R. R. Bowker Company (A Xerox Education Company)
1180 Avenue of the Americas, New York, N.Y. 10036
Copyright © 1976 by Xerox Corporation
All rights reserved
Printed and bound in the United States of America

Library of Congress Cataloging in Publication Data

Hoover, Dwight W 1926–
    Cities.

    (Bibliographic guides for contemporary collec-
tions)
    Includes indexes.
    1. Cities and towns—United States—Bibliography.
I. Title.
Z7164.U7H66   016.30136'3'0973   76-2601
ISBN 0-8352-0790-0

Contents

Foreword

The concept of the Bibliographic Guides for Contemporary Collections Series was derived from a realization that many librarians, students, teachers, and laypersons lack indepth guidance to subjects of current interest. Too often, librarians are faced with inadequate, or even a total lack of selection assistance when developing specific areas for their libraries or individual studies. "Contemporary Collections" seeks to help fill this need. The word "contemporary" refers to a subject, old or new, that is now experiencing a high level of interest throughout America and across the educational spectrum. A sudden upsurge of interest in a specific area emphasizes the lack of guidance, in many instances, to the best and most necessary materials for reading and research. The "Contemporary Collections" series will attempt to meet such information crises by presenting the reader with a selective basic guide to the literature. Each book will be written by an expert or group of experts who will develop each subject through selection, annotation, and commentary. The emphasis is on in-print materials but, obviously, some subjects cannot be adequately explored without citing titles of landmark quality and some of these may be out of print. Where appropriate media other than books will be included for most titles in the series. These bibliographic guides will give librarians, students, scholars, and the general public a frame in which to approach certain immediate topics with solid organization.

Cities everywhere, as we all know, are in trouble today. Through a long and committed involvement, Dr. Dwight Hoover, Professor of American History at Ball State University, has covered the past, present, and future of the American urban experience in its entire spectrum. Architecture, economics, education, ghettoes, life styles, sociology, immigration, are all themes brought into focus as one reads the succinct introductions and annotations. A useful feature of the book is the inclusion of games, discs, films and filmstrips, and other media which enhance our grasp of the contemporary plights or blights of American cities. Dr. Hoover's selections give lucid explanations of the current state of American cities.

Peter Doiron
Series Editor

Preface

The basic criteria for inclusion in this bibliography were contemporaneity and availabilty of materials. However, such criteria are easier to state than to define. Although it was decided to exclude out-of-print books and films or filmstrips more than ten years old, this rule was occasionally violated. Some visual media, issued in the fifties, are listed because of their quality. They may be difficult to secure and will not be suitable to some libraries. Titles of films and filmstrips were taken from releases of producing companies or from compilations of film collections made by university audiovisual aid departments, particularly the very fine Indiana University Film Catalog. By the time this bibliography is printed, some of the titles may be withdrawn from these sources.

In the case of books, certain classics are included on the theory that they may be obtained through interlibrary loan or may even be reprinted. In any case, reference librarians ought to be aware of their existence. Several of the older, more famous titles are available in more than one edition. An attempt was made to list the least expensive edition and to match it with the correct Library of Congress Catalog number. The acquisitions librarian should be aware that prices may have changed since preparation of this manuscript.

Generally, the audience for whom the title is best suited is indicated in the annotation. Materials most specifically aimed at younger students are labelled "elementary," "junior high," or "high school" level; those designed for an older audience, and yet not technically slanted, are designated "average reader" or "general reader"; and those which assume considerable prior knowledge in a certain field are indicated by the terms "specialist" or "advanced reader." Where no audience level is given, such titles, in the author's opinion, appeal to a wide variety of persons.

Within an annotation, other titles may be mentioned. These are not cross-referenced; however, the reader may locate such titles in the bibliography by referring to the Title Index, which is divided into two parts: Books and In-print Materials and Other Media. It should be noted that listings in both Author and Title Indexes refer to the entry number, not to the page number.

A Producer/Distributor Directory is supplied as an aid to the librarian or teacher who wishes to purchase or rent nonprint materials. The list of Journals on Urban Themes gives frequency of publication, price, and source of availability. Again, interested subscribers should be aware that prices are subject to change.

The author wishes to express gratitude to the persons who made this book possible. Peter Doiron, Series Editor, offered a number of useful suggestions and provided the needed encouragement and enthusiasm for the completion of the project. My daughter Polly spent the better part of one summer checking and correcting references, a tedious task which I greatly appreciate having been spared. My able secretary, Anita Sharp, deciphered my handwriting and cheerfully typed the manuscript. The History Department of Ball State University generously provided release time for the research. To each of these people, a hearty thanks.

Dwight W. Hoover
Ball State University

Cities

PART I

The City in Practice

One of the most persistent themes in the media today is the crisis of American cities. Perhaps no other topic generates as much anxiety as the image of the city as a smoldering volcano about to erupt and to destroy its population as Pompeii was destroyed. This section includes books, games, films, and filmstrips on this theme.

This section goes beyond the assumed crisis of the moment to expose the roots of American urban experience. It contains works that trace the history of Blacks and other ethnic groups in the city; of the continuing struggle to provide adequate urban housing, government, and services; of the attempted solutions and the projected future of present-day dilemmas; and of the violence that occasionally has torn apart the fabric of urban society.

In these roots, the thoughtful reader can perceive that what are thought to be current problems are not really new, but are, instead, a product of certain assumptions about the best kind of social and economic systems that have been present for a considerable length of time. Viewed in this perspective, the assumption that the American city is in a pathological state loses part of its force.

General Urban Problems

The problems confronting American cities are manifold. They include physical difficulties—water and air pollution, poor housing, and unsafe working conditions—as well as difficulties connected with essential services—police and fire protection, garbage collection, and urban transit. These problems call for solutions that involve greater public expenditures, but economic recession and taxpayer resistance make the raising of additional funds for the city increasingly difficult. The prognosis for these problems hence must remain in doubt.

Other problems have less tangible solutions. These problems are products of the psychological stress inherent in urban life and of the influx of people of differing national origins and ethnic extraction into central cities. How can individuals cope with the stress engendered by population crowding, unemployment or underemployment, and with the social disorganization demonstrated by crime or drug abuse? How can a sense of community be derived from individuals caught in such conditions and lacking a sense of roots in the city? These problems are less likely to be solved by increases in tax dollars for American cities.

This section contains materials on all these problems; it is designed for an overview of the present urban dilemma. Hopefully, it will provide a beginning point from which these problems can be explored.

1. **America's Urban Crisis.** Society for Visual Education, 1971. (Group 1-A Series.) 6 filmstrips. 15 min. each. Sale $11.50 each; $51.50 for set of filmstrip and records; $57.00 for set of filmstrip and audiotapes.

This series studies urban problems at the intermediate and high school student level. The titles are "The Air Pollution Menace" (64 frames), "The Housing Crisis" (53 frames), "The Roots of Our Urban Problems" (63 frames), "The Transportation Crisis" (60 frames), "Water Pollution—A Complex Problem" (63 frames). They constitute a good introduction to a number of urban problems, but are not very sophisticated.

2. Berkowitz, Marvin. **The Social Costs of Human Underdevelopment: Case Study of Seven New York City Neighborhoods.** New York: Praeger, 1974. LC 73-19440. $16.50.

As the title suggests, this is an in-depth look at the problems of poverty and unemployment in selected areas of New York City. A specialized study aimed at sociologists and economists, it is recommended to libraries with this kind of clientele.

3. Cities and People. Warren Schloat Productions, 1972. 2-part filmstrip. Color. $40 with disc, $46 with audiotape.

A study of the impact of urban life on human populations and the kinds of urban problems city living engenders.

4. City Life. Indiana University, 1972. (WTTW *Earthkeeping Series.*) 16mm. Color. Sound. 29 min. Rent $11.50.

Taken from a television broadcast in which Lewis Mumford focuses upon the causes of urban blight and the need for citizen education and involvement. The level is adult, although mature high school students will profit from it.

5. The City of Necessity. Chicago City Missionary Society, United Church Board for Homeland Ministries and the National Council of the Protestant Episcopal Church, 1963. 16mm. Color. 25 min. Sale $260, rent $16.

Depicts the problems of population and traffic congestion, segregation in housing, and unemployment in the moden American city with Chicago as the specimen case. While the topics are grim, the film does convey a sense of the city's vitality in spite of its difficulties.

6. The Community. Indiana University, 1964. (America's Crises.) 16mm. b/w. Sound. 60 min. Sale $200, rent $10.90.

Examines two communities, Provincetown, Mass., and San Jose, Cal. Provincetown wishes to keep its tradition in the face of an influx of tourists on Cape Cod, while San Jose wants to build a tradition in an area where most residents are strangers.

7. Community Disaster, rev. ed. Western Publishing Co., 1970. Sale $30. (Available from Social Studies School Services or Didactics Corporation.)

This simulation game represents an urban crisis and is suitable for high school students as well as adults. It can be played by as few as six or as many as 16 people; playing time runs from two to six hours. The game does show the kinds of problems engendered by massive civil difficulties and would be an effective tool for training persons in thinking about disasters.

8. A Community Project. Av-Ed Films, C-B Films, 1962. 16mm. Color. Sound. 11 min. Sale $115.

Deals with the need for cooperation in the community in order to obtain better services and living conditions. Appropriate for primary as well as junior and senior high schools.

9. Disaster, 1906. Studio 16 Educational Films, 1961. 16 mm. b/w. Sound. 30 min. Sale $150.

A recounting of the San Francisco earthquake and fire and the reconstruction of the city. Helpful for those interested in city planning and development.

10. The Embattled Metropolis. New York Times Co., 1971. Color. 17 min. 67 fr., disc. Sale $9.

Intended to show the multiplicity of problems encountered by cities today, it does succeed in conveying a sense of urgency about the solutions to these problems.

11. The First Mile Up. McGraw-Hill, 1963. 16mm. b/w. Sound. 27 min. Sale $150.

The first mile up is polluted, and the extent of pollution as well as possible cures for it are the topics of this film, which is suitable for the average student.

12. Glazer, Nathan, ed. **Cities in Trouble.** New York: Franklin Watts, 1970. 276 pp. LC 71-78321. $6.95, pap. $2.45.

A *New York Times* publication that focuses on city crises, concentrating primarily on New York City. The selections are astute, and the level is the same as Ginger's *Modern American Cities*.

13. Gordon, Mitchell. **Sick Cities: Psychology and Pathology of American Urban Life.** Baltimore: Penguin Books, 1963. 444 pp. LC 63-14600. pap. $2.45.

A popularly written account of the problems of the cities as seen from the vantage point of the mid-1960s. As the title indicates, the tenor is pessimistic; but since the reading level is easy, it is recommended as an introduction to urban pathology.

14. Haar, Charles. **Federalism: The Troubled Cities and Urban America.** Washington, D.C.: Audio Educational Associates. 1 audiotape reel. 21 min.

An interview with the urbanologist Charles Haar on the kind of federal help needed by American cities. The interview was done in the late 1960s and contains material of historical as well as of current value. It is recommended as a well-informed discussion of the intellectual base of the new federalism.

15. Halacy, D. S., Jr. **Your City Tomorrow.** New York: Four Winds Press, 1973. 224 pp. LC 72-77818. $5.88.

Four Winds Press is a subsidiary of Scholastic Magazines, and this book reflects that connection. It is simply written and contains numerous illustrations—both photographs and drawings. It covers more territory than the title indicates in that it discusses today's cities and their problems as well as makes projections into the future. The book can be used for high school students and might well be in most libraries' general circulation.

16. The House of Man—Our Changing Environment. Conservation Foundation. Encyclopedia Britannica Films, 1965. 16 mm. Color. Sound. 17 min. Rent $7.50.

The ecological emphasis is obvious here in the portrayal of wasted resources in cities and country. Water and air pollution are discussed. Suitable for the average student.

17. Kennedy, Robert. **The City; Pressure Points in Our Society.** Doubleday. 4-track stereo tape. 15 min.

Senator Robert Kennedy discusses the urban crisis, and reveals how far his thinking had come since his entry into public life. Historically valuable in addition to its timely topic, it is recommended.

18. Levine, Robert A. **The Poor Ye Need Not Have with You: Lessons from the War on Poverty.** Cambridge, Mass.: MIT Press, 1970. LC 70-103899. $7.95.

Levine's analysis of the war on poverty shows the numerous errors of commission and omission that were made. It is an essential book for understanding the approach to urban problems taken by the Johnson administration in the mid-1960s.

19. Lindsay, John V. **The City.** New York: New American Library, 1970. 240 pp. LC 68-54968. pap. $1.25.

John Lindsay discusses some of his experiences as mayor of New York City. Lindsay first tells of his 1969 election campaign and of the problems he encountered as mayor. In the second part he comments upon the urban dilemma and on poverty, welfare, crime, and intergovernmental relations. Popularly written, it shows quite well the issues confronting large cities today.

20. Liston, Robert A. **Downtown: Our Challenging Urban Problems.** New York: Delacorte, 1970. 192 pp. LC 79-102001. $5.95.

A clearly written and easily understood overview of urban problems from the point of view of a political scientist. Liston includes slums, crime, poor housing, congestion, and bad government among urban difficulties, as well as examples of how some communities have overcome these. Recommended as a basic introduction suitable for most libraries.

21. Lowe, Jeanne. **Cities in a Race with Time.** New York: Random House, 1967. 601 pp. LC 66-21478. $12.50, pap. $2.95.

The twin problems of race and poverty are discussed. Lowe maintains there is only a short time left for Americans to solve these problems before the cities explode. Written at a level easy enough for high school students to handle.

22. **Man and the Cities (City Problems and Alternatives).** BFA Educational Media. 6 filmstrips. Sale $78.00 with records, $90 with cassettes.

A series for intermediate and high school students to introduce the ideas of planning and urban problems. The titles are "A New Town," "Planning Our Cities," "Pollution—The Cities' Air," "Pollution—Water and Garbage," "Transportation in the City," and "Urban Ghettos—Isolation and Unemployment." Emphasis is on problems rather than on alternatives, but the series is a good one.

23. **Man and the City.** Warren Schloat/Prentice-Hall Media, 1972. 161 frames. Color. 26 min. $42 FS/discs, $48 FS/cassettes, $95 slides/cassettes.

Useful and recommended for junior high through college level students, this set explores theories of why cities are overcrowded and seem to be unlivable. The demographic aspect is significant.

24. Mills, James. **The Panic in Needle Park.** New York: Farrar Straus & Giroux, 1966. 212 pp. LC 66-14153. $6.95. New American Library. pap. $1.95.

Mills was a reporter for *Life* magazine who spent 60 days among addicts in New York City. Utilizing material from this experience, he wrote of the problems addicts have. The account, neither pleasant nor curative, is powerful.

25. Moynihan, Daniel Patrick. **Coping: Essays on the Practice of Government.** New York: Random House, 1974. 430 pp. LC 73-3983. $10.

A collection of Moynihan's essays written and published since 1962, it is concerned with urban problems such as welfare, education of the poor, race relations, urban decay, and traffic. Moynihan believes that these problems will not be completely solved, largely because of their nature and definition. At best, only limited success can be had; at worst, society can barely cope with them. Of general interest and should be in most libraries.

26. New York City: An Environmental Case Study. Denoyer-Geppert Audio-Visuals, 1970. 2 filmstrips (103 and 100 fr.) Color. 35 min. 2 discs. $34.

The emphasis is ecological and concerns the mutual interaction of technology and natural surroundings. It is well done and is aimed at audiences from the junior high level on up. It could be used to show ecological principles or urban problems.

27. Overlord in the Cities. New Concept Productions/Doubleday and International Communications Corp. Films, 1969. 16mm. Color. Sound. 15 min. Sale $210.50, rent $21.

Useful as an introduction to contemporary problems, it concentrates on urban decay and the strategies of urban leaders.

28. The Pollution Game: A Simulated Problem. Boston: Houghton Mifflin, 1971. $9.

As the name suggests, this game is based upon the current concern with air, water, and waste pollution. The minimum number of players needed is 10, divided into two teams of five persons each. The number of teams can be expanded considerably if desired. The minimum time needed is 1 to 2 hours, but the game can be played longer. It is a good game to show present problems and deserves consideration if an institution is desirous of beginning a collection.

29. Population Ecology. American Institute of Biological Sciences/McGraw-Hill, 1963. (AIBS Secondary School Biological Science Film Series, Unit 9, Ecology, No. 2.) 16mm. Color. Sound. 28 min.

Peripheral to studying the city, but it does consider natural balance and the population explosion—problems that are exaggerated in the city.

30. Leinwand, Gerald, ed. Problems of American Society. New York: Washington Square Press.

Urban materials aimed at the secondary school student. All in paper, they consist of narrative and readings, and were developed in collaboration with the curriculum committee of the Trenton, New Jersey, public schools. The titles, each priced at $.95, are:

> *The Negro in the City*, 1968 LC 78-1502
> *The City as a Community*, 1970 LC 73-12586
> *Air and Water Pollution*, 1968 LC 78-11219
> *Governing the City*, 1971 LC 77-29121
> *Slums*, 1970 LC 74-9238
> *The Traffic Jam*, 1969 LC 72-62339
> *Minorities All*, 1971 LC 78-21989
> *Crime and Juvenile Delinquency*, 1968 LC 70-1977
> *The Consumer*, 1970 LC 79-17483
> *Poverty and the Poor*, 1968 LC 70-3135
> *Prisons*, 1970 LC 72-200963

31. Problems of Cities. New York Times/Teaching Resources Films, 1968. 1 filmstrip (74 fr.) Color. 16 min. Book, disc. Sale $10.

Urban renewal, transportation tie-ups, educational defects, high tax rates, and high crime rates. Suited to junior and senior high students.

32. Problems of Our Cities. Urban Media Materials, 1972. 6 filmstrips. Color. Sound. 3 discs. Sale $61.50 with records, $67.50 with cassettes.

On the intermediate–junior high level, titles are "Introduction," "Housing," "Pollution," "Traffic," "Social Problems," and "Urban Renewal & City Planning." The elementary level limits their value, although libraries could acquire this set if needed for this age group.

33. Quantitative Studies of Urban Problems. Washington, D.C.: American Association for the Advancement of Science, 1969. 4 stereo cassettes.

Tapes taken at the 1969 meeting of the American Association for the Advancement of Science. The titles are "Criminal Justice Systems," "Urban Dynamics," "Urban Housing," and "Water Resource Management." The level is high, geared toward a sophisticated and informed audience.

34. The Restless City Speaks. Audio-visual Material Consultation Bureau/ Wayne State University, 1958. 16mm. b/w. Sound. 15 min. Rent $7.

Tries to show the causes and effects of complex living in a vast urban area. Suitable for less advanced students.

35. Schachter, Esther Roditti. **Enforcing Air Pollution Controls.** New York: Praeger, 1974. 104 pp. LC 73-8165. $11.

A case study of how well the New York standards for diminishing air pollution worked. It was published in cooperation with the Center for Policy Research. Although a slim volume and very specialized, it could be of use to interested people.

36. Simpolis. ABT Associates. $30.

This simulation game requires a large number of players—30 to 50—and is complex, so that it is suitable for high school students and above. The time necessary to complete the game varies according to the time available. The game provides a look at seven major urban problems—transportation, education, housing, civil rights, poverty, crime, and pollution—and is most suitable for libraries that cannot afford a more expensive game.

37. Superfluous People. CBS News/McGraw-Hill Films, 1962. 16mm. b/w. 56 min. Parts I and II. Sale $150 each, $275 set.

This CBS documentary touches on the lives of people who cannot or have not adjusted to city life.

38. The Troubled Cities. National Educational Television/Indiana University Audio-Visual Center, 1966. (American Crises.) b/w. Sound. 60 min. Rent $12.

This documentary probes attempts being made to solve problems brought about by the urban population explosion, including slums, racial imbalance in schools, and the needs of untrained or illiterate rural immigrants.

39. United States History Transparencies. Hammond, 1968. Color. 32 transparencies. Sale $234. 24 sets, $7.96 each.

Two titles of special interest to those involved in the study of cities are "Modern Urban Problems" (4 overlays) and "US—Growth of Industry & Cities" (4 overlays). These transparencies are not complex, as they are designed for intermediate through high school students.

40. Urban Alternatives. Arthur Barr Productions, 1973. 16mm. Color. Sound. 19 min. Sale $250, rent $20.

Ways of coping with today's urban problems. Not particularly sophisticated, it is recommended for those libraries who wish a simple introduction to the topic.

41. Urban Crisis. Paul S. Amidon Associates. 6 monaural cassettes. 180 min. Sale $39.75.

Designed for high school and college students, focusing upon urban problems. Titles are "City—Key to Changing Life Styles," "City—What It Has Become," "Political Implications—Emergence of New Power Structures," "Racial Implications—Analysis of American Race Relations," "Urban Growth—Its Economic Significance," and "Urban Planning—Stimulus for Growth and Change." As might be expected from the attempt to reach several levels of audience capability, they are not very sophisticated. They do provide a clear, introductory look at the topic, however.

42. The Urban Crisis Series. Hammond. Color. Transparencies. Sale $18.

This set focuses on a number of urban problems: "An Alarming Trend," "A Dramatic Population Shift," "Federal Expenditures in Three Areas," "Life in the Ghetto," "One City Planner's Reconstruction of a City," "Problems of Today's Cities," "Rapid Transit System Proposed for Seattle," "Recommendations of the National Advisory Council on Civil Disorders," "A Significant Factor in the Formation of Racial Ghettoes," "Some Factors Contributing to the Financial Crisis of the Cities," "Steps Taken by the Private Sector," "Urban Centers of the Year 2000." An illustrated look into the problems facing cities, although the extent of the urban crisis seems overstated.

43. Urban Impact on Weather and Climate. Davidson Films in Cooperation with American Meteorological Society/Learning Corporation of America, 1971. 16mm. Color. Sound. Sale $245, rent $20.

The American Meteorological Society collaborated in producing this film. The thesis is that urban growth affects the climate adversely through increased cloudiness, water runoff, downwind pollution, etc. Directed toward a junior high and up level.

44. Urban Slurb: Prophets and Men of Action Comment on the U.S. Environment. The Center for Cassette Studies, 1971. Audiotape cassette. 28 min. Sale $12.95.

Statements by both theoretical and practicing urbanologists about the condition of American cities insofar as quality of life and physical environment are concerned. The commentators do not always agree with each other and some of the ideas expressed are not new, but the tape does show the wide variety of opinions on the subject.

45. The Urban Spaceship. CBC Learning Systems. Audiotape cassette. 30 min. Sale $8.

Originally a Canadian Broadcast Co. program, the discussion topics are the design of cities, the problems of pollution and overcrowding, and the solution to urban dilemmas. The references to Canadian cities and circumstances are not too numerous nor inappropriate so as to render the tape less desirable for audiences in the United States. The discussion level is high and the tape is highly recommended.

46. Urban Studies. Society for Visual Education, 1972. 8mm loops. Color. Silent. Sale $25.95 each, $250 set.

The titles are "City: Aerial View," "City: Cross Section," "City Contrasts," "City: Population," "City: Occupation," "City: Recreation," "City: Culture," "City: Government," "City: Transportation," "City: Industry," and "City: Commerce." This set offers visual images without extensive commentary. It is aimed at high school students and lay adults and is technically well done, but does not offer any analytical comment.

47. The Urban World: An International Study. Warren Schloat Productions, 1972. 2 sets of 4 filmstrips each. Color. Sound. Sale $66 with disc, $78 with audiotape.

The first set includes "Housing," "Neighborhoods and Communities," "Transportation," and "Problems and Pollution." The second set covers "Business and Trade," "Jobs and Production," "Government and Services," and "Communication and Education." The level of sophistication is low, but the sets do offer a visual introduction to different kinds of urban solutions to these problems.

48. Urofsky, Melvin I. **Perspectives on Urban America.** Garden City, N.Y.: Anchor, 1973. 307 pp. LC 71-186056. pap $2.95.

Essays on such urban problems as crime, racism, poverty, poor education, and polluted environments. The contributors are not convinced that these problems are confined to cities and do hold out hope for the future of American cities.

49. Venetoulis, Theodore G., and Ward Eisenhower, eds. **Up Against the Urban Wall.** Englewood Cliffs, N.J.: Prentice-Hall, 1971. 546 pp. LC 78-135406. pap. $5.95.

Senator Muskie introduces this collection on urban problems. The areas covered are "The Urban Concept," "The Urban Condition," "The Brutality of Urban Politics," "The Scars of Urban Alienation," "The American Response to the Urban Crisis," and "Toward a New Urban America." The collection is intended for use in college-level courses in urban studies and is recommended for the smaller library that lacks the original material from which this has been taken.

50. Weaver, Robert C. **Dilemmas of Urban America.** Cambridge, Mass.: Harvard University Press, 1965. 138 pp. LC 65-22056. $3.50. Atheneum, pap. $1.95.

Weaver, a Negro, was the first cabinet officer specifically named to handle urban affairs. He is critical of certain aspects of urban renewal but recognizes that the race problem is crucial in cities. Valuable for special projects.

51. Wilson, James Q., ed. **The Metropolitan Enigma**, rev. ed. Garden City, N.Y.: Doubleday, 1968. 426 pp. LC 68-25620. pap. $2.95.

Twelve well-known specialists in urban problems discuss the difficulties with single-pronged efforts to resolve these problems. In this collection, edited by a well-known political scientist, the systems approach is advocated for the cities. All the factors need to be recognized and dealt with appropriately. Sophisticated and more suited to the informed person than to the beginner.

Blacks in the City

Blacks have been residents of American cities since the origin of the Republic. In the towns of Boston, Philadelphia, Charlestown, and New York, both free Blacks and slaves lived and contributed to urban culture these towns gradually developed.

Recent events, however, have focused attention on Blacks in the cities in a different and compelling way. The urbanward migration of southern Blacks to northern and southern cities has given the central parts of these cities a Black core. Students of the migration and the subsequent formation of urban ghettoes have been divided over whether this movement was but the last wave of migration of immigrants to the city or whether it was a unique population movement similar to no other one. In any case, the encounter of Blacks with urban poverty, segregation, and prejudice has been a major theme in post-World War II urban history.

This section examines the Black experience through history, biography, music, film, and prose. It contains materials on cultural development and on freedom tactics. It shows the impact of urban life on Black development.

52. Aberbach, Joel D., and Walker, Jack L. **Race in the City**. Boston: Little, Brown, 1973. 293 pp. LC 72-9786. pap. $5.95.

The authors have concentrated on Detroit, and, through the use of political science survey techniques, have attempted to assess the racial attitudes of a selected sample of citizens of the Motor City. A useful case study of one metropolis where racial tensions usually have been high.

53. Armstrong, Louis. **Satchmo: My Life in New Orleans**. Englewood Cliffs, N.J.: Prentice-Hall, 1954. 240 pp. LC 54-9628. Signet, pap. $.95.

Louis Armstrong's story can be used to supplement a course in urban history. His recollections of his youth are interesting as well as informative. Suitable for junior and senior high school students.

54. Bennett, Lerone, Jr. **Confrontation: Black and White**. Chicago: Johnson Publishing Co., 1965. 321 pp. LC 65-21952. $5.95. Penguin Books, pap. $2.45.

Popularly written, this concentrates on the civil rights movement. Bennett evaluates and discusses such leaders as William Monroe Trotter in Boston, A. Philip Randolph in New York City, and Martin Luther King, Jr. His insights are keen and his prose pungent. Useful for high school students.

55. Bennett, Lerone, Jr. **Pioneers in Protest.** Chicago: Johnson Publishing Co., 1966. 267 pp. LC 68-55366. $5.95. Penguin Books, pap. $1.25.

Benjamin Banneker, Prince Hall, Richard Allen, and Frederick Douglass are some of the Black leaders to be found here. The essays are short and popularly written and are illustrated; ought to appeal to high school students.

56. **The Black Eye.** Charles Dorkins Productions/PACT of Wayne State Community College, 1968. 16mm. Color. Sound. 33 min. Sale $10.

The producers are Black nonprofessionals who look at Detroit through the eyes of natives. Suitable for Black or white students, though it may be more eye-opening for whites.

57. **Black Heritage: A History of Afro-Americans.** Holt, Rinehart & Winston, 1970.

The entire series has 108 half-hour lectures on Black history. Those pertinent to urban history include E. U. Essien-Udom's lectures on "Marcus Garvey and His Movement," four lectures on the "Harlem Renaissance," Horace Mann Bond's "Urbanization: The Expansion of the Ghetto," and the lectures contained in "The Freedom Movement: America and Beyond," in "Protest and Rebellion in the North," and in "The Cultural Scene: From 1954 to the Current Mood." Holt also has a series of 27 paperbacks under the same title with film transcripts, illustrations, and a questions and projects section. A comprehensive collection.

58. Blassingame, John W. **Black New Orleans, 1860–1880.** Chicago: University of Chicago Press, 1973. 301 pp. LC 72-97664. $9.95.

A social history of the Black community in New Orleans during the crucial decades of the Civil War and Reconstruction. He touches upon the family and religious activities as well as the educational and economic opportunities available.

59. Bontemps, Arna, and Conroy, Jack. **Anyplace But Here.** (Revised and expanded edition of *They Seek a City.*) New York: Hill & Wang, 1966. 372 pp. LC 66-15898. $6.95, pap. $2.25.

The first chapter discusses the life and career of Du Sable, the Black trader who first built his trading post on the Chicago River in 1779. The chapter is helpful because it not only suggests the varied activities of a trader but also because the trader was Black. The second chapter recounts the hectic life of Jim Beckwourth, Indian fighter and trapper. Beckwourth started as a blacksmith's apprentice in St. Louis and had an adventurous life. He settled down for a time as a store operator in Denver. Suitable for junior and senior high school students.

60. Bracey, John H., Jr., Meier, August, and Rudwick, Elliott, eds. **Black Nationalism in America.** American Heritage. Indianapolis: Bobbs-Merrill, 1970. 568 pp. LC 79-99161. $8.50, pap. $3.25.

This reader should be used to supplement *Negro Protest Thought in the Twentieth Century* by August Meier and Francis Broderick. It is also part of the

American Heritage series but concentrates on Black solidarity. The book covers the entire American experience, but approximately half of it is devoted to the 20th century. Representative selections have been taken from the works of Alain Locke, Kelly Miller, A. Philip Randolph, Elijah Muhammed, Malcolm X, Eldridge Cleaver, Stokely Carmichael, and others. Comprehensive and informative. For advanced students and special projects.

61. Bracey, John H., Jr., Meier, August, and Rudwick, Elliott, eds. **The Rise of the Ghetto.** Belmont, Cal.: Wadsworth, 1971. 222 pp. LC 78-154818. pap $3.95.

Centers upon the Black experience in America, primarily in the 20th century. The book was intended as a reader in Black history classes and ought to be understood by the average reader. For general circulation and not for scholarly use.

62. Broderick, Francis L., Meier, August, and Rudnick, Elliott, eds. **Black Protest Thought in the Twentieth Century,** 2nd ed. American Heritage. Indianapolis: Bobbs-Merrill, 1971. 648 pp. LC 79-119007. $8.50, pap. $3.95.

The best reader on civil rights movements down to 1965. The selections are original statements by Black leaders. Highly recommended for high school students.

63. Brooks, Gwendolyn. **Gwendolyn Brooks Reading Her Poetry with an Introductory Poem by Don L. Lee.** Caedmon Records, 1969. 2 discs. $6.98 each, cassettes $7.95 each.

Among the poems read by Gwendolyn Brooks is "A Street in Bronzeville," which gives insight into a Black woman's view of the urban experience. Can be used for audiences ranging from those first beginning school through adults.

64. Brown, Letitia Woods. **Free Negroes in the District of Columbia, 1790–1846.** New York: Oxford University Press, 1972. 226 pp. LC 77-186497. $7.95.

Brown tells much of the original Black settlers of the capital city from its inception to just before the Mexican War. The free Black community existed along with a slave society which it helped to subvert. The book is of value to those interested in the roots of Black life in an important American city.

65. Buerkle, Jack V., and Barker, Danny. **Bourbon Street Black: The New Orleans Black Jazzman.** New York: Oxford University Press, 1973. 244 pp. LC 73-77926. $7.95, pap. $2.95.

A survey done by a sociologist of 51 jazzmen in New Orleans who are members of the Black musicians' union. It also includes a short history of jazz in the city. The book has some general interest as well as an attraction for jazz buffs.

66. Bureau of Municipal Research, Philadelphia. **Law Administration and Negro-White Relations in Philadelphia; A Study of Race Relations.** Westport, Conn.: Negro Universities Press, 1970 (originally published in 1947). 183 pp. LC 76-111567. $10.50.

This reprint of research done in Philadelphia at the end of World War II shows the depth of concern that the events in that war and the first wave of civil rights efforts had engendered. Shows the kinds of connections that were then being made between the framing and enforcing of laws and prejudicial treatment. Should be in collections on Black history.

67. Carter, Edward Randolph. **The Black Side; A Partial History of the Business, Religious and Educational Side of the Negro in Atlanta, Ga.** Westport, Conn.: Greenwood Press. 1971 (originally published in 1894). 323 pp. LC 78-170692. $24.75.

Like many of this genre, this reprint contains many laudatory remarks about persons in the city described. Despite this puffery, the book serves as a resource for those interested in urban history and middle-class Blacks of the 19th century.

68. **The Cities.** CBS News/Bailey Films, 1968. 3 16mm films. Color. Sound. 54 min. each. Sale $575 each, $1,550 set.

This series, made for television, includes "A City Is to Live In," "Dilemma in Black and White," and "To Build the Future." Stressing urban and racial problems, all are suited for the high school to adult audience.

69. Cleaver, Eldridge. **Soul on Ice.** New York: McGraw-Hill, 1969. 210 pp. LC 67-27277. Dell, pap. $1.95.

Cleaver's best-selling book remains very controversial in view of his prison record and association with the Black Panthers. It reflects the anger of a Black man with American society. Recommended for mature students.

70. Commission of Inquiry into the Black Panthers and the Police. **Search and Destroy; A Report by Roy Wilkins and Ramsey Clark.** Chicago: Metropolitan Applied Research Center, 1973. 284 pp. LC 73-7068. $5.95.

Wilkins and Clark chaired a commission to investigate the raid of the Chicago police on Black Panther headquarters in December 1969. The commission worked three years investigating the attitudes and events leading to the raid, including the state of police-community relations in Chicago, the thinking behind the police raid, the circumstances of the raid, and the process of official—state, city, and county—justification of the raid. The commission had conclusions of its own which are presented here. Necessary for those with a theoretical or practical interest in police systems, and ought to be read by the general public.

71. Cronon, E. David. **Black Moses: The Story of Marcus Garvey and the Universal Negro Improvement Association.** Madison, Wis.: University of Wisconsin Press, 1969. 278 pp. LC 76-101503. $12.50, pap. $2.50.

This definitive study of Garvey's back-to-Africa movement shows the interrelationship between Harlem and the Garveyites. Useful for research and special studies.

72. Cruse, Harold. **The Crisis of the Negro Intellectual.** New York: Morrow, 1967. LC 67-25316. $10. Apollo, pap. $3.50.

Deservedly acclaimed. Cruse's theme is that the 1920s was a watershed for the Black community in Harlem, and that the Marxists prevented the community from becoming culturally conscious. Difficult.

73. Cullen, Countee. **The Poetry of Countee Cullen.** Caedmon Records. 1 disc. $6.98, cassette $7.95. Read by Ruby Dee and Ossie Davis.

Can be used to illustrate the Harlem Renaissance. The poems of Countee Cullen are lyrical and give both emotional and intellectual insight into the urban world of the 1920s. They can be and have been enjoyed by a general audience.

74. Dabney, Wendell Phillips. **Cincinnati's Colored Citizens: Historical, Sociological and Biographical.** Westport, Conn.: Negro Universities Press, 1970 (originally published in 1926). 440 pp. LC 73-100287. $19.

A list of Black persons of notice in Cincinnati that is of more than antiquarian interest. The reprint is of help to the researcher in Black history, especially in social history, and in urban history, especially in comparing the patterns of occupations and mobility of Blacks and whites.

75. Daniels, John. **In Freedom's Birthplace; A Study of the Boston Negroes.** Westport, Conn.: Negro Universities Press, 1969 (originally published in 1914). 496 pp. LC 68-55880. $15.50.

Daniels' study is about the conditions among Boston's Blacks on the eve of World War I. It is in the muckraking tradition and shows how far from equality, social or economic, Boston's Blacks were. The reprint ought to be included in research collections for Black history or for urban history.

76. Davis, Edwin Adams, and Hogan, William Ransom. **The Barber of Natchez.** Baton Rouge, La.: Louisiana State University Press, 1973. 272 pp. LC 77-159069. pap. $3.50.

A reprint of a 1954 volume on the life of a free Negro in antebellum Natchez who became a barber and a prosperous landowner prior to his murder. The book is based upon the diary of William Johnson and gives an unorthodox view of a southern town as seen by a free Black. The book is an interesting one which has broader appeal than the title would indicate.

77. Davis, Edwin Adams, and Hogan, William Ransom, eds. **William Johnson's Natchez: The Ante-Bellum Diary of a Free Negro,** 2 vols. Port Washington, N.Y.: Kennikat, 1973 (originally published in 1951). 812 pp. LC 68-25203. Set $34.50.

Davis and Hogan based their *The Barber of Natchez* on this diary. It is expensive and is recommended as an addition to *The Barber of Natchez* only to libraries who expect students to utilize their resources for research purposes.

78. Dobler, Lavinia, and Toppin, Edgar A. **Pioneers and Patriots.** Garden City, N.Y.: Doubleday, 1965. 118 pp. LC 65-17241. pap. $1.45.

Pictures and essays on Peter Salem and Benjamin Banneker, Black figures of the Revolutionary era. Junior high level.

79. Douglass, Frederick. **Life and Times of Frederick Douglass.** Adapted by Barbara Ritchie. New York: Crowell, 1962. 210 pp. LC 66-7048. $4.50. Collier Books, pap. $2.45.

Douglass' final autobiography (written in 1892). In it he views his long life as slave and free man. There is not as much concerning Douglass' city impressions as one might expect; still the book is a significant resource for research.

80. Drake, St. Clair, and Cayton, Horace C. **Black Metropolis: A Study of Negro Life in a Northern City,** revised and enlarged ed., 2 vols. New York: Harcourt Brace Jovanovich, 1970. 814 pp. LC 62-52869. pap. $2.85 each.

Drake and Cayton wrote and published this study of Chicago's Bronzeville in the 1930s. This revision contains an introduction by Richard Wright and E. C. Hughes and is recommended to libraries as a classic of the older sociology.

81. **Equality.** Lakeside, Cal.: Interact, 1971. $10.

Equality is a simplified version of *Sunshine* and is designed for students in grades 4 through 6. In involves 20 to 35 players who play the game for three weeks in one-hour rounds. While primarily designed for schools, the game might have drawing power for a program to attract children aged 9 to 11.

82. Essien-Udom, E. U. **Black Nationalism: The Search for an Identity in America.** Chicago: University of Chicago Press, 1962. 367 pp. LC 62-12632. $10, pap. $3.45.

Essien-Udom is an African who has studied the Black Muslims, among others, and is on the whole sympathetic to the idea of a Black identity. For research projects.

83. **Felicia.** Stuart Roe/University of California Extension Media Center, 1965. 16mm. b/w. Sound. 13 min. Sale $70.

The life of a Black girl in Watts is documented to illustrate the problems of a segregated community. The technique should involve students and help them understand the difficulty of slum life.

84. Felton, Harold W. **Jim Beckwourth: Negro Mountain Man.** New York: Dodd, Mead, 1966. 173 pp. LC 66-6676. $4.50. Apollo, pap. $.95.

This biography of Beckwourth relies on his own autobiography. For junior high school students.

85. Forten, Charlotte. **The Journal of Charlotte L. Forten; with an Introduction and Notes by Ray Allen Billington.** New York: Collier, 1961. 286 pp. LC 63-16754. pap. $2.45.

Charlotte Forten was born in Philadelphia a free Negro. She went to school in Salem, Massachusetts, in 1854, then taught in Salem, but because of poor health returned to Philadelphia. During the Civil War, she taught in Port Royal, South Carolina. Her journal ought to interest high school students as it provides an interesting insight into the mores of the day as well as the expectations of a Black girl in a white society.

86. Fox, Stephen R. **The Guardian of Boston: William Monroe Trotter.** New York: Atheneum, 1970. 307 pp. LC 78-108822. $7.95, pap. $3.45.

Trotter was a pioneering Black journalist in Boston whose newspaper, *The Guardian*, proved influential in the late 19th and early 20th centuries. Trotter fought against discrimination and for greater autonomy for Blacks in this northern city. The book is recommended for libraries with an interest in minorities in cities, in urban newspapers, or in civil rights movements. It is not a particularly difficult book and ought to prove of interest to many people.

87. **Free at last.** National Educational Television/Indiana University, 1965. (History of the Negro People.) 16mm. b/w. Sound. 30 min. Rent $6.75. Ossie Davis narrator.

Covering the period from 1865 to 1945, shows glimpses of Frederick Douglass, Booker T. Washington, Marcus Garvey, W. E. B. DuBois, and others. It is excellent on the growth of Harlem and the Harlem Renaissance of the 1920s. Highly recommended for junior and senior high school students.

88. **The Future and the Negro.** National Educational Television/Indiana University, 1965. (History of the Negro People.) 16mm. b/w. Sound. 3 reels. 75 min. Rent $14.25. Ossie Davis, narrator.

A panel discussion, it is excellent but too long to fit the usual class pattern.

89. Garfinkle, Herbert. **When Negroes March: The March on Washington Movement in the Organizational Politics for FEPC.** Glencoe, Ill.: Free Press, 1959. 224 pp. LC 58-6482. $4.95. Atheneum, pap. $2.95.

A paperback reissue of Garfinkle's original work with a new preface by Lewis M. Killiam, it is the definitive study of A. Philip Randolph's attempt to pressure Franklin D. Roosevelt and the Congress into granting a number of demands to Blacks just before World War II. Randolph proposed to generate pressure by a mass movement on Washington; this march never materialized, as a nervous president succeeded in stopping it by compromise. The book is essential for an understanding of the 20th century American civil rights movement.

90. **Ghetto, rev. ed.** New York: Western Publishing Co., 1969. $24.

Ghetto attempts to replicate the experiences of the urban poor in making life choices through the medium of a simulation game. Seven to 10 players are necessary for the game, which takes two to four hours. It is not difficult, and can be played by junior high students through adults. It is recommended for middle-class white persons wanting to learn more of the problems of the Black poor.

91. **Ghettoes of America.** Warren Schloat Productions, 1967. 4 filmstrips. Color. Sound. $70 with disc, $85 with cassettes.

Harlem and Watts are studied through an effective multimedia approach. The level is simple enough for slow students. Includes *Anthony Lives in Watts* (68 and 72 fr.), 26 min., and *Jerry Lives in Harlem* (67 and 57 fr.), 20 min.

92. Graham, Shirley. **Your Most Humble Servant.** New York: Julian Messner, 1949. 235 pp. LC 49-11346. $4.29.

A biography of Banneker aimed at a juvenile level. It recounts Banneker's efforts as an astronomer, almanac maker, and surveyor in Baltimore and Washington.

93. Green, Constance McLaughlin. **The Secret City: A History of Race Relations in the Nation's Capital.** Princeton, N.J.: Princeton University Press, 1967. 389 pp. LC 66-26585. $10, pap. $3.95.

This study of Negro Washington from 1791 to 1961 is a pioneer effort. It shows the growth of a community within a community over the span of the nation's history. The development of urban Black institutions and the limits placed upon them by white power structures are themes which ought to be read by teachers and used by students for research.

94. Gregory, Susan. **Hey, White Girl!** New York: Norton, 1970. 221 pp. LC 79-90978. $5.95.

Susan Gregory was a white girl who spent a year as the only white person in a ghetto high school. This account is a diary of that experience. Highly recommended for general circulation to high schoolers and adults.

95. Handlin, Oscar. **The Newcomers.** Cambridge, Mass.: Harvard University Press, 1959. 171 pp. LC 59-1475. $5. Doubleday, pap. $1.95.

An old study about Blacks and Puerto Ricans in New York City, still valuable although the assumption that the two groups are the last wave of immigrants which duplicated the experiences of earlier ones is debatable.

96. Hansberry, Lorraine. **A Raisin in the Sun.** Caedmon Records, 1972. 3 discs. $21.94 for discs, $23.85 for cassettes.

Starring Ossie Davis, Ruby Dee, Claudia McNeil, and Diana Sands. Lorraine Hansberry's play depicts life in a Black, urban ghetto and the tensions engendered by such a life. The struggle to escape from lower-class life into middle-class respectability may seem dated, but the emotional impact has not diminished. For junior and senior high school students and adults.

97. Hansberry, Lorraine. **To be Young, Gifted, and Black,** adapted by Robert Nemeroff. Caedmon Records, 1971. 3 discs. $21.94 for discs, $23.85 for cassettes.

Starring James Earl Jones, Barbara Baxley, and Claudia McNeil. Lorraine Hansberry died before she could finish this play and her husband, Robert Nemeroff, completed it. Reveals much of the tragedy and the joy of Black life. High school students and adults can profit from this vital work.

98. **Harlem Wednesday.** Contemporary Films/McGraw-Hill, 1959. 16mm. Color. Sound. 10 min. Sale $120.

Paintings by Gregorio Prestopino and jazz by Benny Carter liven this film that purports to show how it was nearly 20 years ago during an ordinary midweek day in Harlem. For junior and senior high school.

99. Harris, M. A. **A Negro History Tour of Manhattan.** New York: Greenwood Press, 1968. 113 pp. LC 68-54217. $3.95.

A slim volume denoting places of interest to Blacks in New York City. It does have use as a guide to tourists or as a reference work for scholars of Blacks in the city. Because of its narrow confines, it is for a limited audience.

100. History of the Negro in America Series. Niagara Films/McGraw-Hill, 1965. 16mm. b/w. Sound. Series of 3 films.

Part I: 1619–1860: Out of Slavery. 20 min. Sale $180, rent $15.

Traces the development of Negro history up to the Civil War. It is superficial in that it tends to accept the orthodox views of slavery and causes of the Civil War.

Part II: 1861–1877: Civil War and Reconstruction. 19 min. Sale $185, rent $15.

Traces the roles of the Black man in the Civil War and in Reconstruction. Useful for junior and senior high school students as it contains the pictures of many of the leaders of the Black community.

Part III: 1877–Today: Freedom Movement. 20 min. Sale $180, rent $15. Third in the series, gives a quick overview of the civil rights movement and looks at urban problems as well. It tries to cover too much in too little a time and thus tends to oversimplify. But it is good as an introduction to the whole problem of Blacks in the cities, particularly for average students.

101. Hoover, Dwight W., ed. **Understanding Negro History.** New York: Franklin Watts, 1968. LC 68-26441. $12.50, pap. $2.95.

Articles attempting to set a theoretical base for the study of Negro history. It is selective and provides a framework for further work. Recommended for senior high school students.

102. House on Cedar Hill. Artisan Productions, 1953. 16mm. b/w. Sound. 17 min. Rent $4.80.

Frederick Douglass' life is traced through the use of drawings, old photographs, and mementoes of his home in Washington, D.C. The film catches the flavor of 19th-century life, particularly as lived by this famous Black abolitionist.

103. Hughes, Langston, and Meltzer, Milton. **A Pictorial History of the Negro in America,** 3rd rev. ed. New York: Crown, 1968. 380 pp. LC 68-9096. $6.95.

A standard reference tool with pictures of individuals and their environments. It can be used to compare Black living conditions from the Revolution to the present.

104. Hughes, Langston. **Simple Stories.** Caedmon Records, 1968. 2 discs. $6.50 for discs, $7.95 for cassette. Read by Ossie Davis.

Simple, a character created by Hughes, responded honestly to the situations in which he found himself. Among the poems included in this anthology are "A Toast to Harlem" and "Golden Gate." All are reflective of the kind of cultural ferment that characterized the Harlem Renaissance of the 1920s and can be appreciated by persons of different ages and educational backgrounds.

105. Johnson, James Weldon. **Black Manhattan.** New York: Arno Press, 1968 (originally published in 1930). 284 pp. LC 68-29003. $13. Atheneum, pap. $3.75.

Johnson wrote his history of the Negro in New York City from the time of the original Dutch community down to the Harlem Renaissance in the 1920s.

106. Jones, William Henry. **Recreation and Amusement among Negroes in Washington, D.C. A Sociological Analysis of the Negro in an Urban Environment.** Westport, Conn.: Negro Universities Press, 1970 (originally published in 1927). 216 pp. LC 72-88440. $13.75.

An example of the second generation of urban sociologists. A research possibility for those interested in the specific topic of recreation and also for those interested in the development of ideas in sociology.

107. Katznelson, Ira. **Black Men, White Cities: Race, Politics, and Migration in the United States, 1900–30, and Britain, 1948–68.** New York: Oxford University Press, 1973 (Institute of Race Relations). 219 pp. LC 72-92828. $9.95.

An interesting attempt at a cross-cultural study of black urbanization in the first three decades in the United States and the last two in England. It sheds light on how American developments compare with those in England, and should intrigue urban historians, sociologists, and planners.

108. Keil, Charles. **Urban Blues.** Chicago: University of Chicago Press, 1966. 231 pp. LC 66-13876/MN. $7.50, pap. $2.95.

Another classic, this attempts to show the relation between blues and the Black urban style of life. It has been widely read and admired. Recommended for students interested in music and in life-styles.

109. Kempton, Murray. **The Briar Patch: The People of the State of New York v. Lumumba Shakur et al.** New York: Dutton, 1973. 282 pp. LC 73-190698. $7.95.

Murray Kempton is a noted liberal editor and commentator who has written here a popular account of the trial of certain Black Panthers at New Haven, Connecticut. Interesting, and ought to appeal to a wide audience.

110. King, Coretta Scott. **My Life with Martin Luther King, Jr.** Caedmon Records. 3 discs. $14.98 for discs, $20.94 for cassettes.

Ms. King relates her impressions of the great civil rights leader of the 1950s and 1960s. Her view was an inside one which conveys much of the emotional flavor of those trying times.

111. King, Martin Luther, Jr. **Why We Can't Wait.** New York: Harper & Row, 1964. 178 pp. LC 64-19514. $6.95. New American Library, pap. $.95.

Should be assigned to students who are interested in King's ideas. Makes a case for immediate improvement in racial relations as well as for nonviolent means to attain equality. Recommended for special projects and for research.

112. Kiser, Clyde Vernon. **Sea Island to City: A Study of St. Helena Islanders in Harlem and Other Urban Centers.** New York: AMS Press, 1967 (originally published in 1932). 272 pp. LC 70-29898. $10. Atheneum, pap. $3.45.

A reissue with a new preface by Joseph S. Himes. It is a pioneering work that focuses upon the migration of rural Blacks from an island off Georgia to various northern cities. As such, it belongs in libraries with collections on Black migration to or Blacks in cities.

113. Kochman, Thomas, ed. **Rappin' and Stylin' Out: Communication in Urban Black America.** Urbana, Ill.: University of Illinois Press, 1972. 464 pp. LC 75-177896. $12.50, pap. $4.95.

This collection includes essays by scholars, popular writers, and political figures such as Charles Keil, Claude Brown, and H. Rap Brown. These essays focus on the ways in which Black Americans communicate with each other—verbally and nonverbally, through jokes and playing the numbers—in restaurants, amusement centers, and on the street. Of interest to both the scholar and the general reader and should have wide circulation.

114. Little, Malcolm. **The Autobiography of Malcolm X.** New York: Grove Press, 1965. 455 pp. LC 65-257331. $7.50, pap. $1.95.

Malcolm X's autobiography has become a classic. The topics he wrote about are controversial, but they offer enormous insights into urban Black life and Black power movements. Black students in particular are impressed by it.

115. Litwack, Leon F. **North of Slavery: The Negro in the Free States, 1709–1860.** Chicago: University of Chicago Press, 1961. 318 pp. LC 61-10869. $6, pap. $2.45.

Almost all of this study is concerned with the treatment of Blacks in the North before the Civil War. Since numbers of Blacks were in cities, Litwack's book is significant in showing the social arrangements in northern cities and the discrimination visited upon Blacks there. Highly recommended for senior high school students.

116. Lynch, Hollis R. **The Black Urban Condition.** New York: Crowell, 1973. 469 pp. LC 72-13822. $12.50.

Lynch has collected documents consisting of the remarks of Black leaders on life in the American city from 1866 to the present. Head of Columbia University's African Studies program, he has included 40 authors, among them W. E. B. Du Bois, Booker T. Washington, and Thurgood Marshall. Best suited to smaller libraries that lack the sources from which these documents were drawn.

117. Martin, Asa Earl. **Our Negro Population; A Sociological Study of the Negroes of Kansas City, Missouri.** Westport, Conn.: Negro Universities Press, 1971 (originally published in 1913). 189 pp. LC 71-89043. $11.

One of the first generation of studies by American sociologists on Blacks in American cities. Martin tells much of the conditions that made Kansas City the home of the blues. Should appear on shelves of libraries with sections on urban history and the Black urban experience.

118. Meier, August. **Negro Thought in America, 1880–1915: Racial Ideologies in the Age of Booker T. Washington.** Ann Arbor, Mich.: University of Michigan Press, 1963. 336 pp. LC 63-14008. $8.95, pap. $2.25.

Meier is one of the foremost historians of the Black man in America. In this study he touches on the competing ideas of the period. His conclusion is that the "new Negro" movement had its roots in an earlier period which already had developed ideas. Good for research and for talented students.

119. Meier, August, and Rudwick, Elliott, eds. **Black Protest in the Sixties.** New York: Franklin Watts, 1970. 355 pp. LC 76-116082. $8.95, pap. $2.95.

The latest collection put together by Meier and Rudwick is the most up to date in the area of recent civil rights movements. Highly recommended for senior high school students.

120. Meier, August, and Rudwick, Elliott. **From Plantation to Ghetto.** New York: Hill & Wang, 1966. 280 pp. LC 66-26030. $6.95, pap. $2.45.

This interpretive history of the Negro in America is the best to date. Chapter 3 is an excellent summary of the Black man in antebellum cities, North and South. Not too difficult for high school students.

121. **The Negro in Civil War and Reconstruction.** University Films/McGraw-Hill, 1965. (The History of the American Negro.) 41 frames. Color. Sale $8.50.

Covers the era 1861–1877 and is recommended for high school students.

122. **New Mood.** National Educational Television/Indiana University Audio-Visual Center, 1965. (History of the Negro People.) 16mm. b/w. 30 min. Rent $6.75. Ossie Davis, narrator.

This third film in the *History of the Negro People* series concerns civil rights movements from 1954 to 1964. Martin Luther King, Jr., Malcolm X, and Medgar Evers, among others, appear and their programs are described. Highly recommended for junior and senior high school students.

123. Newton, Huey P. **To Die for the People.** New York: Vintage Press, 1972. 232 pp. LC 72-529. $7.95, pap. $1.95.

Newton's essays and speeches prior to his change to political action provide a good example of the thinking that helped create and foster the Black Panthers.

124. Newton, Huey P., and Blake, J. Herman. **Revolutionary Suicide.** New York: Harcourt Brace Jovanovich, 1973. 333 pp. LC 72-93749. $8.95. Ballantine, pap. $1.95.

Newton is a functionary of the Black Panthers who has turned from direct action to political action. This is his latest volume, which outlines his more recent philosophy of what Blacks should do in order to achieve equality in America. The book is recommended for sections on Black protest movements.

125. Orleans, Peter, and Ellis, Russell, Jr. **Race, Change, and Urban Society.** Beverly Hills, Cal.: Sage Publications, 1971. 640 pp. LC 70-127992. $22.50, pap. $7.50.

This, the fifth volume of *Urban Affairs Annual Reviews*, resembles the second in that the focus is partially on race. The articles contained in this volume include material on cross-cultural assessment of race conflict, on Puerto Ricans in cities, and on the persistence of tradition in the Oaxaca Valley, as well as much historical and sociological evaluation of the dilemma of urban Blacks in the United States. There are articles on law enforcement, education, legal aid, and community control. Like the others in the series, this belongs on the shelf of all but the smallest libraries.

126. Osofsky, Gilbert. **Harlem: The Making of a Ghetto.** New York: Harper & Row, 1966. 259 pp. LC 66-10913. $8.95, pap. $2.95.

The best history of Negro Harlem, but specialized and probably should be used only in advanced student projects.

127. Ottley, Roi, and Weatherby, William J., eds. **The Negro in New York: An Informal Social History.** New York: New York Public Library and Oceana Publications, 1967. 328 pp. LC 67-21389. $7.50. Praeger, pap. $2.95.

This collection of writings includes essays, poems, and miscellaneous items. While it is best on later periods, it contains some material of the pre-Civil War era. For special studies only.

128. Ovington, Mary White. **Half a Man: The Status of the Negro in New York.** New York: Hill & Wang, 1969. 128 pp. LC 74-86819. $4.95, pap. $1.95.

Originally published in 1911, this is a paperback reissue in the *American Century* series and contains an introduction by Charles Flint Kellogg. Ms. Ovington was a pioneering social worker in New York City and a resident of Greenwich House, the first neighborhood association in the city. She joined the Niagara Movement and helped found the NAACP. This book is the result of her seven-year study of the condition of Negroes in New York City in the Progressive Era.

129. Portrait of the Inner City. Vision Associates/McGraw-Hill, 1965. (Teaching the Disadvantaged Child.) 16mm. b/w. 16 min. Sale $125.

This film discusses growing up in the slums and portrays both the strengths and weaknesses that this experience provides.

130. Quarles, Benjamin. **Black Abolitionists.** New York: Oxford University Press, 1969. 310 pp. LC 69-17766. $6.75, pap. $1.95.

Quarles has written perhaps the best study of the Black abolitionists, which takes into account the educational, organizational, and propaganda efforts of the movement and makes clear its urban setting. A useful reference tool.

131. Racism and the Urban Crisis. Berkeley, Cal.: Pacifica Tape Library, 1970. Reel or cassette. 49 min. $10.

A taped interview with Congresswoman Shirley Chisholm, the Black woman candidate for the 1972 Democratic presidential nomination. Representative Chisholm outlines her views on how racial attitudes have helped create and continue urban problems. She is a controversial and outspoken person; this tape reflects those qualities.

132. Sellers, Cleveland, and Terrell, Robert. **The River of No Return.** New York: Morrow, 1974. 279 pp. $7.95, pap. $3.50.

A Black militant shows much of the history of SNCC, including its gradual demise in the late 1960s and early 1970s. Valuable for both its insights in the Black urban experience and the composition of civil rights groups.

133. Shannon, Lyle W., and Shannon, Magdaline. **Minority Migrants in the Urban Community: Mexican-American and Negro Adjustment to Industrial Society.** Beverly Hills, Cal.: Sage Publications, 1973. 352 pp. LC 72-84055. $15.

This work attempts a cross-group comparison of Blacks and Mexicans in urban society. It is a specialized study which is best suited to libraries with a clientele interested in more formal sociological works.

134. **Slavery in a House Divided.** New York: McGraw-Hill, 1965. (The History of the American Negro.) 35mm. 45 fr. Color. Sale $8.50.

Drawings concentrating on slavery on the plantation, but also offering a few insights into the nature of urban slavery.

135. **Soul City.** National Educational Television/Indiana University Audio-Visual Center, 1971. 16mm. b/w. Sound. 13 min. Rent $4.80.

Floyd McKissick is developing an all-Black community in Warren County, North Carolina. This community, called Soul City, hopes to attract Blacks who otherwise would have ventured North to urban areas. This film, shown on NET, provides a look at the construction, as yet still incomplete, of the community.

136. Spear, Allan H. **Black Chicago: The Making of a Negro Ghetto, 1890–1920.** Chicago: University of Chicago Press, 1967. 254 pp. LC 67-21381. $7.50, pap. $3.45.

Specialized study of the beginnings of the sizable Black community in Chicago at the beginning of significant migration from the South. Students will find it useful in special projects.

137. **Sunshine.** Interact, 1968. $10.

Players assume the role of various racial groups in an imaginary city and work out problems. This game is simpler than the others and can be used on the elementary level. It is useful for teaching problems of minorities as well as urban development.

138. Sutker, Solomon, and Sutker, Sara Smith, with the assistance of Karen A. Plax, eds. **Racial Transition in the Inner Suburb: Studies of the St. Louis Area.** New York: Praeger, 1974. 192 pp. LC 78-180855.

Graphic depiction (tables, figures, and maps) of the changing demographic structure of suburbs closest to downtown St. Louis. Of interest to sociologists or urban planners.

139. Taeuber, Karl E., and Taeuber, Alma F. **Negroes in Cities.** New York: Atheneum, 1969. 284 pp. NUC 70-101205. $9.75, pap. $3.95.

The definitive study of the distribution of Negroes in American cities by two reputable demographers. The Taeubers' conclusions on urban Black populations present a base from which to go back into the past to find out why development went as it did. Useful for research data.

140. Wade, Richard C. **Slavery in the Cities: The South, 1820–1860.** New York: Oxford University Press, 1964. 340 pp. LC 64-22366. pap. $2.50.

The definitive statement on slavery in the cities. This much neglected phenomenon, which seemed to be evolving from a system of slavery to one of segregation, had largely been ignored until Wade considered it. Particularly useful in that it details how urban environments can force changes in social institutions. Especially recommended for teachers and for more mature students.

141. Warner, W. Lloyd, *et al.* **Color and Human Nature: Negro Personality Development in a Northern City.** New York: Harper & Row, 1969. (originally published in 1941). 301 pp. NUC 71-65355. Torch, pap. $2.25.

Warner's study of Black personality emerges from his anthropological perspective and his famous "Yankee City" series. In this reprint, Warner attempts to determine the factors that helped create a specific kind of racial personality. For libraries with an interest in Black urban populations.

142. Wesley, Charles H. **Richard Allen, Apostle of Freedom.** Washington, D.C.: Associated Publishers, 1935. 300 pp. LC 36-272. O.P.

Standard biography of Allen, the outstanding pioneer of the Negro Methodist Church in America. His life reflects the problems of the urban Black in Philadelphia and New York. For teacher reference and student projects.

143. William—From Georgia to Harlem. Hank Madler/Learning Corporation of America, 1971. (The Many Americans.) 16mm. Color. Sound. Sale $215, rent $15.

The story is about a southern Black child who migrates from his Georgia farm home to New York City. It depicts ghetto life realistically and sympathetically. Because of this depiction, can be shown to elementary students as well as adults with profit.

144. Woofter, Thomas Jackson. **Negro Problems in Cities.** Westport, Conn.: Negro Universities Press, 1969 (originally published in 1928). 284 pp. LC 70-89064. $11.

An early look at the first waves of Black migration in the 20th century shows how persistent problems have been. Focuses on employment, or rather the lack of it, and housing, as well as on health and sanitation. It is best suited to research sections on Blacks in the city; but, though dated, it also has some popular appeal.

Ethnic Groups in the City

The history of American cities has been unique in that much of the growth has been a product of non-native immigration. The fear and suspicion that native Americans voiced concerning the industrial city in the late 19th and early 20th centuries was in part a reaction against the Catholic, European-born residents of the city. The fear of these persons was that the city dwellers would not adopt American values but would cling to European ones. Hence, the struggle of immigrants was not only a struggle for physical survival but also one for cultural survival as well. The extent to which these immigrants and their descendents succeeded can be attributed to the cosmopolitanism of American cities that reflects cultural elements from various European groups.

This section has materials on specific ethnic groups in America or in various urban centers. It also contains references to the emotional costs and rewards of immigration as well as to those attempts by the migrants to perpetuate an older community or to form a new one. Finally, there are selections showing the paths to assimilation or accommodation and to political and economic power.

145. Adler, Selig, and Connolly, Thomas E. **From Ararat to Suburbia: The History of the Jewish Community in Buffalo.** Philadelphia: Jewish Publication Society of America, 1960. 408 pp. LC 60-15834. $6.

One of several books written in the 1960s on local Jewish communities. While it emphasizes the roles of prominent individuals and families in the city and deemphasize the relationships between the ethnic communities and the trends in the large society, it is of interest to those persons wanting limited studies of particular communities.

146. Allswang, John M. **A House for All Peoples: Ethnic Politics in Chicago, 1890–1936.** Lexington, Ky.: University Press of Kentucky, 1971. 253 pp. LC 76-119810. $8.95.

Allswang has attempted to reconstruct ethnic political behavior in Chicago using statistical data on elections. Unfortunately, his data are not as useful as they might be, either because of his methods of categorizing or because the data are incomplete, and the book has flaws for the specialist. It is too difficult for the general reader so it can only be recommended as a book for a researcher specifically interested in the manipulation of voting results.

147. **America, the Melting Pot.** Hearst Metrotone News, 1964. (Screen News Digest.) 16mm. b/w. Sound. 15 min.

The mutual impact of the immigrant on America and of America on the immigrant forms the basis of this film. Suitable for high school students.

148. Amfitheatrof, Erik. **The Children of Columbus: An Informal History of the Italians in the New World.** Boston: Little, Brown, 1973. 371 pp. LC 72-12684. $8.95.

A collection of biographies of successful or notable Italians in America. Included are Vanzetti of the Sacco-Vanzetti case and LaGuardia of New York City. The treatment is a popular one and offers little for the serious ethnic scholar.

149. Carpenter, Niles. **Nationality, Color, and Economic Opportunity in the City of Buffalo.** Westport, Conn.: Negro Universities Press, 1970 (originally published in 1927). 194 pp. LC 70-107480. $17.

Containing representative ideas about ethnicity in Buffalo in the 1920s, this reprint is recommended for research libraries primarily.

150. Children of the Inner City. Society for Visual Education. 6 filmstrips. Color. Sound. 6 discs. Sale $56.75 with discs, $60.75 with cassettes.

A teacher's guide comes with the set which includes "Jose, Puerto Rican Boy" (69 frames), "Ernesto, Mexican-American Boy" (70 frames), "Gail Ann, Kentucky Mountain Girl" (68 fr.), "Eddie, American Indian Boy" (61 fr.), "Fred, Black American Boy" (67 fr.), and "Cynthia, Japanese-American Girl" (66 fr.).

The level is elementary and the set does little more than introduce the individuals whose lives are the subjects.

151. City That Cares. Mayor's Office, City of Chicago, 1957. 16mm. Color. Sound. 30 min. Free.

The topic is human relations work in Chicago, and its focus is on the efforts of the city government to maintain racial peace in the city. The film details the kinds of activities and devices used to accomplish the goal of better human relations. The success of these efforts is less firmly established.

152. Clark, Dennis. **The Irish in Philadelphia: Ten Generations of Urban Experience.** Philadelphia: Temple University Press, 1974. 246 pp. LC 72-95884. $10.

Scholars have argued for some time that the studies of the Irish which have concentrated upon Boston have taken an atypical case for the typical one. Clark looks at this ethnic group in the City of Brotherly Love. The case study is of interest to the student of urban history and the history of the Irish in America.

153. Cogan, Sara G. **The Jews of San Francisco and the Greater Bay Area, 1849–1919: An Annotated Bibliography.** Berkeley, Cal.: Western Jewish History Center, Judah Magnes Memorial Museum, 1973. 127 pp. LC 74-151208. $22.50.

A rather specialized item which may be purchased by those libraries interested in studies of ethnicity in the Bay area.

154. Coleman, Terry. **Going to America.** New York: Pantheon, 1972. 317 pp. LC 39-39602. $8.95. Anchor, pap. $2.50.

Migration from Great Britain—England and Ireland primarily—in the 1850s. Coleman's account is a popular one which focuses upon the physical and social hardships encountered by the new Americans in their journey and settlement. For the general reader, not the specialist.

155. Davis, Allen F., and Haller, Mark H., eds. **The Peoples of Philadelphia: A History of Ethnic Groups and Lower Class Life, 1790–1940.** Philadelphia: Temple University Press, 1973. 301 pp. LC 72-95879. $9.95.

The authors have put together an interesting collection of social history centered upon the changing composition of Philadelphia's population. Scholarly and filling the need for ethnic materials, it should be useful for all but the most complete research libraries.

156. Ernst, Robert. **Immigrant Life in New York City, 1825–1863.** New York: King's Crown Press, 1949. 331 pp. LC 49-9759. $9.50.

Ernst studied the social conditions which faced the immigrant Irish and Germans in New York City down to 1863. He is particularly good on the living conditions in tenements. For reference only.

157. Fein, Isaac M. **The Making of an American Jewish Community: The History of Baltimore Jewry from 1773–1920.** Philadelphia: Jewish Publication Society of America, 1971. 348 pp. LC 76-136258. $6.50.

Baltimore has had a significant Jewish community almost from its inception. Fein describes the growth and achievements of that community in this book which is part of a series on the history of Jews in a number of American cities.

158. Goldner, Norman. **The Mexican in the Northern Urban Area: A Comparison of Two Generations.** San Francisco: Rand & Research Associates, 1972. 123 pp. LC 72-86400. pap. $7.

A study of the adaptation of Mexicans according to generations. As a case study of the process of urbanization, it is a valuable addition to libraries attempting to create ethnic sections.

159. **Good Night, Socrates.** Contemporary Films/McGraw-Hill, 1963. 16mm. Sale $235, rent $17.50.

An American of Greek descent reflects on his boyhood in a Greek neighborhood as the section is being torn down. Recommended for its appeal and impact. For junior and senior high school students.

160. **Goren, Arthur A. New York Jews and the Quest for Community, 1908–1922.** New York: Columbia University Press, 1970. 361 pp. LC 76-129961. $12.50.

Details the efforts made by Jews in New York to set up Kehillah, or community councils, in order to develop a sense of community between the newly arrived East European Jews and the already present German ones. Like Nelli's book on the Italians in Chicago, this describes how immigrants to America did turn to group efforts in order to soften the often overwhelming pressures of American city life.

161. Handlin, Oscar. **Boston's Immigrants,** rev. and enlarged ed. Cambridge, Mass.: Harvard University Press, 1959. 382 pp. LC 59-7653. $10. Atheneum, pap. $3.25.

The period covered is 1790 to 1865, and the subtitle, "A Study in Acculturation," reveals clearly what it is about. Handlin is especially good on the factors that contributed to the creation of Irish slums in North End and Fort Hill. Recommended for projects and research.

162. Harlem Crusader. NBC/Encyclopaedia Britannica Films, 1966. 16mm. b/w. Sound. 29 min. Sale $150, rent $7.75.

The subject of this NBC study is a social worker in Spanish Harlem who worked with Puerto Ricans over a five-year period. Shows how this particular social worker operated, and is useful in understanding the problems and goals of the profession. For senior high school students.

163. The Inheritance. Harold Mayer Productions and Amalgamated Clothing Workers/Anti-Defamation League, 1965. 16mm. b/w. Sound. 35 min. Rent $15.

Looks at both sides of the labor movement and immigration from the standpoint of the Amalgamated Clothing Workers. Shows the exploitation of workers in clothing manufacturing as well as the poor living conditions which were common among newcomers to America. Excellent.

164. Jones, Maldwyn Allen. **American Immigration.** History of American Civilization. Chicago: University of Chicago Press, 1960. 359 pp. LC 60-8301. $6, pap. $2.45.

Eminently readable and the best survey of the subject. The chapter "Immigrants in Industrial America" is a superlative summary of the problems of urban life.

165. Jordan, Terry. **German Seed in Texas Soil.** Austin, Tex.: University of Texas Press, 1966. 237 pp. LC 66-15703. $7.50.

Jordan treats of German immigrants to Texas in the 19th century and does speak of town development in the Southwest. The book is a good one and is recommended for those libraries with a regional interest as well as one in immigration patterns in the United States.

166. Korman, Gerd. **Industrialization, Immigrants, and Americanizers: The View from Milwaukee, 1866-1921.** Madison Wis.: State Historical Society of Wisconsin, 1967. 225 pp. LC 67-63001. $4.50.

Korman interweaves three topics in this fine study, which includes the history of a number of ethnic groups. He discusses the enticements offered the immigrant by businesses and the attempt to socialize the immigrant after his arrival. Invaluable in understanding the migration of Germans, the growing industrial society in America in the 19th and early 20th centuries, and the climate of opinion in one Midwestern urban area.

167. Korn, Bertram Wallace. **The Early Jews of New Orleans.** Waltham, Mass.: American Jewish Historical Society, 1969. 382 pp. LC 70-86334. $12.50.

While there were individual Jewish families scattered throughout the urban South, few Southern cities have Jewish communities of a size making a history possible. New Orleans is an exception as this history makes clear, and this exception adds to the value of the study.

168. Kurtz, Donald V. **The Politics of a Poverty Habitat.** Cambridge, Mass.: Ballinger Publishing Co., 1973. 243 pp. LC 73-9595. $12.50.

Kurtz's study is of an urban Mexican-American community by an anthropologist. Scholarly and leans to the behavioral approach. As such, it is most suited to research libraries with a university clientele.

169. Lewis, Oscar. **La Vida: A Puerto Rican Family in the Culture of Poverty—San Juan and New York.** New York: Random House, 1966. 669 pp. LC 66-11983. $12.50, pap. $2.95.

This justly famous study by a sensitive anthropologist helped popularize the idea of a culture of poverty, an idea that has recently been attacked. Lewis does view the struggles of recent Puerto Rican emigrants to New York City with much sympathy and understanding. Useful for an understanding of urban poverty and an appreciation of the impact of a large city upon a migrant population.

170. Lieberson, Stanley. **Ethnic Patterns in American Cities.** New York: Free Press of Glencoe, 1963. 230 pp. LC 63-7551. $7.95.

A demographic look at the children of immigrants who have settled in American urban areas. It is not easy, but can be used as a reference work.

171. A Nation of Immigrants. Wolper Productions/Anti-Defamation League of New York, 1967. 16mm. b/w. Sound. 53 min. Sale $420, rent $25. Richard Basehart, narrator.

Based on the book of the same title by John F. Kennedy, this is basically a history of immigration to the United States, although it also includes descriptions of the contributions made to American society by various ethnic groups. Shows the shape and size of the immigrant ghettoes in American cities and is recommended for that reason.

172. Nee, Victor G., and Nee, Brett de Bary. **Longtime Californ': A Documentary Study of an American Chinatown.** New York: Pantheon, 1973. 401 pp. LC 72-12389. $10.

The Nees have written about San Francisco's Chinatown, their account largely based upon personal interviews in the area in 1971 and 1972. The Nees see three kinds of Chinese societies, each based on a particular immigrant period. These include old bachelors from the 19th century, families with small businesses from the 20th century, and new immigrants who came after 1965. Quite interesting and has much popular appeal.

173. Nelli, Humbert S. **The Italians in Chicago, 1880–1930: A Study in Ethnic Mobility.** New York: Oxford University Press, 1970. 300 pp. LC 76-123610. $8.50, pap. $2.50.

Reflects the growing interest of urban historians in the problems of both social and residential mobility. Nelli suggests that the Italians in Chicago created a community which was lacking in the rural parts of Italy from which they came. His study is of the Italian community in Chicago during a period of accelerated city growth. Excellent, and should have wide circulation even though its intended audience is scholarly.

174. Niehaus, Earl F. **The Irish in New Orleans, 1800–1860.** Baton Rouge, La.: Louisiana State University Press, 1965. 194 pp. LC 65-27709. O.P.

There are few histories of ethnic groups in southern cities; this is an exception to the rule. Niehaus traces the growth of the Irish community in New Orleans from the first influx to the greater numbers who came as a result of the potato famine in Ireland. His book also includes the tensions between Blacks and Irish and the impact the Irish had upon the already existing Catholic churches in New Orleans. Recommended for its scholarly approach and its unique topic.

175. **Our Immigrant Heritage.** Paul Burnford Film Productions/McGraw-Hill, 1966. 16mm. Color. Sound. 32 min. Rent $12.

While emphasizing the later immigration and the cultural values brought by immigrants, there is some treatment of the earlier immigration and the conditions in cities. For junior and senior high school students.

176. Price, John A. **Tiajuana: Urbanization in a Border Culture.** South Bend, Ind.: University of Notre Dame Press, 1973. 195 pp. LC 72-12641. $7.50, pap. $2.95.

Price's study shows the impact of two cultures on one border city done under the sponsorship of the U.S.-Mexico Border Studies Project at the University of Notre Dame and paid for by the Ford Foundation. While the study indicates the presence of major social problems, it also demonstrates that the Mexican city is far more than a slum. Scholarly and for specialists.

177. Rudolph, B. G. **From a Minyan to a Community: A History of the Jews of Syracuse.** Syracuse, N.Y.: Syracuse University Press, 1970. 314 pp. LC 74-11565. $7.50.

Like the Adler and Connolly study, Rudolph's traces the expansion of the Jewish sector of Syracuse. The account is a special one, but can be treated as a not untypical example of Jewish settlement in cities in New York State.

178. Sandberg, Neil C. **Ethnic Identity and Assimilation: The Polish-American Community.** New York: Praeger, 1974. 88 pp. LC 73-10955. $12.50.

Sandberg's study is on metropolitan Los Angeles and, as a dissertation, won the Kosciuszko Foundation Award for 1972. Shows the extent to which the Polish community has retained its cultural heritage and the forces which have operated to diminish that heritage. Recommended for libraries that maintain collections on urban ethnic groups.

179. Shannon, William. **The American Irish,** rev. ed. New York: Macmillan, 1966. 484 pp. LC 66-2047. $9.95, pap. $4.95.

Shannon writes well and his account is exciting. It details the Irishman's paths of mobility in the Catholic Church and the city machine. Highly recommended.

180. Stockyards: End of an Era. Amalgamated Meat Cutters & Butcher Workmen of American and WTTW-TV/Indiana University Audio-Visual Center, 1973. 16mm. Color. Sound. 59 min. Rent $20.50. Studs Terkel, Narrator.

A documentary about the Chicago stockyards from the beginning of the 20th century down to the time these stockyards were phased out. Evokes many images of the ethnic communities around the stockyards' perimeter.

181. Uprooted and the Alien-American. Encyclopaedia Britannica Films, 1963. (Structure and Function of the American Government.) 16mm. b/w. Sound. 30 min. Sale $150.

Closely relates to the film *The Golden Door*. The conflict between immigrant and American values is the basis of the discussion. Sheds light on the problems of urbanization and Americanization. The films in the series are all about the same level of difficulty.

182. Urban Lives—The People Within the City. Westinghouse Learning Corp. and Bruner Productions/Westinghouse Learning Corp, 1971. 4 filmstrips, (35 fr. each), color. 4 discs. $66.50 with discs or cassettes.

Suited for audiences from junior high to college. The topics included are "Change and Difference—Chicanos in Los Angeles," "Cleaning Up Other Peoples's Messes—Indians in Phoenix," "East Harlem Is Very Rough—Puerto Ricans in New York City," "Passing Through—Applications in Chicago." As the titles indicate, they may be used to illustrate urban problems or ethnic differences as well as urban living conditions.

183. Vorspan, Max, and Gartner, Lloyd P. History of the Jews of Los Angeles. San Marino, Cal.: Huntington Library, 1970. 362 pp. LC 71-111799. $8.50.

More scholarly than the comparable histories about Jewish communities in American cities. The case of Los Angeles is different in that the community itself grew rapidly in the late 19th and early 20th centuries, making it a community with less than normal traditions in a society with less than normal ones.

Housing in the City

Since the Civil War American cities have experienced increasing segregation based upon income levels. Poor persons steadily have been restricted to the center core of cities where once adequate housing now has become dilapidated and inadequate. The combination of poor services and overcrowded housing has led to physical decay and social pathology. Part of the problem of the cities is how to provide housing for their poor at a cost which they can afford. The problems of poverty and Black migration are thus inextricably tied to the problem of housing.

This section contains books and films detailing the problems of urban housing and the attempts to resolve these problems, mainly through urban renewal. It also has information on the tactics of the poor to attract attention to poor housing through rent strikes and mass demonstrations as well as on the practices of major private developers. The role of legislation in making possible low cost urban housing and in facilitating urban desegregation can also be found. Finally, the economic and political forces which resist change are described.

184. Abandonment of the Cities. NBC Educational Enterprises/Indiana University Audio-Visual Center, 1971. (First Tuesday Series.) 16mm. Color. Sound. 12 min. Rent $7.25. Garrick Utley, narrator.

A segment taken from a commercial television production suitable for high school students and adults. The emphasis is upon neighborhood deterioration in New York City, St. Louis, and Cleveland, and includes in the areas studied comparatively modern low-income public housing. Illustrates the dilemma of those left in the areas and their attempts to cope.

185. Abrams, Charles. Man's Struggle for Shelter in an Urbanizing World. Cambridge, Mass.: MIT Press, 1964. 307 pp. LC 64-16506. $10, pap. $2.95.

Abrams, a well-known urbanologist, looks at shelter and urban land use throughout the world. His book is nontechnical and, while limited to housing, is an excellent introduction to some of the economic problems of the cities.

186. Challenge of Urban Renewal. NBC/Encyclopaedia Britannica Educational Corp., 1967. 16mm. b/w and color. Sound. 28 min. Sale b/w $150, color $300.

Originally an NBC production called *America, the Beautiful.* Like *The House of Man—Our Changing Environment*, it castigates urban decay and suburban sprawl.

It also contains a plan for rebuilding American cities. Simple enough for average abilities.

187. Davies, Richard O. **Housing Reform During the Truman Administration.** Columbia, Mo.: University of Missouri Press, 1966. 197 pp. LC 65-25641. $5.50.

Davies concentrates on the Housing Act of 1949. He touches on the political horsetrading which made the act possible and on the thinking behind the legislation itself. A good starting place to judge the intersection of political forces and social legislation.

188. **The Dehumanizing City . . . and Hymie Schultz.** Honley Thompson/ Learning Corporation of America and Twyman Films. (Searching for Values: A Film Anthology.) 16mm. Color. Sound. 15 min. Rent $25.

A 15-minute segment taken from the commercial film *The Tiger Makes Out.* Available either singly or in the Searching for Values series. Eli Wallach plays the protagonist, Hymie Schultz, who tries to get some satisfaction from urban bureaucracy and fails. He first tries to persuade his landlady to repair his apartment, then the Housing Authority. Neither ploy works and his attempt to go higher is also frustrated. Suitable for high school students and adults.

189. **Detroit—A City Rebuilds.** Society for Visual Education, 1972. (Focus on America—The Midwest.) 1 filmstrip (84 fr.). Color. Sound. Sale $15 with disc, $16.50 with cassette.

Aimed at intermediate and high school students. Shows the efforts in Detroit to solve housing problems by eliminating or repairing substandard units and by building new ones.

190. Dietz, Albert George Henry. **The Building Industry: A Report Prepared for the Commission on Urban Problems.** Cambridge, Mass.: Commission on Urban Problems, 1968. 263 pp. LC NUC 72-4564.

An overview of the construction industry and the problems of providing adequate housing for city dwellers, particularly those with low incomes. A summary of the thoughts of various experts on the subject.

191. Downie, Leonard, Jr. **Mortgage on America.** New York: Praeger, 1974. 243 pp. LC 73-18751. $7.95.

Downie discusses the machinations of housing developers, in the central city and in the suburbs, in order to derive profits through federal tax loopholes. Among the persons he mentions are such failed speculators as Zeckendorf and Wolman. The book is popularly written, and offers insights into why federal low income housing has had such a sorry record and recommendations for controls to improve the situation. Should have wide appeal to a general audience.

192. Ford, James. **Slums and Housing, with Special Reference to New York City: History, Conditions, Policy.** Westport, Conn.: Negro Universities Press, 1971 (originally published in 1936). LC 76-142935. $45.

Reprint of Ford's two-volume work which contains an architectural evaluation in an appendix by I. N. Phelps-Stokes. The study gives an excellent view of the housing problems connected with, and exaggerated by, the Depression. It belongs in libraries with sections on urban problems, particularly housing.

193. Friedman, Lawrence M. **Government and Slum Housing: A Century of Frustration.** Chicago: Rand McNally, 1968. 206 pp. LC 67-21414. $9.95, pap. $4.35.

Using an historical perspective, Friedman details the reasons why governmental intervention to eliminate slums has been unsuccessful. He takes a longer, more historical view of the problem of decrepit housing and consequently is less optimistic about easy panaceas.

194. Greer, Scott. **Urban Renewal and American Cities: The Dilemma of Democratic Intervention.** Indianapolis: Bobbs-Merrill, 1965. 201 pp. LC 65-26544. $5.95, pap. $1.95.

Greer looks at urban renewal with a somewhat critical eye. He is good at pointing to problems and future prospects. Necessary for any study of the process of urban renewal. Can be handled by superior students.

195. Harvard University, Graduate School of Design. **Park Plaza: Impact Prediction and Evaluation of Urban Renewal Proposals.** Cambridge, Mass.: Harvard University Press, 1972. 142 pp.

A product of the Urban Design Program at Harvard during the fall term 1971-72, it is an attempt to set up standards by which projects in urban renewal can be judged. Recommended only for those libraries able to afford extensive collections in design materials.

196. Haar, Charles M., and Iatridis, Demetrius S. **Housing the Poor in Suburbia: Case Studies in Public Policy at the Grass Roots.** Cambridge, Mass.: Ballinger, 1974. 430 pp. LC 73-11477. $12.50.

An examination of the Boston-Providence area and of the reaction in five communities to attempts by federal and state authorities to place housing for low income persons in the suburbs. Specialized one, but useful to those thinking about problems of welfare and of lessening lines of demarcation in housing.

197. Hecht, James L. **Because It Is Right: Integration in Housing.** Boston: Little, Brown, 1970. 290 pp. LC 74-121436. $7.50.

A popularly written defense of integration in housing. Hecht believes in using legal as well as moral pressures to achieve the desired goal. His account is a short one and is suited for general circulation but is unlikely to evoke much scholarly interest.

198. **How to Close Open Housing.** Sunburst Communications. (Mind Blowers.) 1 filmstrip. Color. Sound. 15 min. 1 disc.

Aimed at students on the high school level. The problem raised is discriminatory housing. Interesting, and could be included profitably in an audiovisual department.

199. Lipsky, Michael. **Protest in City Politics: Rent Strikes, Housing, and the Power of the Poor.** Chicago: Rand McNally, 1970. 214 pp. LC 74-98440. $5.95, pap. $4.95.

Lipsky describes how direct action works to achieve the goals of the urban poor in this study of the problems of housing. The volume can be used in a section devoted to housing or to techniques of political action.

200. The Living City. Encyclopaedia Britannica Films and Twentieth Century Fund, 1953. 16mm. b/w. Sound. 26 min. Rent $7.25.

The object here is to explain urban renewal and to stress the need for proper land use. It does advocate urban redevelopment in a simpler fashion than more recent films do.

201. Lubove, Roy. The Urban Community: Housing and Planning in the Progressive Era. American Historical Series. Englewood Cliffs, N.J.: Prentice-Hall, 1967. 148 pp. LC 67-10119. $3.95, pap. $1.60.

Introduces urban planning as well as selected primary sources from the period. Recommended for those who like to go directly to sources.

202. McDonnell, Timothy. The Wagner Housing Act. Chicago: Loyola University Press, 1957. 410 pp. LC 57-12416. $2.95.

The Wagner Act was one of the first to demonstrate concern for public housing. This account delves into the background of the act and the political currents which helped to shape it. Recommended for those libraries which are concerned with housing policies.

203. Mandelker, Daniel R., and Montgomery, Roger, eds. Housing in America; Problems and Perspectives. Indianapolis: Bobbs-Merrill, 1973. 527 pp. LC 73-7689. $16.50, pap. $9.95.

Readings designed for college students. While the selections are scholarly, there is no bibliography, making the book of more limited use. It does center upon the market factors which influence housing and is thus most useful to readers who are interested in the economic area. Should be in those sections of libraries devoted to urban housing and urban economics.

204. Meyerson, Martin, and Banfield, Edward O. Politics, Planning and the Public Interest. New York: Free Press, 1955. 353 pp. LC 55-7335. $7.95, pap. $2.95.

The authors studied the problems inherent in planning Chicago's public housing. Their analysis of the political factors which come into play is an important one.

205. Moore, William. The Vertical Ghetto: Everyday Life in an Urban Project. New York: Random House, 1969. 265 pp. LC 69-20029. pap. $3.95.

As the name suggests, this is a popular account of daily life in a high-rise apartment house. Useful, and ought to attract the attention of the general reader.

206. Neighborhood. Games Central, ABT Associates, 1963. $16.

This simulation game requires four teams consisting of 24 to 36 players, and is specifically designed for students in the elementary grades. The amount of time used in playing the game varies according to the time available. The game derives from the experience of urban development in Boston's North End and is recommended for libraries with a clientele of younger school-age children.

207. **New Chicago.** Graphics Division, Urban Renewal Department, City of Chicago, 1965. 16mm. Color. Sound. 30 min. Free.

A report on the activities and accomplishments of urban renewal in Chicago. While it does place urban renewal in a more favorable light than perhaps is warranted, its depiction of the kinds of changes desired show the purpose of the program quite well despite the slant.

208. **New York (City). Museum of Modern Art. Another Chance for Housing: Low-rise Alternatives; Brownsville, Brooklyn, Fox Hills, Staten Island.** New York: Institute for Architecture and Urban Studies for the New York State Urban Development Corp., 1973. 38 pp. LC 73-78278.

Architectural design shows how modern urban apartments can be had without the problems commonly associated with high-rise buildings. Quite specialized but will appeal to design-oriented readers.

209. **Northwood, Lawrence K., and Barth, Ernest A. T. Urban Desegregation: Negro Pioneers and Their White Neighbors.** Seattle: University of Washington Press, 1965. LC 65-14840. O.P.

A scholarly work attempting to describe the characteristics of those Blacks who first moved into integrated neighborhoods and those whites who greeted or resisted them. Reveals much about the dimensions of the problem in open housing.

210. **Rainwater, Lee. Behind Ghetto Walls: Black Families in a Federal Slum.** Chicago: Aldine, 1970. 446 pp. LC 77-113083. $12.50, pap. $4.95.

Rainwater discusses the problems in a publically subsidized housing development with crime, physical deterioration, and continuing poverty. He concludes that the provision of housing alone is insufficient to solve Black urban dilemmas and that the real need is more money. He urges income redistribution, which he feels will be the only way to dissolve pockets of urban poverty. Rainwater's account is thoughtful, but controversial, and should have wide distribution.

211. **Rowland, Norman, with the special assistance of Margaret Drury. Reston Low Income Housing Demonstration Program.** Reston, Va.: 1969. LC 79-603847.

Reston is a "new" town in Virginia and this report summarizes the attempt to fill in housing for low income families. The conclusions are of interest to planners and urban theorists.

212. **Rubinowitz, Leonard S. Low-Income Housing: Suburban Strategies.** Cambridge, Mass.: Ballinger, 1974. 323 pp. LC 74-1182. $13.50.

Rubinowitz shows how zoning laws, local building codes, and the cost of construction interact to prevent the spread of low income housing to suburban areas. After considering the obstacles, Rubinowitz next indicates what federal, state, and local governments can do to help remove these obstacles. This is not for beginners; it is, however, useful for those interested in dehomogenizing suburban communities.

213. Sagalyn, Lynne B., and Sternlieb, George. **Zoning and Housing Costs: The Impact of Land-Use Controls on Housing Price.** New Brunswick, N.J.: Center for Urban Policy Research, Rutgers—the State University, 1973. 132 pp. LC NUC 73-98540. $8.

This study shows graphically the connections between the regulation of urban land and the resultant prices which individuals have to pay for houses and apartments. The study is best utilized by economists but is a valuable reference work for libraries with sections on urban planning.

214. Schussheim, Morton J. **The Modest Commitment to the Cities.** Lexington, Mass.: Lexington Books, 1974. 232 pp. LC 73-18185. $13.50.

Schussheim writes about housing in cities primarily; however, he also delves into such value-laden topics as to what national goals are and the nature of the social cement that holds American society together. A scholarly account most suited to specialized libraries.

215. Sternlieb, George, and Center for Urban Policy Research Staff. **Housing Development and Municipal Costs.** Urban Policy Research Center. New Brunswick, N.J.: Rutgers—the State University Press, 1973. 378 pp. $12.95.

Based upon empirical, statistical data, this study shows how common sense expectations about housing development and its relation to municipal costs revenue can be wrong. Recommended for research libraries and for professional ones in economics or planning.

216. Sternlieb, George. **The Tenement Landlord.** New Brunswick, N.J.: Urban Studies Center, Rutgers—the State University, 1966. 269 pp. LC 67-63498. $6, pap. $2.95.

A profile of the owners of tenements in one city, Newark, New Jersey. Although limited to this one city, admittedly a bad one in terms of rundown housing, the study does show why slums persist and why it is so difficult to improve the buildings or to remedy the neglect.

217. **The Tenement.** CBS News/Instructional Media Center, Michigan State University and Carousel Films, 1967. 16mm. b/w. Sound. 40 min. Sale $240, rent $8.20.

An attempt to catch the aura of hopelessness which goes with slum life, it succeeds in large measure. The locale is Chicago but it could be any large American city.

218. Von Furstenberg, George, Horowitz, A. R., and Harrison, Bennett, eds. **Patterns of Racial Discrimination.** 2 vols. Lexington, Mass.: Lexington Books, 1974. $16 each, $32 set.

First volume is on housing and the second concerns employment and income. The editors have tried to synthesize as much of the latest research on discrimination as possible, both descriptive and analytical. A valuable reference for scholars and should be ordered with this use in mind.

219. Wilson, James Q., ed. **Urban Renewal: The Record and the Controversy.** Cambridge, Mass.: MIT Press, 1966. 683 pp. LC 66-14344. $12.50, pap. $4.45.

Well-balanced presentation of the pros and cons of urban renewal. Useful for reference and for special assignments.

220. Yes, But Not Here. New York: Macmillan, 1970. $12.

Simulates group conflict in an urban renewal context. This game takes two to three hours to play as well as 20 to 40 participants divided into four to five teams. The level is junior to senior high. Suitable for circulation and is an interesting one to play.

Education in the City

Public education has been regarded as a necessary element in American life since the late nineteenth century. The purpose of public education in the city has been a changing one. It was the institution which transformed the children of immigrant parents into Americans. It taught habits of work necessary for industry and moral virtues essential for participation in American political processes. It also inculcated students into the social categories utilized by the outside community, sometimes consciously but often unconsciously. With the influx of Blacks to the city, the emphasis shifted from Americanizing the immigrant to making the rural Black a middle-class American. The schools in the city reflected the increasing residential and economic segregation characteristic of the times.

This section contains materials on the history of urban education, the problems of urban education, and on some of the techniques which might solve those problems. There are books on busing, on decentralization, on failures of the schools, and on the possibility of social mobility through education.

221. Abbott, Edith, and Breckinridge, Sophonsiba P. **Truancy and Non-attendance in the Chicago Schools: A Study of the Social Aspects of the Compulsory Education and Child Labor Legislation of Illinois.** The Rise of Urban America. New York: Arno Press, 1970. (originally published in 1917). 472 pp. LC 74-112526. $18.

Abbott and Breckinridge were both early social workers and reformers in Chicago. This study contains a history of the fight to obtain compulsory school attendance laws, a description of how the laws were operating in practice, and recommendations for additional changes. The latter included the raising of the minimum working age to 16, the creation of a girl's reform school, and a continuation school to educate illiterate minors. A valuable source for the history of urban education.

222. Ayres, Leonard Porter. **The Cleveland School Survey.** New York: Arno Press, 1970. (originally published in 1917). 363 pp. LC 72-112539. $13.

The summary volume of a set of 26 underwritten by the Cleveland Foundation of the Cleveland school system. This gives an excellent insight into the problems of an urban school system at the turn of the century, confronted as it was with large numbers of immigrant children for whom English was a foreign language. Recommended to libraries wanting source materials in urban history and urban education.

223. Bolner, James, and Shanley, Robert. **Busing: The Political and Judicial Process.** New York: Praeger, 1974. 257 pp. LC 72-86842. $17.50.

Details the problems in desegregating urban schools through busing, particularly as concerns the popular resistance through politics and the legal entanglements which delay the process. It is a scholarly study mainly suited for experts.

224. Channon, Gloria. **Homework: Required Reading for Teachers and Parents.** New York: Outerbridge & Dienstfrey, distributed by E. P. Dutton & Co., 1972. 128 pp. LC 70-126585. $5.95. Dell, pap. $.75.

An account of one teacher's experiences in an East Harlem school and how this teacher, through experimental activities, was able to reach the children in that school. While it does plead a special case, it is an eye-witness account revealing a few of the barriers in urban education.

225. Cohen, Sol. **Progressives and Urban School Reform: The Public Education Association of New York City, 1895-1954.** New York: Teacher's College, Columbia University, 1964. 273 pp. LC 64-18682. $9.95.

Progressive education was closely tied to other reform elements in American society. A demonstration of this can be found in Cohen's study on the Public Education Association of New York City. This organization represented the progressive thrust toward a more democratic and responsible educational establishment. Its growth and ultimate demise provide an insight into the political pressures which beset educational as well as other reforms.

226. Fuchs, Estelle. **Teachers Talk: A View from Within Inner City Schools.** Garden City, N.Y.: Doubleday, 1969. 224 pp. LC 69-13701. pap. $1.45.

A digest of tapes made from the discussions of beginning teachers of their first semesters in inner city schools. The study was funded by Project TRUE (Teachers and Resources for Urban Education) at Hunter College.

227. Greer, Colin. **The Great School Legend.** New York: Basic Books, 1972. LC 74-174824. $7.45. Viking, pap. $2.25.

Greer attacks the idea that the schools have provided the most significant path of mobility for urban minorities such as European immigrants and southern Blacks. He claims the schools have always functioned as agencies for reenforcing social stratification. Can be managed by the general reader and does have valuable insights into the continuing problems of urban education.

228. Greer, Colin, ed. **The Solution as Part of the Problem: Urban Education Reform in the 1960's.** New York: Harper & Row, 1973. 119 pp. LC 73-9081. pap. $1.25.

Articles arguing that the preferred solutions given for problems of urban schools —desegregation, decentralization, and deschooling—have not succeeded. They also go on to suggest why these panaceas failed. The collection is a good one and ought to enlighten almost every reader with a concern over the future of American urban education.

229. Harlan, Louis R. **Separate and Unequal: Public School Campaigns and Racism in the Southern Seaboard States, 1901–1915.** New York: Atheneum, 1968 (originally published in 1958). 290 pp. LC 68-16414. pap. $2.75.

Harlan's study of the controversy over funding Black schools in Virginia, North Carolina, South Carolina, and Georgia during the Progressive Era. Harlan effectively demonstrates how southern white educators argued, on the one hand, for increased funds for education but, on the other hand, were willing to accept lesser amounts of money for Black schools. A necessary historical account of the origins of the problems of urban education.

230. Haskins, James. **Diary of a Harlem Schoolteacher.** New York: Grove Press, 1969. 149 pp. LC 75-101385. pap. $.95.

Haskins presents the experiences of a teacher assigned to a ghetto school in New York City. He graphically shows what the problems are and how much needs to be done in order to achieve a higher quality of education of life. Should appeal to a wide audience.

231. Herndon, James. **The Way It Spozed to Be.** New York: Simon & Schuster, 1968. 188 pp. LC 68-12171. $6.95. Bantam, pap. $.95.

Herndon taught for a year in a Black ghetto school in California. This contains some of his more memorable encounters, giving an insight into the problems of urban Black education as well as the rewards in it. He proposes no easy solutions to existing problems, but does convey a sense of the emotional issues involved.

232. Holt, John. **The Underachieving School.** New York: Pitman, 1969. 209 pp. LC 78-79048. Dell, pap. $.95.

John Holt is a popular and controversial critic of today's schools. In this account, a characteristic one, Holt attacks testing and the high priority placed upon college education and gives his views on why ghetto schools have failed and why students do not learn.

233. Kaestle, Carl F. **The Evolution of an Urban School System, New York City, 1750–1850.** Cambridge, Mass.: Harvard University Press, 1973. 205 pp. LC 72-93950. $12.50.

Kaestle's study is important for those interested in the genesis of the Manhattan educational system. Shows how forces outside the school shaped it into what it was.

234. Katz, Michael B. **Class, Bureaucracy, and Schools: The Illusion of Educational Change in America,** rev. ed. New York: Praeger, 1975. 158 pp. LC 74-9401. $8.50, pap. $3.50.

Like Katz's earlier book (see next title), this one denies that much meaningful change has occurred in education circles and attributes this lack to the conservatism of the educational bureaucracy and to the desires of the significant social groups which control the schools. Easily read and helps explain why educational reform seems so difficult to achieve.

235. Katz, Michael B. **The Irony of Early School Reform: Educational Innovation in Mid-Nineteenth Century Massachusetts.** Cambridge, Mass.: Harvard University Press, 1968. 325 pp. LC 68-17626. $10. Beacon Press, pap. $2.95.

The irony of which Katz speaks in this significant study is that educational reform designed for immigrants and the laboring class was rejected by them but was put through by the social groups composed of those earlier immigrants from England who were now in control. Katz uses three examples: the argument about teaching methods advocated by Horace Mann, the proposal for public high schools at Beverly and Groton, and the attempt to humanize reform schools. A thoughtful look at a past often forgotten.

236. Lazerson, Marvin. **Origins of the Urban School: Public Education in Massachusetts, 1870–1915.** Joint Center for Urban Studies, Cambridge, Mass.: Harvard University Press, 1971. 278 pp. LC 77-168433. $10.

Lazerson studied 10 large Massachusetts school systems, and has a bad opinion of the schools. Moralism of the late 19th century was replaced with vocationalism and patriotic citizenship training. Vocationalism did not accomplish the goal of bringing the schools closer to the practical world of industry; instead, it segregated the classrooms of the poor from those of the middle class.

237. Lutz, Frank W., ed. **Toward Improved Urban Education.** Worthington, Ohio: C. A. Jones, 1970. 343 pp. LC 75-116552. $10.95.

Articles on both theory and practice. Neither seems quite attuned to the realities of the classroom. Recommended only for small libraries in a pinch.

238. Moore, G. Alexander, Jr. **Realities of the Urban Classroom: Observations in the Elementary Schools.** Garden City, N.Y.: Anchor Books, 1967. 188 pp. LC 67-10423. pap. $1.45.

Based on three inner city schools where the students are products of low income homes of ethnic parents. It is aimed at teachers and others who have not had extensive experiences in these areas.

239. Raviteh, Diane. **The Great School Wars: New York City, 1805–1972, A History of the Public Schools as Battlefields of Social Change.** New York: Basic Books, 1973. 449 pp. LC 73-81136. $12.95.

Raviteh has written a history of New York City public schools which reflects the problems the schools have had. She shows how the schools have been connected to the pressing social and political issues of the day. She also shows how little peace the schools have had. Best suited to those with an intensive interest in urban education and the history of education but also will attract a few who are interested in political processes.

240. Resnik, Henry S. **Turning on the System: War in the Philadelphia Public Schools.** New York: Pantheon, 1970. 299 pp. LC 69-20186. $6.95.

Some of the problems which plagued the schools of Philadelphia. Resnik shows sympathy for the people caught in the system but not too much for the system itself. Designed for general audiences and should be acquired with those persons in mind.

241. Rist, Ray C. **The Urban School: A Factory for Failure; A Study of Education in American Society.** Cambridge, Mass.: MIT Press, 1973. 265 pp. LC 73-15580. $12.50.

Rist's study of the socialization of Black ghetto children was based on research he conducted in the St. Louis public schools from 1967 to 1970, and on his resultant doctoral dissertation. The students studied were in kindergarten, first, and second grades and attended de facto segregated schools. Rist's thrust is that the schools not only teach their pupils to read and write but sort them out into the social categories in which they are expected to go. In addition to the research finding, Rist suggests ways in which the latter function of the school can be changed. The major part of this study is technical, but the recommendations are significant enough to have wide circulation.

242. Rogers, David. **110 Livingston Street: Politics and Bureaucracy in the New York City Schools.** New York: Random House, 1968. 584 pp. LC 68-14499. $8.95; pap. $2.45.

A highly critical description of an urban school. Rogers believes much of the school system is devoted to stultifying individual growth and to making automatons of the students. Lively and controversial.

243. Rudman, Herbert C., and Featherstone, Richard L., eds. **Urban Schooling.** New York: Harcourt Brace Jovanovich, 1968. 296 pp. LC 68-55459. $6.95; pap. $4.95.

The focus of the 12 essays is on urban school problems—finance, race, and administration. A useful addition to small libraries, although the authors intended it to be a reader for college students, if they lack other sources on the topic.

244. Schultz, Stanley K. **The Culture Factory; Boston Public Schools, 1789–1860.** New York: Oxford University Press, 1973. 394 pp. LC 72-92297. $11.50.

Schultz examines the goals and methods of public schools in Boston from the inception of the Republic down to the Civil War. Shows how much these urban schools reflected the changing attitudes of the larger Boston community, and is of interest to those concerned with the history of urban education and of American schools in general.

245. Seybolt, Robert Francis. **The Private Schools of Colonial Boston.** New York: Arno Press, 1969 (originally published in 1935). LC 77-89232. $4.

The origins of urban education in the town of Boston. Useful for those interested in the beginnings of schools in American cities as well as in colonial history.

246. Silver, Catherine Bodard. **Black Teachers in Urban Schools; The Case of Washington, D.C.** New York: Praeger, 1973. 222 pp. LC 72-92467. $15.

Silver relies upon questionnaires distributed to Black elementary teachers in Washington, D.C., in 1967. As such, she concentrates upon the reactions of these teachers to the classroom situations in which they find themselves. There is much sociological jargon, thereby limiting appeal to those interested in the sociology of education.

247. Toffler, Alvin, ed. **The Schoolhouse in the City.** New York: Praeger, 1968. Published in cooperation with Educational Facilities Laboratory. LC 68-23358. $5.95; pap. $2.50.

Toffler gained fame through his *Future Shock*; this earlier book is an anthology on urban education. Like *Future Shock*, this emphasizes that there is a crisis in America, one that may have long-range consequences for both its institutions and inhabitants.

248. United States Commission on Civil Rights. **Civil Rights U.S.A.: Public Schools, Cities in the North and West, 1962; Staff Reports.** Westport, Conn.: Greenwood Press, 1968 (originally published in 1962). LC 63-60249. $18.

This reprint discusses the progress of school integration in selected northern and western cities in the early 1960s. A useful report for people researching minority rights, urban education, and urban history.

249. U.S. Urban Education Task Force. **The Urban Education Task Force Report; Final Report of the Task Force on Urban Education to the Department of Health, Education, and Welfare.** New York: Praeger, 1970. 369 pp. LC 74-128106. $12.50.

The Urban Education Task Force's chairman was Wilson C. Riles and the report contains a foreward by Jeffery Cohclan. The Task Force attempted to survey the problems of urban education as they appeared at the end of the 1960s and to make recommendations for the future. Primarily of interest to those doing research or making policy in urban education or urban problems.

250. Wise, Arthur. **Rich Schools, Poor Schools: The Promise of Equal Educational Opportunity.** Chicago: University of Chicago Press, 1968. 228 pp. LC 68-54485. $9, pap. $2.25.

Wise describes in some detail one of the major problems facing urban schools: unequal financing. His account is in some ways a sequal to Conant's *Slums and Suburbs* which touched on the same theme. Rich suburbs with broad tax bases are able to support schools far more lavishly than are urban areas with poverty-stricken inhabitants. Wise takes a position favorable to equal educational resources but admits that the achievement of this goal will be quite difficult.

251. Zimet, Melvin. **Decentralization and School Effectiveness; A Case Study of the 1969 Decentralization Law in New York City.** New York: Teacher's College Press, 1973. 186 pp. LC 73-78731. $8.50, pap. $4.95.

Zimet's analysis is of a school district in the South Bronx which is 65% Puerto Rican and 30% Black. He traces the impact of the 1969 decentralization law upon the school administration and does not claim unqualified success for the concept which was compromised from the start. Vital for those interested in urban education.

Transportation and the Cities

American cities grew as a result of the development of water and land transport. New York City became great because of its port facilities and its tapping of the trans-Appalachian frontier through the Erie Canal. Chicago grew because of the railway network which radiated out from it. Los Angeles' shape today is a function of its freeways and its streetcar system.

Internally, American cities have been greatly affected by the automobile, which, in large measure, drove out competing forms of transportation. The impact of highways and streets crowded with cars has concerned urbanologists, even those of differing philosophical leanings. The search for alternate means of moving people to work in the cities has become almost a separate science in itself. The increasing awareness of the finite limits of fossil fuels has served to intensify that search.

This section, then, concerns the way in which transportation facilities have helped to make American cities in the past and how these facilities are complicating the design and function of contemporary ones.

252. Albion, Robert G. **Square Riggers on Schedule: The New York Sailing Packets to England, France, and the Cotton Ports.** Princeton, N.J.: Princeton University Press, 1938. 371 pp. LC 38-16737. O.P.

Albion discusses the beginnings of scheduled service out of New York City to Europe and its economic impact. While old, it is interesting and ought to appeal to senior high school students who are interested in maritime development.

253. **Anglo America Set H—Industry, Cities, and Transportation.** New York: McGraw-Hill, 1969. Color transparencies.

Transparencies for use mainly in intermediate and high school classes. The titles of the applicable transparencies are "Aviation," "Cities," "Highways," "Manufacturing Areas," and "Railroads and Waterways." The level is not one of great sophistication and the transparencies are recommended only for audiences with limited backgrounds.

254. **Chicago—Transportation Community.** Society for Visual Education, 1970. (Working in U.S. Communities.) 1 filmstrip (57 fr.). Color. Sound.

Shows the connection between the transportation facilities in Chicago and its growth. Grade level is junior high.

255. **Era of Water Commerce.** Affiliated Films/McGraw-Hill, 1960. (American Adventure.) 16 mm. b/w and color. Sound. 11 min. $70 b/w, $140 color.

Covers the period from 1750 to 1850; shows the interaction between water commerce and economic growth, including city development. For junior and senior high school.

256. Gilchrist, David T., ed. **The Growth of Seaport Cities, 1790–1825.** Charlottesville, Va.: University of Virginia Press, 1967. 227 pp. LC 67-21658. $5.

This specialized collection focuses upon the most significant American cities in the first few decades of the Republic. The growth of New York, Boston, and Philadelphia as centers of maritime enterprises tells much about economic inputs into urban development.

257. Gruen, Victor. **The Heart of Our Cities.** New York: Simon & Schuster, 1969. 368 pp. LC 64-13607. $8.50, pap. $3.75.

While primarily concerned with the inner city, Gruen's work is also valuable for its attention to traffic flow. Not too difficult reading.

258. Harvard University. Graduate School of Design. **Movement Systems in the City.** Cambridge, Mass: Harvard University Graduate School of Design, 1965. 39 pp. LC NUC 66-65548.

The academics at the Harvard Graduate School of Design have put together their thoughts on urban transit. Written at a challenging level, of value to those struggling with the problem of automobile traffic in the city.

259. Hilton, George W., and Due, John F. **The Electric Inter-urban Railways in America.** Stanford: Stanford University Press, 1960. 463 pp. LC 60-5383. $15.

Although they have passed from the American scene, the interurbans have a devoted following of antiquarians. Interurbans did not directly change the patterns of city life, but they did tie cities together and affect city design. This history of the movement is recommended for special projects and for railroad buffs.

260. Jensen, Vernon H. **Strife on the Waterfront: The Port of New York since 1945.** Ithaca, N.Y.: Cornell University Press, 1974. 478 pp. LC 73-14137. $18.50.

Jensen's account of labor-management relations in the Port of New York begins with the strike of 1945 and considers a dozen major confrontations. The history of the Port has not been a peaceful one, and Jensen does suggest solutions for the hostility. Admittedly for specialists, *Strife* does shed light on problems beyond that of the docks.

261. Keefer, Louis E., and Witheford, David K. **Urban Travel Patterns for Hospitals, Universities, Office Buildings, and Capitols.** Washington: Highway Research Board, Division of Engineering, 1969. 144 pp. LC 74-601108.

This Highway Research Board report shows traffic flow and is of special interest to those with responsibility for planning or revamping traffic patterns. Because of its highly specialized nature, this publication is most suited to libraries which have urban planners and research persons as clients.

262. Leavitt, Helen. **Superhighway–Superhoax.** Garden City, N.Y.: Doubleday, 1970. 324 pp. LC 70-86890. $6.95.

As the title suggests, this is not an unbiased look at the problem. Leavitt attacks the highway lobby and argues that urban freeways were a mistake. She claims that Americans were sold a bill of goods and that the money for highways would have been better spent elsewhere. Popularly written, and of interest to a wide variety of readers.

263. **Los Angeles—City of Automobiles.** Society for Visual Education, 1972. (Focus on America—The Pacific States.) 1 filmstrip (83 fr.) Sound. 16 min. Sale $10, $5 with disc, $6.50 with cassette.

Aimed at junior high and adult audiences, theme is the congestion, problems, and adjustments which the motorcar has forced upon this southern California metropolis.

264. Lupo, Alan, Colcord, Frank, and Fowler, Edmund P. **Rites of Way: The Politics of Transportation in Boston and the U.S. City.** Boston: Little, Brown, 1971. 294 pp. LC 72-167850. $7.95, pap. $4.95.

A popular account of a dispute between a Boston community where an urban freeway was to be located and the highway planners who wanted to put it there. The study is not objective but it shows the emotions which can be aroused by such planning. Since it speaks to current urban problems, it should be attractive to a number of readers.

265 **Megalopolis.** Indiana University Audio-Visual Center, 1972. (WTTW Earthkeeping Series.) 16mm. Color. Sound. 29 min. Rent $11.50.

Park Forest South in Illinois shows the problems of land use created by the automobile. It is suitable for high school students as well as adults, and is an excellent case study of urban sprawl.

266. Murray, James J., ed. **Urban and Regional Transportation: Surveys and Readings.** Durham, N.C.: Planning-Transportation Associates, 1973. 472 pp. LC NUC 73-114624.

This collection of materials centered on transportation is of most significance to those specializing in planning or upgrading rapid transit systems. It is not designed for the lay reader and, hence, should be included only in libraries with sections on the area.

267. **A New Era in Urban Transportation.** University of Minnesota Audio Visual Library Service, 1973. 1 filmstrip (82 fr.). Color. Sound. Audiotape (5"reel). 35 min.

Suitable for high school to college level audiences. Features planned and recent developments in rapid transit systems and provides visual impressions of these systems.

268. Organization for Economic Cooperation and Development. **Future Directions for Research in Urban Transportation.** Paris: Organization for Economic Cooperation and Development, 1969.

This is a projection of possibilities which ought to be explored in the realm of urban transit. While the report is not confined to American cities, it does have relevance for them. The report is suggested for research libraries as well as for those with collections concentrating upon urban transportation.

269. Rae, John B. **The Road and the Car in American Life.** Cambridge, Mass.: MIT Press, 1971. 390 pp. LC 70-148972. $12.

Rae's fine history of the automobile in America illustrates how technological innovation changed the shape and style of urban life and is an excellent place to begin on the shifting image of the city in the 20th century. Because of its general interest, recommended for most libraries.

270. Reed, Merl E. **New Orleans and the Railroads: The Struggle for Commercial Empire, 1830–1860.** Baton Rouge, La.: Louisiana State University Press, 1966. 172 pp. LC 66-12768.

Reed shows how a city tied to the Mississippi River failed to expand with enough vigor to meet the competition of northern cities. This useful reference tool clearly presents the case that too much reliance on past success means future failure.

271. Rubin, Julius. **Canal or Railroad: Imitation and Innovation in the Response to the Erie Canal in Philadelphia, Baltimore, and Boston.** Philadelphia: American Philosophical Society, 1961. 106 pp. LC 61-16538.

One of the most significant books in the unit because it describes how various urban communities reacted to the challenge of technological advance. For sophisticated students only.

272. **Saga of the Erie Canal.** Coronet Films, 1966. (Cultural Heritage Series.) 16 mm. b/w and color. Sound. Rental available from Indiana University. Rent, $4.75 color, $3.15 b/w.

Combines technical discussion—the building of canal locks—with the impact of the canal on the popular mind—songs about the canal. Highly recommended for junior and senior high school students.

273. **Santa Fe and the Trail.** Encyclopedia Britannica Films, 1963. 16 mm. Color. Sound. 20 min. Sale $210.

The impact of Spanish culture on the settlements of the Southwest is the theme. A good film in the sense that it shows alternate ways of looking at city planning. For junior and senior high school students.

274. Scheiber, Harry N. **Ohio Canal Era. A Case Study of Government and the Economy, 1820–1861.** Athens, Ohio: Ohio University Press, 1969. 430 pp. LC 68-20936. $12.

Scheiber's interest is in the interplay between government and business, but he also shows how economic growth in cities was dependent upon transport facilities. For research projects.

275. Shaw, Ronald. **Erie Water West: A History of the Erie Canal, 1792–1854.** Lexington, Ky.: University of Kentucky Press, 1966. 449 pp. LC 66-16231. $8.

The definitive work on the Erie Canal and the one which students should read first.

276. Streeter, Floyd B. **Prairie Trails and Cow Towns, The Opening of the Old West**. New York: Devin-Adair, 1963. 214 pp. LC 63-15595. $6.95.

Suitable for junior high school and above, particularly for a sense of town location and design.

277. Taylor, George R. **The Transportation Revolution, 1815–1860**. Economic History of the United States. New York: Harper, 1951. 490 pp. NUC 70-99222. pap. $3.95.

Detailed aspects of transport—canal, rail, and turnpike. For reference only.

278. **Third Avenue El**. Contemporary Films/McGraw-Hill, 1957. 16 mm. Color. Sound. 11 min. Rent $7.50.

Provides a nostalgic ride through old New York City on the elevated railroad, which has since been torn down. Not the least of the attractions is the sound track—the music of Haydn played by Wanda Landowska on the harpsichord. Conveys a sense of the city as might have been experienced by a commuter years ago.

279. Walker, James Blaine. **Fifty Years of Rapid Transit: 1864 to 1917**. New York: Arno Press, 1970 (originally published in 1918). 291 pp. LC 70-112581. $14.

James Blaine Walker was a member of the Public Service Commission of New York City from 1908 to 1934 and, in this reprint he details the problems encountered in the development of the subway from the horse-drawn trolleys to the cable car and the elevated train. The villain is the politician who, more than technological difficulties, hindered and slowed the rise of efficient rapid transit systems. Recommended for collections on urban history and urban transit systems.

280. Warner, Sam Bass, Jr. **Streetcar Suburbs: The Process of Growth in Boston, 1870–1900**. New York: Howard University Press, 1962. LC 62-17228. rev. 2. Atheneum, pap. $2.95.

Well illustrated and not difficult, this study is basic to understanding the beginnings of urban sprawl, the interconnection between transportation and suburbs, and the process of residential segregation by income groups. Highly recommended for senior high students.

281. **You Can't Get There from Here**. National Educational Television/Indiana University Audio-Visual Center, 1965. (The Glory Trail.) 16mm. b/w. Sound. 30 min. Rent $6.75.

Traces the development of transportation and communication facilities in the West. It is good on the impact of the railroad and shows some urban development. For junior and senior high school.

282. Zwerling, Stephen. **Mass Transit and the Politics of Technology: A Study of BART and the San Francisco Bay Area**. New York: Praeger, 1974. 159 pp. LC 73-15202. $14.

The experimental rapid transit system which was to revolutionize the Bay area has not lived up to its advance billing. Zwerling attempts to explain why by showing the problems BART faced and the compromises which the advocates of the system had to make. Belongs in sections on urban transportation and its problems.

Urbanization and Suburbanization

The processes of urbanization and suburbanization extend back in the American past almost to the beginnings of the Republic. After the Revolution, American towns rapidly became cities; the 19th-century growth of these cities equaled that of any other cities in the world. At the same time, however, there was a growth of outlying communities which would be equivalent to suburbs today. Brooklyn was an independent city in its own right in the first half of the 19th century. It functioned in part as a bedroom community for Manhattan and, like later suburbs, was eventually incorporated into a larger entity.

The process of suburbanization accelerated in the last half of 19th century, and by 1920, when the United States Census first showed the urban populace to be a majority, suburbs were growing faster than central cities. A second phenomenon of great consequence was the growing inability of central cities to annex suburbs. By 1950, some central cities had actually declined in population and by 1970, this decline was more marked. By 1970, some of the older suburbs were experiencing the same drop.

This section touches upon a few of the elements which contribute to both urbanization and suburbanization in the United States as well as in other parts of the world. It includes materials on the life and behavior of persons living in cities and in the suburbs, as well as accounts of the difficulties caused by the removal of affluent middle-class taxpayers from central cities to the suburbs. Other materials on the same processes can be found in the sections on urban history and urban sociology.

283. **American Dichotomy—City and Suburb.** A Series. Westinghouse Learning Corp., 1971. 6 filmstrips (130 fr. each). Color. Sound. 6 discs. Sale $76.50 set.

Paterson, New Jersey, is used as an example of the symbiotic relationship between new suburbs and an older central city. Intended to appeal to persons from the junior high school level up, so are somewhat elementary.

284. Arnold, Joseph L. **The New Deal in the Suburbs: A History of the Greenbelt Town Program, 1935–1954.** Columbus, Ohio: Ohio State University Press, 1971. 272 pp. LC 74-141494. $10.

Roosevelt's administration was one of the first to attempt federally planned urban communities which utilized rural settings and urban advantages. This is an account of that attempt, its successes and failures and the public response to it. Necessary for those interested in the origins of New Deal planning.

285. Berger, Bennett M. **Working Class Suburb: A Study of Auto Workers in Suburbia.** Berkeley, Cal.: University of California Press, 1960. 143 pp. LC 60-11846. $7.50, pap. $2.50.

An intensive study of a community bound together by a common occupation by a noted sociologist. While specialized, it does reveal the impact or lack of impact of a suburban environment upon a rather socially homogeneous group.

286. Chandler, Tertius, and Fox, Gerald. **3,000 Years of Urban Growth.** New York: Academic Press, 1974. 431 pp. LC 72-84378. $28.

According to the authors, this study took 30 years to research. It is massive, though not extraordinarily long, and expensive. It has an excellent introduction by Lewis Mumford, but its main value lies in the enormous numbers of statistics the authors have accumulated on cities of the world, past and present. There are, in addition, maps and a bibliography. Highly recommended as a reference tool.

287. **City I.** Urban Systems Simulation, Washington Center for Metropolitan Studies.

The game involves the social, economic, and political relationships of an urban center and its three suburbs. Sophisticated, and recommended for senior high students and adults.

288. **City II.** Urban Systems Simulation, Washington Center for Metropolitan Studies.

Revised version of *City I*, which was based on Feldt's *Cornell Land Use Game*. *City II* attempts to engender a social conscience in the player and adds a construction industry and an adequate transportation system to the economic sector. It also has additional political jurisdictions. The University of Maryland had a contract from the U.S. Office of Education to develop a version of *City II* for high school use. The program was tested in selected high schools in the Washington, D.C., area beginning in the fall of 1969 and is now available for general use.

289. Davis, Kingsley, comp. **Cities: Their Origin, Growth, and Human Impact.** Readings from *Scientific American*. San Francisco: Freeman, 1973. 297 pp. LC 73-2575. $12, pap. $5.50.

Davis has put together a selection of essays from *Scientific American* and has added an introduction of his own. The essays, as might be expected from the nature of the magazine, do reflect recent scholarly opinion on urban development and problems but are written so as to be understood by the educated layperson. Useful for smaller libraries without extensive collections, but will not contribute much to larger libraries with more specialized collections.

290. Douglass, Harlan Paul. **The Suburban Trend.** The Rise of Urban America. New York: Arno Press, 1970 (originally published in 1925). 340 pp. LC 73-124478. $14.

Surprisingly contemporary, Douglass discusses the reasons for suburban growth as well as the problems brought about by this growth. He concludes that suburbs are tied to the city but are not of it. Recommended for students of population trends and city growth.

291. Downs, Anthony. Opening Up the Suburbs: An Urban Strategy for America. New Haven, Conn.: Yale University Press, 1973. 219 pp. LC 76-158984. $7.95, pap. $2.95.

Downs proposes to end residential segregation by income and to integrate low cost housing in middle income residential areas. He feels that his program would diminish the problems of the schools in racial mixture and would eliminate the need for busing. A provocative study which deserves wide circulation.

292. Ecology and Man. McGraw-Hill. $45.00 for each set of 6, $8.50 for each filmstrip.

There are three sets to this program. The first defines ecosystems; the second shows five ecosystems and their structures; and the third shows applied ecology. The last is most appropriate to urban life, though the other two are excellent. High school and adult level. Eighteen filmstrips, three sets:

Set No. 1

"Introduction to Ecology" LC FiA 66-2610
"Changes in Ecosystems" LC FiA 67-2819
"Energy Relationships" LC FiA 66-2631
"Habitats and Niches" LC FiA 66-2636
"Populations and Biomass" LC FiA 66-3419
"Adaptations to Environment" LC FiA 66-2816

Set No. 2

"The Forest Biome" Part 1, LC FiA 67-2827
"The Forest Biome" Part 2, LC FiA 67-2828
"The Grassland Biome" LC FiA 67-2824
"Fresh Water Ecology" LC FiA 67-2829
"Seacoast Ecology" LC FiA 66-3420

Set No. 3

"Man-Managed Ecosystems" LC FiA 66-3416
"The Management of Water" LC FiA 66-3418
"The Management of Soil" LC FiA 66-3417
"The Ecology of Farming" LC FiA 67-2825
"Competitive Land Uses" LC FiA 67-2823
"Human Ecology" LC FiA 66-3413

293. Ecology of the Urban Environment—Air Pollution. Urban Media Materials, 1972. 6 filmstrips (35 fr. each). Color. $4.95 each, $28.50 set.

A set of 6 filmstrips, the topics are "Air Pollution," "Housing Patterns," "Population," "Urban Wildlife," "Water Supply," and "Sanitation." The level is elementary, as the series is designed for elementary and junior high. Recommended only as a basic, simple introduction to the topic.

294. Gans, Herbert J. The Levittowners: Ways of Life and Politics in a New Suburban Community. New York: Pantheon, 1967. 474 pp. LC NUC 71-61631. $10. Random House, pap. $2.95.

Studies reactions of inhabitants of a suburban community which was created after the Second World War.

295. Ginger, Ray, ed. **Modern American Cities.** Chicago: Quadrangle, 1969. 242 pp. LC 70-78318. $6.95, pap. $2.45.

Selections from the *New York Times*, divided into three parts: "Boomtowns and Placid Places," "Some Characteristics of Cities," and "Toward the Future of Cities." A good collection which can be handled by senior high school students.

296. Kramer, John, comp. **North American Suburbs: Politics, Diversity, and Change.** Berkeley, Cal.: Glendessary Press, 1972. 330 pp. LC 70-178881. $7.95, pap. $4.95.

Articles treating the forces operative in suburbs of Canada and the United States and giving a general overview of why these suburbs are what they are. Belongs on the shelves of general libraries, although some of the essays are quite sophisticated.

297. Masotti, Louis H., and Hadden, Jeffrey K., eds. **Suburbia in Transition.** New York: New Viewpoints, 1974. 345 pp. LC 73-5907. pap. $4.95.

The editors of this anthology have tried to achieve balance in the articles and as wide a coverage as possible in the short space available. They have succeeded quite well, and the collection is a useful starting point for readers concerned with changing suburbs.

298. Masotti, Louis H., and Hadden, Jeffrey K., eds. **The Urbanization of the Suburb.** Urban Affairs Annual Reviews. Beverly Hills, Cal.: Sage Publications, 1973. 640 pp. LC 72-98038. $22.50.

This sixth volume in the series explores the way in which suburbs are coming to resemble cities. The articles look at suburbs from historical, sociological, and political science viewpoints. There are, in addition, selections on suburban police, zoning, economic characteristics, and families in the suburbs. A useful book and, like the series, should have wide distribution.

299. **Nineteen Seventy Census of Population.** San Jose, Cal.: Lansford Publishing Co. Color. Transparencies.

This set of transparencies was made to illustrate the census of 1970 and shows population trends quite well. There are four titles which have have an urban emphasis: "Cities of the U.S. Ranked by Size," "Population Density of the U.S.," "Population Distribution in Metropolitan and Non-Metropolitan Areas," and "Urban and Rural Population, 1790-1960."

300. Rosenwaike, Ira. **Population History of New York City.** Syracuse, N.Y.: Syracuse University Press, 1972. 224 pp. LC 75-39829. $12.

New York City's population variation through time as well as the racial, ethnic, and religious backgrounds of that population. The author also treats physical mobility. Among his findings are that New York City lost much of its native born population to the rest of the U.S., that the movement to the suburbs began in 1830, and that poverty and ghettoization were not always correlated with high birth and death rates.

301. Smalltown USA. NBC/Encyclopaedia Britannica Films, 1965. 16mm. b/w. Sound. 27 min. Sale $150.

Looks at four representative small towns which are vanishing because of changing industrial patterns, migration to larger urban areas, and automation. Useful for students who live in cities or small towns, because it shows alternative ways of life.

302. Sobin, Dennis P. **The Future of the American Suburbs: Survival or Extinction?** Port Washington, N.Y.: Kennikat, 1971. 152 pp. LC 72-154034. $8.95.

A popularly written attempt to project present trends into future prospects. The author has put together 10 essays which range from "Suburbs Past and Present" to "The Suburban Mystique," and which are concise, well-written expositions of history and sociology. Ought to attract the general reader and is recommended for most libraries.

303. Suburbia—How America Lives. Audio-Visual Narrative Arts, 1972. 2 filmstrips (73 and 69 fr.). b/w. Sound. 12 and 11 mins.

The first part is "Moving Out—The Dream" and the second is "Moving In—The Reality." The level is that of the intermediate grades up. As the titles suggest, they concern the ideal of the suburb and the reality. They also show how suburbs developed, in what ways they differ, and in what direction they are headed. More descriptive than analytical but they do provide some critical insights.

304. Taylor, Graham R. **Satellite Cities: A Study of Industrial Suburbs.** The Rise of Urban America. New York: Arno Press, 1970 (originally published in 1915). 333 pp. LC 70-112576. $15.

Taylor's study was a pioneering effort to look at the 19th-century industrial suburb. He examined Gary, Indiana, Pullman (near Chicago), Norwood, Ohio, East St. Louis, Illinois, and Fairfield, Alabama. He found that none of these worked very well, that private development and individual initiative both had resulted in less than desirable communities. Should be in sections on urban history and urban planning.

305. United States. President's Task Force on Suburban Problems. **Final Report.** Charles M. Haar, ed. Cambridge, Mass.: Ballinger, 1974. 212 pp. LC 74-9612. $12.50.

The report of President Johnson's task force created in 1967. It is both descriptive and analytical; recommends political and economic programs for the federal government. Not easy to read, but should be available for reader reference.

306. Urban Development. Filmstrip House, 1970. (Culture of Regions: New England.) 1 filmstrip (63 fr.). Color. Sound. 15 min. Series of 4 filmstrips. $45 with discs, $49 with cassettes.

Brief coverage showing the physical features of several New England cities. Must be purchased as a set.

307. Wood, Robert C. **Suburbia: Its People and Their Politics.** Boston: Houghton Mifflin, 1959. 340 pp. LC 58-9078. $6, pap. $4.75.

Wood, a professor of political science at MIT, director of the Harvard-MIT Joint Center for Urban Studies, and a chairman of the President's Task Force on Metropolitan and Urban Problems, analyzes the suburban population and finds it motivated by an older, small town ideology out of keeping with American metropolitan growth. Recommended for the informed reader.

Crime and the Police

Uniformed police in organized police departments made their appearance in American cities in the middle of the 19th century. Prior to that time, crime was controlled, if at all, by an informal segregation of so-called criminal elements to certain parts of the city, by night watchmen or constables, and by private investigators. By the 20th century, cities universally had police departments, but already questions about the role of the police had arisen. What was the interaction between police and criminals? How could or should police be controlled? William Graham Sumner, speaking in opposition to America's imperialistic adventures, asked how natives in a foreign country could be governed if the police in New Haven could not. The questions persisted and assumed new urgency in the 1960s with civil disorder and police reaction. As yet, there have been no definitive answers.

This section includes materials on both sides, criminal and police, with first-hand accounts from representatives of each. It also has information on the history of police in various communities and of attempts to reform and reorganize police systems. There are also selections which point to future problems and trends.

308. Adams, Thomas F. **Law Enforcement, an Introduction to the Police Role in the Community,** 2nd ed. Englewood Cliffs, N.J.: Prentice-Hall, 1973. 366 pp. LC 72-5601. $11.95.

Basically a text used in criminal justice classes and curricula, it is for beginners who wish to understand what the functions, major and minor, of a police department are. Belongs in libraries which lack other materials on this topic.

309. Agar, Michael. **Ripping and Running: A Formal Ethnography of Urban Heroin Addicts.** New York: Academic Press, 1973. 173 pp. LC 72-12214. $9.50.

An anthropological look at hard drug users in cities. Agar's book is an attempt to classify the addicts and to find reasons for their behaviors as well as to describe them. Recommended for libraries with sections on urban problems and urban crime.

310. Ahern, James F. **Police in Trouble: Our Frightening Crisis in Law Enforcement.** New York: Hawthorn, 1972. 260 pp. LC 78-179115. $6.95.

Ahern concludes that the whole police system is in danger of collapse. He overstates the problem but may be of value in alerting readers to some of the difficulties which plague law enforcement officials. Recommended with the above reservation in mind.

311. Astor, Gerald. **The New York Cops: An Informal History.** New York: Charles Scribners Sons, 1971. 249 pp. LC 73-123856. $6.95.

A well-written popular account of New York's finest suited for high school students and the general reader. The book makes no major suggestions nor does the author conclude that New York's Police Department is ready to collapse. Libraries should buy this for readers interested in how the police came to be what they are.

312. Banton, Michael. **The Policeman in the Community.** New York: Basic Books, 1964. 276 pp. LC 64-22857. $7.

Banton is a sociologist who has studied police forces in the field in both English and American cities. He points out how different assumptions regarding the police have worked to create forces of quite different character in these communities. Basic for anyone interested in the social dynamics of law enforcement agencies.

313. Bent, Alan Edward. **The Politics of Law Enforcement.** Lexington, Mass.: Lexington Books, 1974. 203 pp. LC 73-18415. $12.50.

Bent uses an organizational model to study police behavior and he concludes that the police system needs to be tightly controlled to prevent its discretionary authority from being abused. The bureaucratic tendency in the police departments makes such control difficult even though it is necessary. Best suited to those readers familiar with the vocabulary of organization theory, and recommended for libraries with a scholarly clientele.

314. Black, Algernon D. **The People and the Police.** New York: McGraw-Hill, 1968. 246 pp. LC 68-30971. $6.95.

Interaction between the public expectation of police goals and behavior and the police expectation of the same goals and behavior is the topic of this study. Black shows the frustration of the police and the ignorance of the public, both of which lead to tensions and misunderstandings. Can be handled by the general reader, but a familiarity with basic sociological premises would help.

315. Boston. City Council. Joint Special Committee Appointed to Investigate the Official Conduct of the Members of the Board of Police Commissioners. **Reports.** New York: Arno Press, 1971 (originally published in 1881). LC 78-156279. $7.

An 1881 investigation of the police commissioners in Boston showing the intent of urban reformers to rationalize and professionalize police administration. Recommended for libraries with a need for original source materials in urban or police history.

316. Brown, Michael K., and Johnson, Paula. **Evaluation of the UCLA Community-Police Relations Training Program, 1970/71.** Los Angeles: Institute of Government and Public Affairs, UCLA, 1971. LC 72-610679.

The Watts riot of 1965 focused much attention on the bad relations between the Black community and the police of Los Angeles. Since the mid-1960s, the Los Angeles Police Department has made an effort to improve its image in the community and to gain an insight into why the community felt as it did. This report is a look at the effectiveness of the program, and belongs in libraries with sections on urban police problems or practices.

317. Cahalane, Cornelius F. **The Policeman.** The Rise of Urban America. New York: Arno Press, 1970 (originally published in 1923). 354 pp. LC 75-112529. $14.

Cornelius Cahalane was a New York City police inspector in the early 20th century. Cahalane intended his book as a kind of manual for practicing policemen. With this as his goal, he included advice on how to solve the problems which recurred in the everyday life of the police officer. This reprint belongs in research libraries as well as those with collections on police.

318. Chevigny, Paul. **Police Power: Police Abuses in New York City.** New York: Pantheon, 1969. 298 pp. LC 68-26044. Random House, pap. $2.20.

Chevigny wrote from experiences he had as an attorney for the New York Civil Liberties Union. The book is not flattering to the police, as the author documents case after case of police behavior ranging from dishonesty to illegality; it is hard-hitting and shows the seamy side of one metroplitan police force.

319. Cho, Yong H. **Public Policy and Urban Crime.** Cambridge, Mass.: Ballinger, 1974. 224 pp. LC 74-1145. $13.50.

A mathematical study using a multiple regression model for analyzing the impact a policy has on the rate of any particular crime. The study considers crime first, the effects control policies have on crime, and the effects social policies have on crime. A sophisticated study, suited to research and university libraries with informed readers.

320. Christian, Charles. **A Brief Treatise on the Police of the City of New York.** The Rise of Urban America. New York: Arno Press, 1970 (originally published in 1812). 32 pp. LC 76-112548. $5.

Crime in New York City at the beginning of the 19th century. Christian describes the extensive criminal activity in the city and proposes, as solutions, a better police patrol system, a new city prison, a reduction in the number of saloons, a new female penitentiary, more control over pawn shops, and registers for domestic servants. An interesting and valuable book for students of urban and police history.

321. Costello, Augustine E. **Our Police Protectors: A History of the New York Police From the Earliest Period to the Present Times.** Montclair, N.J.: Patterson Smith, 1972. Municipal Police History, (originally published in 1885). 572 pp. LC 79-129324. $16.

Theodore N. Ferdinand has introductory remarks to this reprint that ought to be included in libraries needing source materials on urban history or urban police.

322. Cray, Ed. **The Enemy in the Streets, Police Malpractice in America.**
Garden City, N.Y.: Anchor Books, 1972. 345 pp. LC 72-175408. pap. $2.50.
Cray takes an unsympathetic view of the police in this book, documenting
police failings with examples of false arrests, brutality, and illegal searches.
Popularly written, it is more devoted to revealing problems than to solving them.

323. **Crime in the Cities.** NBC/Encyclopaedia Brittanica Educational Corp.,
1966. 16 mm. b/w. Sound. 28 min. Sale $150, rent $7.75.
Examines the connection between prejudice, segregation, and crime as well as
the distinctions between crimes against persons and property. Timely and useful
in current problems classes.

324. Daley, Robert. **Target Blue: An Insider's View of the N.Y.P.D.** New
York: Delacorte, 1971. 562 pp. LC 73-4258. $8.95. Dell, pap. $1.75.
Problems, real and imaginary, faced by the policeman in New York City. Daley
documents very well the general impression among the police that they are
exposed and vulnerable, that they lack support from citizens whom they are
sworn to protect, and that they are the thin line of defense of society from
barbarians. Has had wide circulation and has interested many readers.

325. Dawley, David. **A Nation of Lords: The Autobiography of the Vice Lords.**
Garden City, N.Y.: Anchor Books, 1973. 200 pp. LC 72-89672. pap. $1.95.
David Dawley, who was an organizer for the Vice Lords, depicts the reasons
for their growth in Chicago, their social organization, their encounters with
other gangs, their attractions, and their transformation into a more positive
group. Dawley is sympathetic to the group and does show the strength of
ghetto gangs. Because of the directness of the oral history approach, this ought
to have wide appeal.

326. Flinn, John J. **History of the Chicago Police.** Municipal Police History.
Montclair, N.J.: Patterson Smith, 1973 (originally published in 1887). 605 pp.
LC 75-172577. $17.50.
Mark H. Haller wrote the introduction to this volume. Flinn's history, like the
others in the series, does not disclose the whole truth about police operations
in the 19th century but does provide insights into the operation of the city
police force as well as the city in general.

327. Folsom, De Francias. **Our Police: A History of the Baltimore Force.**
Municipal Police History. Montclair, N.J.: Patterson Smith, 1974 (originally
published in 1888). LC 75-172585. $17.50.
With a new introduction by Theodore N. Ferdinand, this reprint is the kind of
resource book which libraries wanting collections in urban history ought to
possess.

328. Gardiner, John A. **Traffic and the Police; Variations in Law-Enforcement
Policy.** Cambridge, Mass.: Harvard University Press, 1969. 176 pp. LC 69-
18030. $6.
Gardiner addresses himself to the question of who gets ticketed and arrested
for traffic offenses and why. The variations in charges for the same offense

are amply demonstrated. A short volume belonging in libraries with collections on urban law enforcement.

329. The Godfather—For All the Families. Family Games/Urban Systems, 1971. $15.

A simulation game also available at retail outlets. It parallels the novel and the movie *The Godfather* and the game *Monopoly*. The object is to gain control of neighborhood rackets. The game requires two or more players and is suitable for high school students or adults. Fun, although touching on the sensational.

330. Hansen, David A. Police Ethics. Springfield, Ill.: C.C. Thomas, 1973. 78 pp. LC 72-87003. pap. $3.50.

Handbook designed to guide policemen in the dilemmas they face in their occupation. It can be ordered for the general reader who is interested in the nature of police work.

331. Jacob, Herbert. Urban Justice; Law and Order in American Cities. Englewood Cliffs, N.J.: Prentice-Hall, 1973. 145 pp. LC 73-399. $6.95, pap. $3.95.

Jacob's book is a survey of the problems of administering justice in cities. As such, it is suitable to general readers wanting an overview of the major trends and difficulties. Recommended for smaller libraries which lack resources in this particular field.

332. Juris, Hervey A., and Feville, Peter. Police Unionism; Power and Impact in Public-Sector Bargaining. Lexington, Mass.: Lexington Books, 1973. 228 pp. LC 73-7995. $12.50.

Juris and Feville studied police unions in 22 cities in the United States and based this account on their field experiences. They tried to assess the impact police unions had on the formation of law enforcement policy, on the perogatives of the chief of police, on the professionalization of the police, and on the sensibilities of the community. They conclude that police unions have, for the most part, been beneficial and have not frustrated the goals of the city administrators. Highly recommended for libraries with sections on the urban police.

333. Lane, Roger. Policing the City: Boston, 1822–1885. Cambridge, Mass.: Harvard University Press, 1967. 299 pp. LC 67-17313. $9.50. Atheneum, pap. $3.25.

While Lane covers more than the era under consideration, he does outline in detail the changes in one American city in the organization and function of the police department. Boston had peculiar problems—the mass immigration of the Irish is one—but it was typical in its solution to the pressing dilemma of public order. The best study on the development of modern police for students with this interest.

334. Lipsky, Michael, ed. Law and Order: Police Encounters. Chicago: Transaction Books, 1970. 144 pp. LC 78-115947. $7.95, pap. $2.95.

Lipsky has taken six articles from the semipopular sociology journal *Trans-Action* and put them in a book. These are articles by scholars but written in a popular style; hence they are suited most to an audience of enlightened laypersons. Recommended for libraries which have demands for articulate books on urban social issues.

335. McLennan, Barbara N., ed. **Crime in the Urban Society** [by] Joseph S. Clark [and others]. Port Washington, N.Y.: Kennikat/Dunellen, 1970. 151 pp. LC 73-122595. $8.95, pap. $3.95.

McLennan is a political scientist and her book is edited from that perspective. It contains articles by specialists in the field of law enforcement and criminal problems. Sophisticated, it will appeal only to a specialized audience; it ought to be in those libraries with a college student clientele.

336. Missouri General Assembly. Joint Committee of the General Assembly Appointed to Investigate the Police Department of the City of St. Louis. **Report**. New York: Arno Press and the *New York Times*, 1971 (originally published in 1868). 575 pp. LC 70-154587. $16.

The results of an 1868 investigation of the St. Louis Police Department. In post-Civil War America, reformers were conscious of the problems inherent in policing metropolises and of the need to take as much politics as possible out of the departmental practices. Useful for libraries with collections on urban history or the history of police forces.

337. New York (City) Knapp Commission. **The Knapp Commission Report on Police Corruption**. New York: Braziller, 1973. 283 pp. LC 73-76969. $9.95, pap. $4.95.

This report has aroused considerable interest as well as controversy. It is a study of the New York City Police Department which shows how widespread corrupt activities really are among New York's Finest. While most attractive to specialists on the problems of police in an urban community, it also has much material for the informed lay reader.

338. Niederhoffer, Arthur. **Behind the Shield: The Police in Urban Society**. Garden City, N.Y.: Doubleday, 1967. 253 pp. LC 67-16896. pap. $1.95.

Sociologist Niederhoffer spent 21 years in the New York City Police Department. Using this experience, he considers the correct training for policemen, their exposure and their susceptibility to corruption, their reaction to civilian review boards, and the predilection for conservative politics. Not difficult and quite readable, it is suitable for informed laypersons.

339. Norris, Donald F. **Police-Community Relations: A Program That Failed**. Studies in Social and Economic Process. Lexington, Mass.: Lexington Books, 1973. 136 pp. LC 73-948. $10.

Norris' account is more limited that the title suggests. It is actually the history of an experiment with a police-community unit in Richmond, Virginia. As a sample study, it has some value but it is not a survey of the problem.

340. **Police and Law Enforcement, 1972; An AMS Anthology**, 2 vols. James T. Curran et al., comp. New York: AMS Press, 1973. 432 pp. LC 73-7210. vol. 1 $20, vol. 2 $15, set $35.

A compendium of recent essays on various facets of police work. The book is divided into sections on the police in society, police-community relations, police reform, and police management, education and training. Best suited to smaller libraries which lack the original materials from which these selections were taken.

341. Radelet, Louis A. **The Police and the Community.** Criminal Justice. Beverly Hills, Cal.: Glencoe Press, 1973. 751 pp. LC 72-93310. $12.95.

Radelet is the director of the National Center on Police and Community Relations and this shows the imprint of his experiences. Comprehensive and long, it was designed for use as a college textbook, hence it is most suited to libraries which have only limited sources in the area.

342. **Raid.** ABT Associates. $20.

This simulation game involves the protection rackets in the slums and is the less sophisticated version of the AGIL/COIN model designed for adults. *Raid* is aimed at junior and senior high school students. It takes one hour to play and calls for 5, 10, or 15 players. It does provide insight into the kinds of crimes which occur most frequently in areas of poor housing and poverty. Because of this insight, it is recommended for those libraries desiring to acquaint middle-class persons with the difficulties encountered by poor people.

343. Reiser, Martin. **The Police Department Psychologist.** Springfield, Ill.: C.C. Thomas, 1972. 119 pp. LC 74-190335. $6.75.

A how-to-do-it book for police psychologists about screening materials to use in the employment of policemen. Specialized and probably inappropriate for general city collections.

344. Reiss, Albert, Jr. **The Police and the Public.** New Haven, Conn.: Yale University Press, 1971. 228 pp. LC 78-158143. $12.50, pap. $2.95.

Reiss, along with a team of associates, observed police operations in four cities by riding along with police on their patrols. They found indications that police had little regard for public opinion and that one in five did take illegal gifts even while they knew they were being watched. A significant sociological study of the police which ought to be in nearly every library.

345. Richardson, James. **New York Police: Colonial Times to 1901.** New York: Oxford University Press, 1970. 332 pp. LC 78-83049. $10.

Traces the development of the professional police force in New York City from early beginnings down to the turn of the century, including the changing problems and conflicting jurisdictions of city and state governments. An excellent title for special studies.

346. Ruchelman, Leonard, ed. **Who Rules the Police?** New York: New York University Press, 1973. 298 pp. LC 72-96430. $11.95.

Excerpts taken from scholarly journals, books, and commission reports which focus upon the problem of the limits of police power and supervision of the police. The collection provides opinions from several vantage points, but takes no definitive position of its own. Smaller libraries might find it useful.

347. Saunders, Charles B., Jr. **Upgrading the American Police; Education and Training for Better Law Enforcement.** Washington, D.C.: Brookings Institution, 1970. 182 pp. LC 70-108836. $6.95.

Saunders' report contains recommendations for improving urban police enforcement largely through increased professionalization, better screening of recruits, and the imposition of higher standards of education for entrance. It is partly responsive to the urban disturbances of the 1960s which revealed many glaring weaknesses in city police departments. Should be in libraries whose readers are interested or involved with the improvement of the human element in police work.

348. Savage, Edward H. **Police Records and Recollections: or Boston by Daylight and Gaslight for 240 Years.** Municipal Police History. Montclair, N.J.: Patterson Smith, 1970 (originally published in 1873). 406 pp. LC 74-154048. $12.50.

Roger Lane has an introduction to this reprinted reminiscence of a former Boston chief of police. Essential for a library which is building a primary source collection in urban history or in police systems.

349. Shoup, Donald C., and Mehay, Stephen L. **Program Budgeting for Urban Police Services, with Special Reference to Los Angeles.** New York: Praeger, 1972. 341 pp. LC 72-83009. $17.50.

A model budget for a police system. This budget may not fit all communities, especially those which are more compact and less oriented to the automobile than Los Angeles, but it is an essential aid to those police officials who are attempting to create their own program budgets.

350. Sprogle, Howard O. **The Philadelphia Police, Past and Present.** Municipal Police History. Montclair, N.J.: Patterson Smith, 1971 (originally published in 1887). 671 pp. LC 70-172570. $17.50.

An inside look at the creation and early operation of a police force in a major American city.

351. Stark, Rodney. **Police Riots, Collective Violence and Law Enforcement.** Belmont, Cal.: Wadsworth, 1972. 250 pp. LC 78-178816. $7.50, pap. $4.50.

Stark's slant on the police is that of a social observer who concerns himself with the reasons why at times police seem to become a kind of mob and engage in violent, destructive behavior. He uses as examples excesses of the police in urban disturbances of the last decade. A serious study of the tensions which grip the modern police officer, this is not recommended for beginners.

352. Steadman, Robert F., ed. **The Police and the Community.** Baltimore: Johns Hopkins University Press, 1972. $6, pap. $2.25.

Steadman's emphasis in this collection is upon the interaction between the police in large urban areas with the residents of the inner city. Three of the background papers helped influence the Committee for Economic Developments' policy statement on crime and justice. Best suited for small libraries lacking material on police-community relations.

353. Teeters, N.K. **The Cradle of the Penitentiary: The Walnut Street Jail in Philadelphia, 1773–1835.** Philadelphia: Pennsylvania Prison Society, 1955. 152 pp. LC 55-2515.

The evolution of Philadelphia's main jail. The conception of crime, police, and detention can be found here. For research only.

354. United States. President's Commission on Law Enforcement and Administration of Justice. **Task Force Report: The Police.** New York: Arno Press, 1971 (originally published in 1967). LC 73-154585. $10.

Report of a commission appointed by President Johnson to improve the quality of law enforcement and justice in the 1960s. Racial and urban tensions of the period are so evident that the recommendations come as no surprise. For serious scholars and involved laypersons.

355. Walling, George W. **Recollections of a New York Chief of Police, with a Historic Supplement of the Denver Police.** by A. Kaufmann. Municipal Police History. Montclair, N.J.: Patterson Smith, 1972 (originally published in 1890). 698 pp. LC 70-129311. $17.50.

A two-titles-in-one package recommended for libraries interested in building sources on urban history or the history of the police.

356. Wambaugh, Joseph. **The New Centurions.** Boston: Little, Brown, 1970. 376 pp. LC 77-131254. $8.95. Dell, pap. $1.50.

A novel that captures quite well the world of the policeman as Wambaugh sees it. Wambaugh, once a Los Angeles detective sergeant, retains an active interest in the operations of LAPD.

357. Warren, John H., Jr. **Thirty Years' Battle with Crime, or the Crying Shame of New York, As Seen Under the Broad Glare of an Old Detective's Lantern.** New York: Arno Press, 1970 (originally published in 1875). 400 pp. LC 73-112582. $16.

An excellent first-hand report on how the police viewed crime in the mid-19th century. Warren considered prostitution the most pressing problem and urged the licensing and inspection of prostitutes. He also discusses abortion, begging, food adulteration, and confidence games. Best suited for sections on police history and on crime in the city.

358. Westley, William A. **Violence and the Police: A Sociological Study of Law, Custom, and Morality.** Cambridge, Mass.: MIT Press, 1970. 222 pp. LC 75-110236. $10, pap. $2.95.

Westley's basic frame of reference here is that the police department constitutes a subculture which can be understood best in terms of its own value system. He believes that the rookie is socialized into a profession which formulates a code of behavior all its own. While primarily designed for scholars, it also has appeal for the average reader.

359. Wilson, James Q. **Varieties of Police Behavior: The Management of Law and Order in Eight Communities.** Cambridge, Mass.: Harvard University Press, 1968. 309 pp. LC 68-54027. $10.

Political scientist Wilson specializes in urban and police problems. Written from the perspective of the university, this is a comparative look at how eight cities have attempted to provide and control law enforcement agencies. Basic for those who wish to understand the workings of police systems.

Civil Disorders

The 1960s were years of considerable disorder in the cities which at the time seemed to threaten to destroy the fabric of urban society and to presage decades of continuing racial conflict. The riots lessened in number and in extent of violence, and the 1970s, by contrast, appeared to go down in history as a quiet decade. Political conventions now were held without great challenges from the street and Black suffering did not result in urban conflagration.

Upon close scrutiny, it became apparent that racial riots or urban violence was not an invention of the 20th century. Mobs rampaged through American cities in the 19th century as well, carrying out judgments on morality, crime, and racial qualities. Because of this retrospect, the disorders of the 1960s are less threatening and the future is somewhat brighter. However, the reasons for the eruption of riots or for their demise are still not clearly understood. This section contains materials which constitute a first step toward that understanding.

360. Boesel, David, and Rossi, Peter, eds. **Cities Under Seige: An Anatomy of Ghetto Riots, 1964–1968.** New York: Basic Books, 1971. 436 pp. LC 77-147019. $12.95.

The urban disturbances of the 1960s predictably created much interest in the conditions that caused such disturbances. The editors of this collection have tried to and succeeded in putting together representative opinions on the origin of urban riots.

361. Boskin, Joseph, ed. **Urban Racial Violence in the Twentieth Century.** Beverly Hills, Cal.: Glencoe Press, 1969. 148 pp. LC 78-75964. pap. $2.95.

Boskin's anthology focuses quite strongly on the disturbances of the 1960s but is otherwise quite balanced. The articles are a sober assessment of the causes and consequences of riots. Mainly aimed at those who have some background in urban studies.

362. California Governor's Commission on the Los Angeles Riots. **Violence in the City—An End or a Beginning?** Los Angeles, 1965. 101 pp. spiral bound $1.

One of the first government reports on the riots of the 1960s and touches primarily on the disturbance in Watts. The report is intriguing for its basic assumptions and its use of the organic metaphor of a sick society. Belongs primarily in research libraries.

363. **Civil Disorder: The Kerner Report.** National Educational Television/ Indiana University Audio-Visual Center, 1968. 16mm. b/w. Sound. 56 min. Parts I and II. Sale $265, rent $15.25.

The format of this three-part film (parts I and II are recommended) is a discussion of the report among James Baldwin, Charles V. Hamilton, Bayard Rustin, and Kenneth Clark. Not visually stimulating, but the participants do analyze the report quite well. For senior high school students.

364. Cohen, Nathan, ed. **The Los Angeles Riots: A Socio-psychological Study.** New York: Praeger, 1970. 742 pp. LC 73-94248. $20.

This collection also bears the imprint of the Institute of Government and Public Affairs of the University of California, Los Angeles. Experts try to determine the underlying motives for the racial disturbances in Los Angeles in the mid-1960s. Sophisticated essays which require background in sociopsychological principles.

365. Fogelson, Robert M. **Violence as Protest: A Study of Riots and Ghettoes.** Garden City, N.Y.: Doubleday, 1971. 265 pp. LC 72-121579. pap. $1.95.

A study of urban violence in the 1960s by an historian who was a consultant to the President's Crime Commission and the President's Riot Commission. Fogelson attempts to answer the question of who rioted as well as the one about the grievances of the ghetto. He does show quite graphically the dilemma of Black moderates and the difficulties of white liberals in coming to terms with racial violence. He concludes on a pessimistic note.

366. Headley, Joel Tyler. **The Great Riots of New York: 1712-1873.** Indianapolis: Bobbs-Merrill, 1969 (originally published in 1873). 312 pp. LC 78-98275. $10.50, pap. $3.

A reprint including a section on the 1863 draft riots aimed at New York Negroes. A source for student research units on anti-Black feeling in the cities.

367. Heaps, Willard A. **Riots U.S.A., 1765-1965,** rev. ed. New York: Seabury Press, 1966. 214 pp. LC 69-13444. $4.95.

Riots are identified from a composite definition taken from a New York court decision in 1848, from *Le Bon*, and from the dictionary. The section on the Stamp Act Riots is good, and the whole book is valuable showing that urban violence has long been part of American experience. For reference purposes.

368. Horsmanden, Daniel. **The New-York Conspiracy; or, A History of the Negro Plot, with the Journal of the Proceedings Against the Conspirators at New-York in the Years 1741-2,** 2nd ed. Westport, Conn.: Negro Universities Press, 1971 (originally published in 1810). LC 69-16546. $14. Beacon Press, pap. $2.95.

An account of a New York City disturbance which included both white and Black servants and which seemed to threaten general insurrection. For research libraries with collections in urban history or urban riots.

369. Jacobs, Paul. **Prelude to Riot: The Urban Condition from the Bottom Up.** New York: Random House, 1968. 298 pp. LC 66-21487. pap. $1.95.

A fine study of the conditions which lead to urban uprisings. Popularly written, and can be handled by senior high school students.

370. Law and Order: Values in Crisis. Warren Schloat Productions, 1970. 6 filmstrips. Color. 6 discs (manual and automatic). 11 to 16 min per side. Sale $92 with discs, $110 with cassettes.

In this series *Violent Dissent* and *The Establishment Responds* are the most pertinent. The first discusses campus disorders and the second urban riots, including the police response at Berkeley's People's Park demonstration and Chicago's 1968 Democratic National Convention. Recommended for junior and senior high school students.

371. Lee, Alfred McClung, and Humphrey, Norman D. Race Riot: A First-Hand Observation of the 1943 Detroit Riots. New York: Octagon, 1973 (originally published in 1943). 143 pp. LC 68-20841. $9.

Insights into the temper of 1943 Detroit and the social dynamics which produce urban violence. Also shows how little attention was paid to suggested remedies for urban problems.

372. Richards, Leonard L. "Gentlemen of Property and Standing," Anti-Abolition Mobs in Jacksonian America. New York: Oxford University Press, 1970. 196 pp. LC 74-93862. $6.95, pap. $1.95.

Richards looked at urban violence in several northern cities—New York, Philadelphia, Cincinnati, and Utica—in the 1830s and 1840s. He claims that there were two kinds of mobs, the first led by men of substance in the community who were principally interested in attacking white abolitionists, and unorganized ones, which lacked leadership, aimed at Blacks.

373. Skolnick, Jerome. The Politics of Protest. New York: Simon & Schuster, 1969. 419 pp. LC 75-91304. $6.95, pap. $2.95.

Task force report to the National Commission on the Causes and Prevention of Violence concerning the strategy, techniques, and presumed effectiveness of protest movements. For research libraries and for reference.

374. Stein, David Lewis. Living the Revolution: The Yippies in Chicago. Indianapolis: Bobbs-Merrill, 1969. 146 pp. LC 74-81287. $5.

The 1968 Democratic Convention was the scene of considerable disruption. Prominent among the groups central to the disturbances was the Yippies. This is a popular account of the group, their aims and objectives, and the reasons for their growth in urban America.

375. Tuttle, William M., Jr. Race Riot: Chicago in the Red Summer of 1919. New York: Atheneum, 1970. 305 pp. LC 71-130983. $8.95, pap. $3.25.

One of the worst Black-white confrontations in 20th-century America occurred in Chicago immediately after World War I. Tuttle tells how the riot began, expanded, and was finally resolved. Engrossing and should have wide appeal.

376. U.S. Kerner Commission Report. Report of the National Advisory Commission on Civil Disorders. New York: Bantam, 1968. 609 pp. LC 68-7504. $10.

The definitive governmental statement on the urban disturbances of the 1960s. Contains a great number of facts on the riots and stands as a significant reference volume for libraries.

377. Waskow, Arthur I. **From Race Riot to Sit-In, 1919 and the 1960s.** Garden City, N.Y.: Doubleday, 1966. LC 66-11737. Peter Smith, pap. $4.25.

The strategy of civil rights movements via a comparison of the riots of 1919 with the protest techniques of the 1960s. A provocative book which can be handled by college-bound senior high school students.

378. Zobel, Hiller B. **The Boston Massacre.** New York: Norton, 1970. 372 pp. LC 79-77413. $8.50, pap. $3.25.

Zobel is a lawyer who is anti-rebel and who takes a dim view of the behavior of Boston citizens during the Revolution. He claims that the Boston mob ran the city by force and terror and that Sam Adams and Richard Dana were the real villains. Zobel's position is important in that it is conservative, shows how we romanticize violence in the past if it accomplishes what are considered desirable ends.

Urban Poverty

As Michael Harrington has pointed out, American poverty lacks visibility. The poor are hidden by physical circumstance and by the mask of social assumption. In the cities, the poor are concentrated in central areas and nonpoor observers see them as they commute to work. Because of the relative inexpensiveness of clothing, these poor appear to be adequately dressed. Thus the nature of the living conditions of the urban poor and the desperation of their lives remain a mystery to the outsider.

The selections in this section focus upon the questions of who are the urban poor and what circumstances have conspired to produce urban poverty. There are materials contained herein which concern the development of concepts and definitions of poverty as well as first-hand accounts of the costs of poverty. The world of the poor Black and the poor white in blighted urban areas is depicted. Some assessments of the historical dimensions of poverty are here; there are also evaluations of the effects of the recent War on Poverty program and of community participation on the plight of the urban poor.

379. Bloomberg, Warner, Jr., and Schmandt, Henry J., eds. **Power, Poverty, and Urban Policy**. Urban Affairs Annual Review. Beverly Hills, Cal.: Sage Publications, 1968. 604 pp. NUC 69-106286. $22.50.

Articles concentrating on the problems of the poor—unemployment, housing, medical care, justice—and on proposed solutions to these problems. As might be expected from the publication date, much attention is devoted to community action programs and to the acquisition of political power by the poor. There are cross-national comparisons with countries in Africa, Asia, and Europe. This volume, like the others in the series, is a highly recommended reference.

380. Brace, Charles Loring. **The Dangerous Classes of New York and Twenty Years' Work Among Them**. Montclair, N.J.: Patterson Smith, 1968 (originally published in 1880). 468 pp. LC 67-26666. $14. National Association of Social Workers, pap. $5.

This reprint recounts the experiences of Brace, a 19th-century urban reformer. He was concerned about the poor in New York City and proposed to send the children of the poor to rural areas to assimilate moral values. Belongs in libraries with sections on urban history or on social reform.

381. Bremner, Robert H. **From the Depths: The Discovery of Poverty in the United States**. New York: New York University Press, 1956. 364 pp. LC 56-7622. $9.75, pap. $3.50.

A period study of the beginning realization that poverty was not necessarily a transitory stage for everyone but was instead a permanent condition for some. Can be used for research purposes.

382. Brody, Eugene B., ed. **Behavior in New Environments: Adaptation of Migrant Populations.** Beverly Hills, Cal.: Sage Publications, 1970. 479 pp. LC 70-92359. $15.

Collected essays on the problems of migrants to industrial cities. The authors are concerned with how these migrants manage their lives and work. Scholarly, but cuts through the disciplines of history and sociology.

383. Cities and the Poor. National Educational Television and Radio Center/ Indiana University, 1966. (America's Crises Series.) 2 16mm films. b/w. Sound. 60 min. each. Rent $12 each.

Studies the problem of the urban poor, attempts by government and private agencies to help, and the rise of militant groups.

384. Clark, Kenneth. **Dark Ghetto: Dilemmas of Social Power.** New York: Harper & Row, 1965. 251 pp. $7.95. LC 64-7834. pap. $1.75.

The noted Black director of the Social Dynamics Research Institute of the City College of New York did this study of Harlem which covers such areas as the social dynamics, psychology, pathology, and power structure of the ghetto. Recommended for research into ghetto life.

385. Downs, Anthony. **Who Are the Urban Poor?**, rev. ed. New York: Committee for Economic Development, 1970. 64 pp. LC 77-133484. pap. $1.50.

Downs analyzes the social characteristics of those persons in America who live below the poverty level. He shows the factors which have contributed to this state—ill health, lack of education, lack of opportunity, and broken homes. A necessary volume for understanding the reasons for the persistence of poverty in this country.

386. Eames, Edwin, and Goode, Judith Gronich. **Urban Poverty in a Cross-Cultural Context.** New York: Glencoe Press, 1973. 299 pp. LC 72-90545. $8.95.

Eames and Goode distinguish three societies in their study—agrarian, transitional, and contemporary. They compare poverty in these three societies and conclude that there is a culture of poverty. Fairly difficult and more appropriate for the sophisticated reader.

387. Gitlin, Todd, and Hollander, Nanci. **Uptown: Poor Whites in Chicago.** New York: Harper & Row, 1970. 435 pp. LC 69-15309. $10.95, pap. $3.45.

Chicago has become a center for a number of poor whites from Appalachia. The authors describe their life-styles, their problems in getting employment, and in just staying alive. There is a feel for urban poverty and thus is recommended for that reason.

388. Hansen, Niles. **Rural Poverty and the Urban Crisis; A Strategy for Regional Development.** Bloomington, Ind.: Indiana University Press, 1970. 352 pp. LC 72-108207. $12.50.

Hansen outlines a proposed solution for both the lack of economic opportunity for landless rural people and for urban economic difficulties. He proposes that governmental assistance be given to enable persons to go to those cities of between 250,000 and 750,000 which have jobs and which are now growing. Hansen's proposal is an unconventional one but has attracted attention as a possibility of alleviating some of the hardships of the poor.

389. Howell, Joseph T. **Hard Living on Clay Street: Portraits of Blue Collar Families.** Garden City, N.Y.: Anchor Books, 1973. 381 pp. LC 73-79736. pap. $2.95.

Howell lived on Clay Street, a white working-class neighborhood, for a year as a kind of participant-observer. He catches quite well the problems, frustrations, and the strengths of the two working-class families with whom he associated. Although the study was funded by the National Institute of Mental Health, it does cover more ground than just psychological adjustment.

390. Levitan, Sar A. **Programs in Aid of the Poor in the 1970's.** Baltimore: Johns Hopkins University Press, 1969. 117 pp. LC 74-108383. $7, pap. $2.50.

A projection of possible choices social planners can make in the 1970s. While a scholarly effort, it also contains ideas of value to the average social or community worker and is recommended for libraries with sections on urban welfare systems.

391. Lewis, Oscar. **A Study of Slum Culture; Background for La Vida.** New York: Random House, 1968. 240 pp. LC 68-11969. $7.95.

Written by a well-known anthropologist who pioneered the concept of a culture of poverty in his studies of Puerto Ricans in New York City and San Juan. Several decades of Lewis' thinking are summed up. Essential for scholars interested in urban themes.

392. Lyford, Joseph P. **The Airtight Cage: A Study of New York's West Side.** New York: Harper & Row, 1966. 356 pp. LC 65-14687. pap. $2.25.

A case study of poverty in New York City, particularly as it is experienced by Puerto Ricans and Blacks. Conveys a sense of the desperation and lack of hope common to many inhabitants of this blighted area. Can be understood by the average reader, yet has material sophisticated enough for more advanced ones.

393. Marshall, Dale Rogers. **The Politics of Participation in Poverty; A Case Study of the Board of the Economic and Youth Opportunities Agency of Greater Los Angeles.** Berkeley, Cal.: University of California Press, 1971. 210 pp. LC 79-121192. $10.

A case study of the Board of the Economic and Youth Opportunities Agency of Greater Los Angeles. The primary concern is with the composition of the board, how the persons who claim they represent the community got on the board, and how the board acts to influence the behavior and opinion of its members.

394. Mohl, Raymond A. **Poverty in New York, 1783–1825.** New York: Oxford University Press, 1971. 318 pp. LC 72-140913. $10.

Mohl claims that there was much poverty in New York City at the beginning of the Republic. He discusses how what started out as charity motivated by altruistic motives became benevolence dominated by a desire for social control. Essential for understanding changing American attitudes toward poverty and the poor.

395. The Newcomer. Board of Global Ministries/United Methodist Film Service, 1963. 16mm. b/w. Sound, 30 min. Rent $8.

Immigration of a rural family to the city and the problems it encounters in the move. Since it was produced by a church group, it naturally emphasizes how the church as an institution can help in the situation. An accompanying discussion guide outlines a program designed to aid newcomers. Suitable for junior and senior high school students, and useful for inner-city children who may have had the same experience.

396. Poor People's Choice. Academic Games Project, Center for the Study of Social Organization of Schools, Johns Hopkins University.

Originally entitled *Ghetto*, this simulation puts the players in the position of residents of an inner-city slum. The object is to attain economic and social mobility despite the handicaps of the environment. The game can be used in classes from the junior high level on up.

397. Sexton, Donald E., Jr. **Groceries in the Ghetto.** Lexington, Mass.: D. C. Heath, 1974. 141 pp. LC 73-999. $8.50.

The basic question which Sexton asked in this small research study was whether food in ghetto groceries cost more and was of poorer quality than food in groceries in more affluent areas. The study is specialized and will be most appreciated by economists, although activists and others concerned with the urban poor will find data of value to them.

398. Sterne, Richard S., et al. **The Urban Elderly Poor; Racial and Bureaucratic Conflict.** Lexington, Mass: Lexington Books, 1974. 142 pp. LC 73-18014. $12.50.

Concerns the problems of those older people who are the most poverty stricken. It shows how the lack of money affects these persons and suggests what needs to be done to imporve their lot. Belongs in those libraries with collections on urban problems, social welfare, and gerontology.

399. Thomas, Piri. **Down These Mean Streets.** New York: Knopf, 1967. $7.95. New American Library, pap. $1.25.

Much used in college classes, this is an account of Spanish Harlem by a Puerto Rican who engages in criminal activities and is hooked on drugs. Depressing but it does give an insight to urban problems from the point of an insider.

400. Uptown—Portrait of a New York City Slum. Herbert Danska Films/Contemporary Films, 1966. 16mm. b/w. Sound. 27 min.

The camera takes the viewer on a tour of Spanish and Negro Harlem. Descriptive and can be used in the average junior and senior high school class.

401. Valentine, Charles A. **Culture and Poverty: Critique and Counter-Proposals.** Chicago: University of Chicago Press, 1968. 216 pp. LC 68-16718. $7.50, pap. $2.50.

Oscar Lewis' concept of a culture of poverty comes under attack in Valentine's work as a middle-class view of urban poverty which reflects an inability to look at the social structure as it is. Valentine suggests that sociologists ought to study the urban scene on its own terms. He then projects a program which can overcome poverty through "positive discrimination" in favor of the poor. While controversial, his study deserves the praise given it by Ralph Ellison as "one of the most important works of social anthropology to have been published in this country."

Urban Bosses

The era of boss rule in cities used to be considered defunct. Standard accounts of machine control began with Boss Tweed in New York City after the Civil War and ended with the assumption that Franklin Roosevelt's New Deal with its welfare provisions ended the hold of such machines in American cities.

But this view is too simplistic. Tammany Hall began much earlier than Tweed, and Mayor Daley effectively controls Chicago in the 1970s. It became apparent that boss rule had closer ties to the American urban experience than had been supposed. While it was always obvious that city bosses appealed to the European immigrant who was the newcomer to American cities, now it is also apparent that the boss furnished needed services to the business community and to middle-class, native-born Americans as well.

This section contains accounts of both well-known and lesser practictioners of the art of machine politics. It has reflections on bosses of the past as well as those of the present. There are descriptive as well as analytical accounts of this most American phenomenon.

402. Bean, Walton. **Boss Ruef's San Francisco; The Story of the Union Labor Party, Big Business, and the Graft Prosecution.** Berkeley, Cal.: University of California Press, 1952. 345 pp. LC 52-7946. $7.50, pap. $2.45.

Bean describes the alliance between businessmen and the Union Labor Party in San Francisco and details how this alliance was broken by the prosecution of the principal members of the ring. Fits in well with other studies of city machines.

403. Brownell, Blaine A., and Stickle, Warren E., eds. **Bosses and Reformers; Urban Politics in America, 1880–1920.** Boston: Houghton Mifflin, 1973. 252 pp. LC 72-4796. pap. $3.95.

Subtitled "Urban Politics in America, 1880–1920," this report combines primary and secondary source materials. The former includes articles by contemporary journalists and observers and the latter, essays by historians and political scientists. A useful introduction for those libraries which lack extensive resources in the area of machine politics.

404. Callow, Alexander B., Jr. **The Tweed Ring.** New York: Oxford University Press, 1966. 351 pp. LC 66-24440. pap. $3.50.

The most readable account of the Tweed Ring in New York City. It explains why the immigrants supported Boss Tweed and what his function was.

405. Dorsett, Lyle W. **Bosses and Machines in Urban America.** St. Charles, Mo.: Forum Press, 16 pp. LC 73-81060. pap. $.95.

Dorsett's essay, taken from *Forums in History*, evaluates the role of political organizations in cities in the late 19th and early 20th centuries and concludes that these organizations, despite their corruption and venality, did serve a necessary function. Designed for college undergraduates majoring in history, this essay could be used by libraries as an introduction to the subject of boss rule.

406. Dorsett, Lyle W. **The Pendergast Machine.** Urban Life in America. New York: Oxford University Press, 1968. 163 pp. $6, pap. $2.95.

Good, but brief, summary of the lives and careers of the Pendergast brothers. Recommended as a case study in bossism.

407. Gosnell, Harold Foote. **Machine Politics: Chicago Model,** 2nd ed. Westport, Conn.: Greenwood Press, 1969 (originally published in 1937). LC 37-20974. $12.25. University of Chicago, pap. $3.45.

Gosnell demonstrates how the machine met the needs of its constituents and thus was able to remain in power. Belongs in libraries with sections on political machines and in those specializing in material on Chicago.

408. Haeger, John D., and Weber, Michael P., eds. **The Bosses: Daley, Croker, Plunkitt, Tweed.** St. Charles, Mo.: Forum Press, 1973. 82 pp. LC 74-77391. pap. $1.95.

Short collection of readings centering on the evolution of the city boss from Tweed to Daley as seen through the eyes of contemporaries as well as by recent scholars in urban history. An introduction to the problem and is recommended for small libraries with limited resources.

409. Holli, Melvin G. **Reform in Detroit: Hazen S. Pingree and Urban Politics.** Urban Life in America. New York: Oxford University Press, 1969. 269 pp. LC 69-17762. pap. $2.50.

Pingree was not a boss, he was a reform mayor; but the problems of Detroit were similar to those of other cities of the time. The conditions which led to bossism existed in Detroit, and the city suffered government by cronies. Useful view of the Motor City.

410. Ivins, William Mills. **Machine Politics and Money in Elections in New York City.** New York: Arno Press, 1970 (originally published in 1887). 150 pp. LC 71-112553.

Urban reformer and Judge Advocate General of the State of New York, Ivins' thesis was that the availability of money to the machine made challenges to its dominance extremely difficult. He listed the election costs in New York City as well as the use of police as campaigners and estimates on the size of assessments of various political offices. For research collections on urban reformers and on antimachine works.

411. Keller, Morton. **The Art and Politics of Thomas Nast.** New York: Oxford University Press, 1968. 353 pp. LC 68-19762. $14.95, pap. $6.95.

Crusading cartoonist Nast exposed the Tweed Ring with his acid cartoons. This reference contains more than two hundred of his drawings. A useful tool for students who wish to see history visualized and who are interested in cartooning.

412. Mandelbaum, Seymour. **Boss Tweed's New York.** New York: Wiley, 1965. 196 pp. LC 65-16417. pap. $4.50.

Mandelbaum's thesis is that Tweed was an essential link in the communications chain which held New York City together, and that his fall was a result of improved media alternatives. Recommended for special collections only.

413. Miller, Zane L. **Boss Cox's Cincinnati: Urban Politics in the Progressive Era.** New York: Oxford University Press, 1968. 301 pp. LC 68-29722. pap. $2.95.

Cincinnati grew rapidly in the latter half of the 19th century, and developed machine politics similar to other cities. Like Kansas City, Mo., Cincinnati's population did not have a large percentage of immigrants but did have a city boss. Recommended for cross-city comparisons of political machines.

414. Parkhurst, Charles H. **Our Fight with Tammany.** Rise of Urban America. New York: Arno Press, 1970 (originally published in 1895). 296 pp. LC 73-112566. $12.

Parkhurst was the president of the Society for the Prevention of Crime in New York City in the last decades of the 19th century. This reprint chronicles Parkhurst's campaign against vice, a campaign which involved the police and the municipal administration and finally resulted in the appointment of the Lexow Commission. Of interest to urban historians and political scientists.

415. Riordon, William L. **Plunkitt of Tammany Hall: A Series of Very Plain Talks on Very Practical Politics, Delivered by Ex-Senator George Washington Plunkett, The Tammany Philosopher, From His Rostrum—The New York County Court House Bootblack Stand.** New York: Dutton, 1963. LC 63-2468. pap. $1.25.

Classic account of one leader of the Democratic machine in New York City. Plunkitt is interesting enough to stimulate even the casual reader.

416. Royko, Mike. **BOSS: Richard J. Daley of Chicago.** New York: Dutton, 1971. 215 pp. LC 79-133585. New American Library, pap. $1.50.

Royko is a Chicago journalist, and this popularly written account reflects his disenchantment with the Daley administration in the Windy City. Royko's expose is in the muckraking tradition and has enjoyed a wide audience.

417. Salter, J. T. **The People's Choice: Philadelphia's William S. Vare.** New York: Exposition Press, 1971. 112 pp. LC 72-164867. $5.

Vare was Republican boss of the Philadelphia machine during the 1920s. His administration rested upon the support of such diverse groups as Blacks, Italians, and Russian Jews. The biography of Vare shows quite well how the Democratic appeal to ethnics, beginning with Al Smith and continuing through Roosevelt, eroded the Vare machine in Philadelphia. Scholarly presentation of interest to students of urban politics and history.

418. Shapley, Rufus E. **Solid for Mulhooly: A Political Satire.** The History of Urban America. New York: Arno Press, 1970 (originally published in 1889). 210 pp. LC 76-112572.

Political satire written to support a reform candidate for mayor in Philadelphia in 1881 who subsequently defected to the political machine. Portrays the story of a fictional immigrant Irishman, Mulhooly, who typifies political life in the American city. Mulhooly gains his political education and his seat in Congress from saloon acquaintances. The Arno reprint is of the 1889 edition containing illustrations by Thomas Nast and was chosen in preference to the original 1881 version. Humorous and still delivers the flavor of late 19th century political beliefs.

419. Stave, Bruce M. **Urban Bosses, Machines, and Progressive Reformers.** Lexington, Mass.: D. C. Heath, 1972. 158 pp. LC 76-172912. pap. $2.95.

Contemporary evaluations of the political systems of cities at the turn of the century showing how these judgments have both changed and persisted. College students and informed adults will appreciate it.

420. Steinberg, Alfred. **The Bosses.** New York: Macmillan, 1972. 379 pp. LC 73-190158. New American Library, pap. $1.95.

A journalistic account of the lives of six of America's most notorious city bosses—Frank Hague, Ed Crump, James Curley, Huey Long, Gene Talmadge, and Ed Pendergast. Availability in paperback ought to attract general readers.

421. Tarr, Joel Arthur. **A Study in Boss Politics: William Lorimer of Chicago.** Urbana, Ill.: University of Illinois Press, 1971. 376 pp. LC 72-133945. $12.50.

Mayor of Chicago in the early 20th century, Lorimer successfully manipulated ethnic and religious antagonisms to keep himself in power. This case study deserves a place beside those on Boss Tweed, Cox, and Pendergast.

422. Wendt, Lloyd, and Kogan, Herman. **Lords of the Levee: The Story of Bathhouse John and Hinky Dink.** Bloomington, Ind.: Indiana University Press, 1976 (originally published in 1943). 384 pp. LC 67-25139. pap. $2.95.

Wendt and Kogan's story is of two Chicago machine politicians whose antics seem stranger than fiction. Still tells a lively tale and dissects the urban community very neatly.

Urban Reform
and the Provision of Services

The concern to solve urban problems has co-existed with the urban problems themselves. Certain difficulties with the provision of such services as pure water, adequate sewage facilities, and a public health system early became identified. Cities moved to remedy these problems as they also paved streets, improved lighting, and set municipal building codes. While the provision of these urban services often failed to meet even minimal standards, at least their need was quite uniformly accepted.

Two new developments in the late 19th century encouraged the formation of other reform groups which focused upon the cities. These groups were concerned about the housing available to immigrants and about the social conditions which these immigrants found. Some reformers hoisted the standard of tenement reform; others attacked the saloon. Still others attempted to extend Protestant Christianity in the cities. The tangible institutions created at this time were settlement houses and policitical reform groups—all of this in response to the immigrant from Europe.

With the migration of Blacks from the rural South, groups such as the Urban League responded to the population movement by attempting to mitigate the harshness of the urban environment. The civil rights movements of the 1950s and the 1960s in part originated in the cities, and Black populations in the cities provided the kind of mass support necessary to make the movement the limited success it was.

This section, then, is a mixed bag. It contains materials on civil rights organizations, on settlement houses, on campaigns to control diseases and drinking, on the lives of reformers like Jane Addams, Jacob Riis, and Saul Alinsky, on juvenile delinquency, and on community organization. All concern significant problems as perceived by individuals and groups in different eras.

423. Abbott, Edith. **The Tenements of Chicago, 1908–1935.** New York: Arno Press, 1970 (originally published in 1936). 505 pp. LC 78-112535. $24.

Edith Abbott was a pioneering social worker who, as dean of the University of Chicago's School of Social Service Administration, helped supervise studies of housing in the Windy City. This study concentrated upon accommodations of ethnic groups in Chicago and concluded with a call for federal aid to meet needs which dwarfed private and local resources. This reprint of the original edition remains a valuable source on the roots of urban housing decay.

424. The Alinsky Approach. National Film Board of Canada/McGraw-Hill Films. Rent $80.

Actually a series of 5 films on the veteran community organizer, Saul Alinsky. Alinsky proposed that each seemingly powerless group actually had some weapons which could be used to gain its own ends. Valuable for those involved in community organization.

425. American Public Health Association. **A Half Century of Public Health.** The History of Urban America. New York: Arno Press, 1970 (originally published in 1921). 461 pp. LC 74-112569. $17.

Studies on housing, sewage and water systems, food supplies, and child welfare, as well as a history of the American Public Health Association. The essays reflect optimism about the possibility of improving municipal public health largely because of the record of achievement after the application of Pasteur's germ theory of disease. Should prove beneficial to those interested in public health and welfare history.

426. Barker, John Marshall. **The Saloon Problem and Social Reform.** Rise of Urban America. New York: Arno Press, 1970 (originally published in 1905). 212 pp. LC 76-112521. $8.

Urban reformer Barker viewed saloons with alarm. He believed they contributed to social evils such as crime and poverty, to political evils such as corrupt politicians, and to private misery. His book gives an idea of the motivation of prohibitionists in the Progressive Era.

427. Blake, John B. **Public Health in the Town of Boston, 1630–1822.** Cambridge, Mass.: Harvard University Press, 1959. 278 pp. LC 59-10314. $11.

The development of public health in Boston from the beginnings to a modern system is the theme of this work. It is a significant effort and can be used to show the evolution of public concern and the displacement of private efforts.

428. Blake, Nelson M. **Water for the Cities: A History of the Urban Water Supply Problem in the United States.** Syracuse, N.Y.: Syracuse University Press, 1956. 341 pp. LC 56-13576. $7.50.

Definitive work on the development of water systems in the United States. Like Duffy's on public health, Blake's is the one with which to begin. A needed reference tool.

429. Blodgett, Geoffrey. **The Gentle Reformers: Massachusetts Democrats in the Cleveland Era.** Cambridge, Mass.: Harvard University Press, 1966. 342 pp. LC 66-13178. $10.95.

One of the major characters in this study of post-Civil War Massachusetts is Mayor Josiah Quincy of Boston. Quincy was a reform mayor who increased the number of city playgrounds and who initiated both a public bath house and a publicly owned printing plant. Contains much material on Boston, and, though scholarly, is a useful addition to libraries with large collections.

430. Breckinridge, Sophonisba, ed. **The Child in the City: A Series of Papers Presented at the Conference Held During the Chicago Child Welfare Exhibit.** Rise of Urban America. New York: Arno Press, 1970 (originally published in 1912). 502 pp. LC 70-112541. $20.

Papers presented by such pioneer social and settlement house workers as Lillian Wald, Jane Addams, Florence Kelly, and Julia Lathrop. A valuable source for the early history of social work as well as urban history. Recommended for those libraries acquiring original materials.

431. Breckinridge, Sophonisba, and Abbott, Edith. **The Delinquent Child and the Home.** New York: Arno Press, 1970 (originally published in 1912). 355 pp. LC 70-112525.

Breckinridge and Abbott, two Chicago social workers, studied the wards of Chicago's juvenile court. These reformers' interests were in the relationship of delinquency to conditions in homes utilizing data from the records of persons connected with the courts. As an early study of urban juvenile delinquency, this is a classic which ought to be included in libraries with sections on urban problems or with specialties in the history of welfare institutions in the United States.

432. Buenker, John D. **Urban Liberalism and Progressive Reform.** New York: Charles Scribners Sons, 1973. 299 pp. LC 73-1314. $8.95.

Buenker attempts to trace the elements in American cities which helped create and mold reform movements. He shows how ethnic politics ties into reform politics and how significant urban political movements were in the genesis of reform.

433. Carey, Mathew. **A Short Account of the Malignant Fever, Lately Prevalent in Philadelphia: With a Statement of the Proceedings That Took Place on the Subject, In Different Parts of the United States. To Which Are Added, Accounts of the Plague in London and Marseilles; and a List of the Dead, From August 1, to the Middle of December, 1793,** 4th ed. Rise of Urban America. New York: Arno Press, 1970 (originally published in 1794). 164 pp. LC 73-112531. $7.

Mathew Carey was an Irish-American newspaperman who, at the time of the Yellow Fever epidemic in Philadelphia, published the *Pennsylvania Herald.* Carey also was a member of the Committee of Health of the city which tried to organize relief measures to meet the crisis. An invaluable source on eighteenth-century American cities and on the history of public health in the United States.

434. Chicago. Vice Commission. **The Social Evil in Chicago: A Study of Existing Conditions with Recommendations by the Vice Commission of Chicago.** Rise of Urban America. New York: Arno Press, 1970 (originally published in 1911). 399 pp. LC 78-112578. $16.

The Chicago Vice Commission was typical of organizations formed by urban Progressives to alleviate problems of the day. In this reprint, the commission reports its findings on prostitution in Chicago with the ultimate aim of eliminating it. Should be considered by libraries which have research sections on urban problems and urban progressivism.

435. Citizen's Association of New York. **Council of Hygiene and Public Health.** New York: Arno Press, 1970 (originally published in 1866). 360 pp. LC 77-112532. $24.

A significant report since the association was responsible for the creation of a board of health in New York City and of the passage of a tenement house law regulating these residences. The report came as a result of the mob violence, the Draft Riots in the poorer sections of the city in 1863, and the investigators found deplorable physical conditions in both housing and inhabitants. A vital acquisition for libraries providing materials in the history of public health and urban reform.

436. Crooks, James B. **Politics and Progress: The Rise of Urban Progressivism in Baltimore, 1895-1911.** Baton Rouge, La.: Louisiana State University Press, 1968. 259 pp. LC 68-21805. $8.50.

Crooks shows how and why Progressivism arose in Baltimore. Through the use of one city and a limited time span, Crooks is able to examine the dynamics of urban politics much more carefully than if he had attempted a broader study. For libraries with sections on political changes in the city.

437. Cully, Kendig B., and Harper, F. Nile, eds. **Will the Church Lose the City?** New York: World, 1969. 256 pp. LC 73-86449.

An anthology about the problems of the church in urban society. As the title indicates, the contributors are more interested in saving the church than the city. The articles do show the interrelationship between religious institutions and urban pressures quite well, although, for the most part, the level of sophistication is not too high, even for the lay reader. Recommended for smaller libraries lacking collections about churches and cities.

438. Davis, Allen F. **American Heroine: The Life and Legend of Jane Addams.** New York: Oxford University Press, 1973. 339 pp. LC 73-82664. $10.95, pap. $3.95.

Davis' biography of Jane Addams, the founder of Hull House in Chicago, is the latest and most definitive. Important to those people looking for the roots of the social work profession in America as well as those of early attempts to ameliorate the impact of the industrial city. As such, it is highly recommended.

439. Davis, Allen F. **Spearheads for Reform: The Social Settlements and the Progressive Movement, 1890-1914.** New York: Oxford University Press, 1967. 322 pp. LC 67-25457. $8.95.

History of the influence which settlement house movement leaders had upon reform politics in pre-World War I years. Davis' interesting study challenges the conventional wisdom that Progressivism was largely a product of businessmen and lawyers from small and medium-sized towns. Shows how much effect city social reformers actually had upon the larger national movement. Recommended to those readers of urban politics and urban reform.

440. DeForest, Robert W., and Veiller, Lawrence, eds. **The Tenement House Problem: Including the Report of the New York State Tenement House Commission of 1900.** 2 vols. New York: Arno Press, 1970 (originally published in 1903). LC 75-112537. set $45.

DeForest was chairman of the New York State Tenement House Commission and, as the result of the 1900 report, became the first commissioner of the New York City Tenement House Department under the provisions of the 1901 building law. The report of 1900 helped create the law with its descriptions of the bad conditions in the houses of the time. This two-volume set includes a history of tenement house legislation and a section on enforcement of the 1901 law. A landmark publication belonging in libraries with collections on housing and reform movements in cities.

441. Douglass, Harlan Paul. **The St. Louis Church Survey: A Religious Investigation with a Social Background.** Rise of Urban America. New York: Arno Press, 1970 (originally published in 1924). 327 pp. LC 77-112540. $14.

Studying the impact of migration to the city and to the suburb, Douglass recounts the trends in St. Louis after 1870 when poor immigrants from Europe or rural America moved into the city's center and the richer natives moved to the outskirts. Only the Catholic Church seemed equipped to meet the challenge as the older Protestant churches either closed their doors or became impoverished. Should be in all collections on religion in the city and the suburb.

442. Dubofsky, Melvyn. **When Workers Organize: New York City in the Progressive Era.** Amherst, Mass.: University of Massachusetts Press, 1968. 225 pp. LC 68-19669. $12.

Dubofsky shows the extent of the effort made by unskilled and semiskilled workers to unionize in New York City prior to the general strike of 1916 which failed. While concentrating mainly on the garment trade, he gives insights about other labor movements of the time. Specialized and appealing to those already involved in the study of urban laboring classes or urban economic development.

443. Duffy, John. **A History of Public Health in New York City, 1625–1866.** New York: Russell Sage Foundation, 1968. 619 pp. LC 68-25852. $20.

The dean of public health historians has written the most significant book on the evolution of public health departments. Students should turn to it first for information on this subject.

444. Duffy, John. **Sword of Pestilence: The New Orleans Yellow Fever Epidemic of 1853.** Baton Rouge, La.: Louisiana State University Press, 1966. 191 pp. LC 66-13659. $5.95.

Part of American antiurban sentiments came from a genuine fear of diseases which seemed to strike harder in urban residents than in rural ones. Duffy describes one 19th-century plague, yellow fever, and its impact upon New Orleans, then one of the largest and most important southern cities.

445. Fish, John Hall, **Black Power/White Control: Struggle of The Woodlawn Organization in Chicago.** Princeton, N.J.: Princeton University Press, 1973. 528 pp. LC 72-5379. $12.50.

TWO (The Woodlawn Organization) began in Chicago in 1961 with leadership from a group of clergymen and advice from the veteran radical and community organizer, Saul Alinsky. Fish himself was active in TWO, which has attempted to preserve a mixed racial community in the Black inner-city area. Fish traces the background of the organization and describes three programs of the organization, the Youth Project, the Experimental Schools Project, and the Model Cities Program. All aroused considerable animosity and trouble. Should be in all libraries with collections on community organizations and on Black urban development.

446. Haas, Edward F. **The Illusion of Reform: De Lesseps S. Morrison and New Orleans Politics, 1946–1961.** Baton Rouge, La.: Louisiana State University Press, 1974. 368 pp. LC 73-90867. $12.95.

Morrison served as mayor of New Orleans and ran unsuccessfully for governor of Louisiana three times. Haas' book has insight on the urban situation in the deep South after the Second World War and before the major civil rights thrust in the 1960s. A scholarly work recommended for students of urban political movements and leaders.

447. Hawes, Joseph M. **Children in Urban Society: Juvenile Delinquency in Nineteenth-Century America.** New York: Oxford University Press, 1971. 315 pp. LC 78-151185. $10.95.

Delineates the changes in attitude toward errant children in America in the 19th century. The century began with the nearly universal belief in good and bad children but it ended with the more contemporary view that such categories were too gross to mirror social reality. The newer view held that each child should be diagnosed and treated individually and that deviant behavior was the result of a number of environmental as well as internal factors.

448. Holden, Arthur C. **The Settlement Idea: A Vision of Social Justice.** The Rise of Urban America. New York: Arno Press, 1970 (originally published in 1922). 213 pp. LC 70-112549. $9.

Holden wrote this account during the 1920s when the impetus of the settlement house movement seemed to be gone. However, he argued that settlement houses had filled a real need and that their usefulness had not ended. In making this point, Holden traced the history of the movement from 1884 and Toynbee Hall to his own time. A necessary title in the history of social welfare movements.

449. Huggins, Nathan I. **Protestants Against Poverty: Boston's Charities, 1870–1900.** Westport, Conn.: Greenwood Press, 1971. 225 pp. LC 70-150980. $11.50.

Huggins shows how the motivating force behind the various charities in Boston at the end of the 19th century was the belief of middle-class reformers that a change in values and behavior through moral uplift would eliminate poverty and achieve a better urban society. Most suited to specialists in welfare history, although it sheds light on several different urban attitudes.

450. Hull House Maps and Papers (by) Residents of Hull House. New York: Arno Press, 1970 (originally published in 1895). 230 pp. LC 78-112519. $10.

These collected essays represent an attempt to do for Chicago what Charles Booth did for London: to survey the poor. The Hull House residents included such well-known people as Florence Kelly, Julia Lathrop, and Ellen Gates Starr. These reformers made a detailed study of ethnic groups in the near west side of Chicago, using a house-by-house survey. Should be in collections on urban reform movements, social welfare history, and ethnic groups.

451. Jacob Riis–Social Crusader. Popular Science Publishing Corp., Audio Visual Division, 1969. 1 filmstrip (42 fr.). Color. $7.50.

An elementary sketch of reporter and tenement house reformer, Jacob Riis, who roamed New York City at the end of the 19th century. While biographical, it throws some light on urban problems of the time.

452. Lubove, Roy. The Progressives and the Slums: Tenement House Reform in New York City 1890–1917. Westport, Conn.: Greenwood Press, 1974 (originally published in 1962). 284 pp. LC 74-4843. $14.75.

The roots of urban planning drawn from social reformers such as Lawrence Weiller are traced by Lubove. Some of the sources used here also appear in his preceding volume. For special collections.

453. Mann, Arthur. La Guardia: A Fighter Against His Times, 1882–1933. Chicago: University of Chicago Press, 1969. 384 pp. LC 71-51901. pap. $2.95.

454. Mann, Arthur. La Guardia Comes to Power. Chicago: University of Chicago Press, 1969. 199 pp. LC 69-128576. pap. $1.95.

In his two-volume biography of La Guardia, Mann describes the influences which made La Guardia a liberal, and his programs to improve the governance of New York City. Although scholarly, his works are also eminently readable and are attractive to a large audience.

455. Mann, Arthur. Yankee Reformers in an Urban Age: Social Reform in Boston, 1880–1900. New York: Harper & Row, 1966. 314 pp. NUC 67-101822. pap. $2.45.

Reform movements, including those of religion and education, in Boston. Mann's conclusion that there was an active reform movement before the Progressive era is an important one. Recommended for special collections.

456. Meier, August, and Rudwick, Elliott. CORE: A Study in the Civil Rights Movement, 1942–1968. New York: Oxford University Press, 1973. 563 pp. LC 72-92294. $15.

Definitive history of the Congress of Racial Equality, founded in Chicago in 1942, written by two well-known historians of Black America. CORE began as an integrated group devoted to nonviolence through Gandhian techniques and became an all-Black one with a self-proclaimed Black nationalist mission. A necessary history for libraries with sections on urban civil rights movements.

457. Mennel, Robert M. **Thorns & Thistles: Juvenile Delinquents in the United States, 1825-1940.** Hanover, N.H.: Published for the University of New Hampshire by the University Press of New England, 1973. 231 pp. LC 72-95187. $10.

A survey of the definition and treatment of juvenile delinquents from the early 19th century to World War II. Mennel also includes two chapters on theories of delinquency and argues that the system of corrections has acted to stigmatize children from poor urban families. Recommended for welfare systems collections.

458. **Old Brewery and the New Mission House at the Five Points, [by] Ladies of the Mission.** New York: Arno Press, 1970 (originally published in 1854). 304 pp. LC 72-112563. $12.

The Mission at Five Points, the most notorious section of New York City in the mid-19th century, was the project of the New York Ladies Home Missionary Society of the Methodist Episcopal Church in 1848. The ladies of the mission began a Sunday School, an elementary school, acted as an employment agency, and embarked on a temperance campaign which succeeded in closing down a liquor store. An excellent view of the state of New York City's slums in the mid-19th century as well as the reform impulse of American churches as expressed in the city.

459. Parris, Guichard, and Brooks, Lester. **Blacks in the City: A History of the National Urban League.** Boston: Little, Brown, 1971. LC 76-161866. $12.50.

This latest history of the Urban League attempts to show why the organization was formed, what factors contributed to its successes and failures, and what caused it to assume its present shape. Of high general interest and should be included in any section on 20th century civil rights movements.

460. Petshek, Kirk R. **The Challenge of Urban Reform: Policies and Programs in Philadelphia.** Philadelphia: Temple University Press, 1973. 336 pp. LC 72-95878. $10.

More limited than the title indicates, Petshek's account consists of an analysis of urban reform in the 1950s and 1960s during the administrations of Mayors Clark and Dillworth. Petshek attributes part of the success of Philadelphia's revival to a combination of private and public efforts and gives credit to city planners. Belongs in comprehensive collections on urban reform history and on urban politics.

461. Pickett, Robert S. **House of Refuge: Origins of Juvenile Reform in New York State, 1815-1857.** Syracuse, N.Y.: Syracuse University Press, 1969. 217 pp. LC 69-19745. $7.50.

Pickett traces the history of a single institution set up to cope with the problems of youth in New York after the War of 1812. The House of Refuge was a pioneering attempt to bring a number of juveniles together under one roof for treatment. Its creation reflected the optimism of the early 19th-century American people. Useful in setting the stage for present theories about treatment of juvenile offenders and can be recommended for urban historians and urban sociologists, although it is probably too sophisticated for the lay reader.

462. Pinkney, Alphonso, and Woock, Roger R. **Poverty and Politics in Harlem**: **Report on Project Uplift 1965**. New Haven, Conn.: College and University Press, 1971. 191 pp. LC 79-116379. $6, pap. $2.95.

An evaluation of how the War on Poverty worked in one community. The specific program examined was the OEO's (Office of Economic Opportunity) Project Uplift 1965, which was designed to employ, educate, and train Black youths in Harlem. The authors are not particularly optimistic about the results, but suggest that future projects should tie into existing programs, employ local residents, and not create the impression that much change is probable.

463. Piven, Francis Fox, and Cloward, Richard A. **Regulating the Poor: The Functions of Public Relief**. New York: Pantheon, 1971. 389 pp. LC 70-135368. $10. Random House, pap. $2.45.

A more radical look at public welfare than is customary. The authors argue that welfare is a device to assure the establishment of a measure of social peace. They indicate that the remarkable expansion of welfare rolls which began in the mid 1960s was significantly influenced by the urban disturbances of the time. A controversial approach, but also a thought-provoking one.

464. Powell, John Harvey. **Bring Out Your Dead: The Great Plague of Yellow Fever in Philadelphia in 1793**. New York: Arno Press, 1970 (originally published in 1949). 326 pp. LC 77-112567. $14.

The yellow fever epidemic in 1793 sorely tried Philadelphia as it killed 10 percent of the inhabitants and forced many others to flee the city. The crisis was severe enough to disrupt the ordinary political and economic life of the community. With the help of an extra-legal committee of volunteers, the situation came under control and the city struggled back to normal. Recommended for sections on urban public health and urban history.

465. Ringenbach, Paul T. **Tramps and Reformers, 1873–1916: The Discovery of Unemployment in New York**. Westport, Conn.: Greenwood Press, 1973. 224 pp. LC 77-175610. $10.50.

Efforts of New York City reformers to rehabilitate tramps is studied by Ringenbach. At first these persons believed the tramps to be voluntarily unemployed but later learned that this was not the case. Quite specialized, but of significance to social welfare history as it helps to understand early attitudes of reformers.

466. Rosenberg, Carroll Smith. **Religion and the Rise of the American City**: **The New York City Mission Movement, 1812–1870**. Ithaca, N.Y.: Cornell University Press, 1971. 300 pp. LC 76-164640. $12.50.

From its inception, the American city has been an object of concern and a field for husbandry for religious groups. Carroll Rosenberg has written a history of one institution created to help transform the city, the mission. She shows the long involvement of the church in the city and is helpful in understanding the currents which were present in both organized society and religion.

467. Rosenberg, Charles E. **The Cholera Years: The United States in 1832, 1849, and 1866.** Chicago: University of Chicago Press, 1962. 257 pp. LC 62-18121. pap. $3.45.

Rosenberg focuses upon one of the dread diseases 19th-century Americans associated with the cities, and shows how the attitudes toward the city changed as the cause of the disease was shifted from personal sin to a more material base. Reflecting more about cities than its title might lead one to believe, it is of uniformly high quality.

468. Saul Alinsky Went to War. National Film Board of Canada/McGraw-Hill, 1969. 16mm. b/w. Sound. 59 min. Sale $405, rent $25.

Saul Alinsky, veteran community organizer who got his start in Chicago, documents the tactics he used in Rochester, New York, in the struggle between F.I.G.H.T., an Alinsky-organized group, and Eastman-Kodak. The issues mainly concerned employment practices. Demonstrates effectiveness of weapons employed by the community organizer.

469. Smith, Stephen. **The City that Was** and **The Report of the General Committee of Health, New York City, 1806.** Metuchen, N.J.: Scarecrow Press, 1973. 211 pp. 90 pp. (History of Medicine, vol. 36). LC 73-1827.

Issued by the library of the New York Academy of Medicine and with a preface by John Duffy, this is a reprint of two early comments on public health in New York City. While mainly useful for research libraries, the titles could be included in more general ones.

470. Sorrels, William W. **Memphis' Greatest Debate: A Question of Water.** Memphis, Tenn.: Memphis State University Press, 1970. 139 pp. LC 74-130973. $5.50.

Sorrels' is one of the few case studies we have on the development of municipal water systems in the 19th century. It should be used in conjunction with Blake's *Water for the Cities*, which is more general.

471. Steffens, Lincoln. **The Shame of the Cities.** New York: Peter Smith, 1948 (originally published in 1904). 306 pp. LC 48-5672. $4. Hill & Wang, pap. $2.25.

This reprint has an introduction by Louis Joughin. Steffens' book consists of a series of six articles he wrote for *McClure's* magazine on the corruption of municipal government in America. Libraries lacking the original edition can purchase this classic of the muckraking tradition.

472. Stewart, Frank Mann. **A Half-Century of Municipal Reform; The History of the National Municipal League.** Westport, Conn.: Greenwood Press, 1972 (originally published in 1950). 289 pp. LC 74-168967. $13.25.

A scholarly history of the reformist National Municipal League indicating the strands of progressive thought which combined to form the league. It belongs in libraries collecting urban reform movements.

473. Strickland, Arvarh E. **History of the Chicago Urban League.** Urbana, Ill.: University of Illinois Press, 1966. 286 pp. LC 66-18826. $7.50.

There are very few studies of Black reformist organizations in particular cities; this is one which does trace the development of a significant organization, the Urban League, in a major city. Recommended for its insights into Black migration to urban areas and into the attempts to ameliorate problems engendered by strange urban circumstances.

474. Trattner, Walter I. **From Poor Law to Welfare State: A History of Social Welfare in America.** Riverside, N.J.: Free Press, 1974. 276 pp. LC 73-2129. pap. $3.95.

Comprehensive survey of social welfare in the United States. Trattner begins in colonial times and ends in the present. A necessary beginning point for those seeking the origins of present welfare practices and problems.

475. Urban Archives Center. **Private Social Services in Philadelphia: A Survey of the Records.** Philadelphia: Temple University Libraries, 1973. pap. $3.

A small volume listing the agencies which have operated in the City of Brotherly Love. Recommended as a reference tool for researchers.

476. U.S. Bureau of Labor. **The Slums of Baltimore, Chicago, and Philadelphia. Seventh Special Report of the Commissioner of Labor.** History of Urban America. New York: Arno Press, 1970 (originally published in 1894). 620 pp. LC 71-112587.

The result of a U.S. Bureau of Labor statistical survey conducted in the slum areas of three American cities. Most of the findings were expected; excepting the statistics for public health. These showed no greater incidence of disease in slums than in other areas. Recommended as a research tool to libraries.

477. Warren, Roland L., Rose, Stephen M., and Bergunder, Ann F. **The Structure of Urban Reform.** Lexington, Mass.: Lexington Books, 1974. 220 pp. LC 73-22155. $14.

Sociological study of how reform movements are created. It shows the structure necessary for beginning urban reform as well as processes essential for sustaining it. There is also a consideration of the role community decision organizations play in instituting and maintaining urban reform. For larger libraries with extensive collections.

478. Weiss, Nancy J. **The National Urban League, 1910–1940.** New York: Oxford University Press, 1974. 402 pp. LC 73-90366. $12.50.

The Urban League was one of the pioneering civil rights groups in the United States. This study takes the Urban League from its foundation down to World War II. The Urban League specializes in ameliorating the impact of the city on Blacks by helping them obtain housing and jobs, and this account describes the evolution of its efforts. Although scholarly, it deserves a place in collections on the history of civil rights groups.

479. Wingo, Lowdon, ed. **Reform as Reorganization.** Governance of Metropolitan Region, #4. Baltimore: Resources for the Future (distributed by Johns Hopkins University Press), 1973. LC 73-19348. pap. $3.

Whether or not to reorganize metropolitan governments in order to achieve solutions to urban problems is the concern here. Several possibilities are considered and a centrist position is taken on the issue of changes in the structure of government. Not too difficult for laypersons.

480. Wolff, Miles. **Lunch at the Five and Ten, The Greensboro Sit-Ins: A Contemporary History.** New York: Stein & Day, 1970. 191 pp. LC 75-104632. $5.95.

The civil rights movement of the 1960s began with a student sit-in at a lunch-counter in Greensboro, North Carolina. This sit-in movement led to the creation of SNCC and to the Civil Rights Acts of 1964 and 1965. This history of that movement is popularly written and suitable for most libraries. It gives the urban background of the civil rights drive of the time.

481. Woods, Robert A., ed. **The City Wilderness: A Settlement Study by Residents and Associates of the South End House.** New York: Arno Press, 1970 (originally published in 1898). 319 pp. LC 70-129319.

South End House was a Boston settlement house in a working-class neighborhood composed of Irish, Jews, Germans, Italians, and Negroes. Its residents, taking their cue from Booth's work in London, surveyed their community in order to determine its problems and needs. Among the problems identified were unemployment, poor housing, and serious political corruption. Libraries collecting primary material on settlement houses will find this volume a necessary purchase.

482. Woods, Robert A. **The Neighborhood in Nation-Building: The Running Comment of Thirty Years at the South End House.** History of Urban America. New York: Arno Press, 1970 (originally published in 1923). 348 pp. LC 78-112586. $14.

Thirty years of essays and speeches made by Woods. They center upon the problems, goals, and methods of settlement houses such as South End House. They constitute a valuable commentary upon the changing ideas and perspectives on the settlement house movement. Like Woods' other works, this one should be on research library shelves.

483. Woods, Robert A., and Kennedy, Albert J., eds. **Handbook of Settlements.** History of Urban America. New York: Arno Press, 1970 (originally published in 1911). 326 pp. LC 74-112585. $13.

Robert Woods was an early leader in the settlement house movement in the United States. He underwent training at Toynbee Hall and helped found South End House in Boston. Along with Kennedy, he collected all kinds of information to create this directory of settlement houses which gives not only house names but also their activities. Most useful as a reference support in research on settlement houses or early social welfare history.

484. Woods, Robert A., and Kennedy, Alfred J. **The Settlement Horizon: A National Estimate.** History of Urban America. New York: Arno Press, 1970 (originally published in 1922). 499 pp. LC 79-112562. $18.

Both a history of the settlement house movement and a projection of the future problems to which the settlement houses should address themselves, this report contains the viewpoint of insiders and is a valuable first-hand account of this early social welfare movement.

485. Zinn, Howard. **SNCC: The New Abolitionists.** Boston: Beacon Press, 1964. 246 pp. LC 64-20493. $4.95, pap. $2.95.

The best study on the founding of SNCC, though dated. Useful for teachers and for student projects.

486. Zurcher, Louis A., Jr. **Poverty Warriors: The Human Experience of Planned Social Intervention.** Austin, Tex.: University of Texas Press, 1970. 442 pp. LC 70-111391. $10.

Analyzing the OEO program in Topeka, Kansas, from the standpoint of a social scientist, Zurcher documents the problems OEO workers found in this Midwestern community and concludes that the results were not far-reaching. The major difficulty he found was in the differing expectations of the poor and of the leaders of the community. More adapted to scholars, although it does contain data of interest to workers in the welfare area whose needs are less theoretical.

PART II

The City in Perspective

Beyond the concern with the American city as a cesspool of pathology is one with the city as a legitimate object of intellectual attention. This concern takes a number of forms. In part, it involves speculation on the origins of the city in human history and in attempts to abstract common elements in the development of cities in various parts of the world. The history of cities results from such a concern as does the geography of cities which often involves the spatial dimensions of urban centers. This interest also stimulates cross-cultural and cross-time studies.

Another way of looking at cities is through the medium of urban images, both visual and poetic. The changing physical shape of cities reflects changing assumptions about the nature and function of these cities and the place of their human inhabitants. The images of the city found in imaginative literature disclose the same kinds of information. Both reveal how the city has been perceived in ideal as well as practical terms. The gap between the real and the ideal, in turn, demonstrates the force of external circumstance on human design.

Closely related to the images of the city is the planning of the city. Although professional city planning is only about 70 years old in the United States, most historic cities have involved some kind of planning assumptions. Views about the total function of the city and ways to facilitate that functioning may not have been explicit but they were at least implicit. Because of this fact, the plans of cities show much about the culture in which they exist.

Social sciences offer several ways of looking at cities. Urban sociology is at least partly concerned with the network of social relations in communities and sociologists do evaluate communities in terms of social function and social pathology. These scholars can determine whether a physically deteriorated environment is also socially deteriorated and the extent to which an ethnic community has been assimilated into a larger one. Political scientists are more concerned with the formal and informal ways in which cities are governed. They are interested in the structure of government as well as its function and in ways of making the system more manageable and cities more governable. Finally, urban economists evaluate the city in terms of economic theory and attempt to explain how a nonprofit firm works. They suggest ways of maximizing services from a fixed amount of dollars and indicate to what extent the problems of the city are due to a lack of resources.

Finally, the biographies of individual cities show what elements have affected growth and/or decline and what alternatives can be derived from the experiences of those living in these urban centers.

Cities of the World

Despite the common sense belief that all cities share certain elements—a belief which does have an element of truth in it—cities have had different origins and different patterns of development. European cities may have been located on rivers and may have shown expansion from East to West, but African cities do not necessarily share these features. In addition, meso-American cities show that it is possible to have cities where few people live and where there is no literate governing group.

This section contains books, films, and filmstrips on cities of the world. The emphasis is upon the origins of cities in history and on their development or demise. Included are materials on African, Chinese, and native American cities as well as general works on preindustrial cities and on European and Near Eastern cities. The data from this section ought to provide a benchmark against which the American urban experience can be set. To what extent do American cities resemble classical ones, and has their history merely replicated those histories of earlier ones?

487. Adams, Robert McC. **The Evolution of Urban Society: Early Mesopotamia and Pre-Hispanic Mexico.** Chicago: Aldine, 1966. 191 pp. LC 66-15195. $7.50, pap. $2.95.

A comparison of city development in Mesopotamia and Middle America. Advanced; probably would serve best as a reference work for research projects.

488. **Angkor—The Lost City.** National Film Board of Canada/Contemporary Films. 16mm. b/w. Sound. 12 min. Rent $4.

Studies the ancient capital of the Khimers, the ancestors of the Cambodians, and shows how an Eastern city was planned and formed. Illustrates the grandeur and frailty of this civilization. Suitable for all grades.

489. Briggs, Asa. **Victorian Cities.** New York: Harper & Row, 1970. 411 pp. 72-39072. pap. $2.95.

Briggs' classic work can be recommended to readers to demonstrate that the problems of American cities are not unique. Briggs studies Leeds, Manchester, London, Melbourne, and other English cities.

490. Childe, Vere Gordon. **What Happened in History?**, rev. ed. Baltimore: Penguin Books, 1954. 300 pp. pap. $1.65.

Includes the orthodox statement of the evolution of Mesopotamian cities from rural surplus. Childe also treats Indian and Egyptian civilizations. Good for most educated readers.

491. Cities of Europe. Encyclopaedia Brittanica Filmstrip, 1958. 7 filmstrips. Color. $6 each, $42 set.

Suitable for junior and senior high school students who should be able to see how these European cities developed in relation to their separate heritages as well as their points of similarity. Titles include:

    Granada and the Alhambra. (45 fr.) LC FiA 59-2270
    London (58 fr.) LC FiA 59-2271
    Madrid (51 fr.) LC FiA 59-2272
    Paris (58 fr.) LC FiA 59-2273
    Rome: The City (56 fr.) FiA 59-2274
    Toledo: Fortress City of Spain (43 fr.) FiA 59-2275

492. The City in History. Educational Dimensions Group, 1973. 2 filmstrips (79 fr. and 84 fr.). Color. Sound. 40 min. Sale $49 with cassettes.

The growth of cities through history. Part I traces the beginning of cities from ancient times until the Renaissance; Part II traces American cities from colonial times to the present. The level is from junior high through adult and the process of historical development is graphically shown.

493. Cottrell, Leonard. Lost Cities. New York: Grosset & Dunlap, 1963. 251 pp. LC 64-6438. pap. $2.25.

This British author examines Nimrud, Nineveh, Ur, Babylon, and Nippur. Good for the average reader.

494. Creel, H. G. The Birth of China. New York: Frederick Ungar, 1937. 402 pp. LC 54-5633. $10.50, pap. $3.45.

Describes cities along the Yellow River. Mainly for reference use.

495. Davidson, Basil. The Lost Cities of Africa. Boston: Little, Brown, 1959. 366 pp. LC 59-11107. $10, pap. $2.75.

Particularly useful in discussing the achievements of urban development in Africa. Suitable for senior high school students.

496. Exploring the Ancient Civilizations. Imperial Film Co., 1965. 6 filmstrips. Color. $7 each, $42 set.

Not highly sophisticated, so they may be used for varying levels. While concentrating primarily upon civilizations, they also show the cities of the past and indicate urban form. The titles are:

    Exploring Rome and Pompeii (40 fr.)
    Exploring Ancient Athens (38 fr.)
    Exploring Ba'albeck and Jerash (38 fr.)
    Exploring Ancient Egypt (38 fr.)
    Exploring Ancient Mexico: Pre-Aztec (38 fr.)
    Exploring Ancient Mexico: The Mayas (38 fr.)

497. History of the Cities. Warren Schloat Productions, 1972. 2 filmstrips (188 fr.). Color. Sound. 25 min. $42 with disc, $48 with cassette.

Designed for students from junior high school through college, the survey is fairly sophisticated and should be basic to any collection on urban history.

498. Man—Builder of Cities. Encyclopaedia Britannica, 1955. (Man and His Fight for Freedom.) 1 filmstrip (43 fr.). Color. $10.

Athens, Rome, Ch'ang-an, Venice, and Florence are viewed as old cities, while modern ones include New York, Paris, and Chicago. Useful for elementary through high school grades. Emphasis is mainly on cities in the Western tradition.

499. Peruvian Archeology. Pan American Union/International Film Bureau, 1951. 16mm. Color. Sound. 108 min. Sale $135, rent $8.

Five periods of Peruvian history are illustrated with examples of architecture, textiles, coverings, the arts, and aesthetic designs. The Inca Temple of the Sun is featured, as is Machu Picchu. Interdisciplinary in nature, and suitable for junior and senior high school students.

500. Pompeii: Once There Was a City. Learning Corporation of America/University of Illinois, 1970. 16mm. Color. Sound. 25 min. Rent $10.60.

Scenes from Pompeii are juxtaposed with those from American cities in the 1960s to emphasize the element of violence and material success in each. The obvious moralism does not intrude. Awarded Columbus Film Festival Chris Statuette. For high school students and above.

501. Roebuck, Janet. **The Shaping of Urban Society.** New York: Charles Scribners Sons, 1974. 256 pp. LC 73-18205. $8.95, pap. $3.95.

A general history of urban development, including economic, technological, social, political, intellectual, and social history.

502. Silverberg, Robert. **Lost Cities and Vanished Civilizations.** Philadelphia: Chilton, 1962. 177 pp. LC 62-8846. pap. $.95.

Silverberg includes a number of cities in the world from the Near East to Chichen Itza. Useful for the general reader.

503. Sjoberg, Gideon. **The Preindustrial City: Past and Present.** Glencoe, Ill.: Free Press, 1960. 353 pp. LC 60-10903. $8.95, pap. $3.95.

Difficult but essential. Sjoberg, a sociologist, attempts to describe preindustrial cities in terms of social class, marriage and the family, and economic, political, and religious structures. He assumes two forms of city life, the industrial and the preindustrial. Provocative and useful for deriving generalizations, but is not for any but the sophisticated reader.

504. The Sumerian Game. Board of Cooperative Educational Services. $12.

The basic economic principles at the time of the neolithic revolution in Mesopotamia are demonstrated in this game. The player assumes the role of Ludriga I, priest-ruler of Lagash in 3500 B.C., and tries to make the most productive decisions about the storage and distribution of grain, the development of crafts, the facilitation of trade, and other problems of economic life. While the game is aimed at the 6th-grade level, it could also be of use as an urban history introduction.

505. Swaan, Wim. **Lost Cities of Asia: Ceylon, Pagan, Angkor.** New York: Putnam, 1966. 175 pp. LC 66-25448. $15.

An account of the cities that have died in Asia. Popularly written and suitable for the average reader.

506. Urban Civilization. Educational Audio-Visual, 1972. 3 filmstrips (75 fr., 84 fr., 80 fr.) Color. 3 discs. $48 with discs, $54 with cassettes.

These filmstrips with commentary are not individually titled but each centers on the growth and development of cities in human history. The level is junior high to college.

507. Vaillant, George. **The Aztecs of Mexico,** 2nd ed. Baltimore: Penguin Books, 1962. 362 pp. LC 69-87819. pap. $2.95.

Comprehensive history of the Aztecs with many illustrations. The first few chapters are the most useful on the development of cities in Mexico. Not for the average reader, but an excellent reference source.

508. Weber, Adna F. **The Growth of Cities in the Nineteenth Century.** Westport, Conn.: Greenwood Press, 1969 (originally published in 1889). 495 pp. LC 69-1412. $18.75. Cornell University Press, pap. $2.95.

Weber's account was remarkable at the time for its sophisticated statistical analysis of city growth. It is still valuable for the present-day student, both as a reference work and as a view of past historical study.

509. Wheeler, Sir Robert Eric Mortimer. **The Indus Civilization,** 3rd ed. Cambridge: Cambridge University Press, 1968. 143 pp. NUC 69-64617. $11.50, pap. $4.95.

Standard work on cities of the Indus Valley. Useful as a reference tool for those who wish to do research on urban development in that area, but not a book for general use.

510. Wolf, Eric. **Sons of the Shaking Earth.** Chicago: University of Chicago Press, 1959. 302 pp. LC 59-12290. $10.50, pap. $2.45.

A cultural history of the people of Mexico and Guatemala with many illustrations and several chapters on urban life and form. Well written and suitable for senior high school students.

Urban Theory

The future of cities and their past development have engaged present-day intellectuals, philosophers, and commentators. These thinkers have struggled with how the good life may be lived in urban areas and what kinds of physical conditions are necessary for the achievement of that good life. They have also tried to key urban existence to human needs. Some have derived grand theory to explain the growth of cities in the past and to predict future patterns. Others have a more limited view, opting to study more limited periods and areas.

Included in this section are the works of such notable urbanologists as Lewis Mumford, both his books and films derived from them. Older theorists such as Ebenezer Howard are also included. Political scientists like Scott Greer and economists like John Kenneth Galbraith appear, but so also do such unaffiliated intellectuals as Konstantinos Doxiadis and Paolo Soleri. These thinkers all project visions about the ideal city, albeit very personal ones. In addition, there are materials inserted on "new" town movements, their past successes and failures and their probable future. Without such visions as these thinkers have, the future of cities would be dim indeed.

511. Bender, Thomas. **Toward an Urban Vision.** Lexington, Ky.: University of Kentucky Press, 1974. 292 pp. LC 74-18930. $14.50.

Bender is concerned with the growth of intellectual and institutional mechanisms coming to terms with the industrial city of 19th-century America. Bender offers a series of case studies on how various Americans adopted new ideas when it became obvious that the Jeffersonian heritage of antiurbanism did not fit the realities of the mid-19th century. Particularly good on Frederick Law Olmsted and is a requisite volume for collections on the history of the idea of urbanism.

512. Berry, Brian J. L. **The Human Consequences of Urbanization.** New York: St. Martin's Press, 1973. 205 pp. LC 73-86361. $9.95, pap. $3.95.

A high-level book on theory. Berry disclaims the idea that urbanization is a single, universal process, maintaining instead that what is called urbanization is composed of several different processes coming out of disparate cultures and historic eras. Not for the ordinary reader but deserves a place in sections devoted to urban theory.

513. Bierman, A. K. **The Philosophy of Urban Existence.** Athens, Ohio: Ohio University Press, 1973. 194 pp. LC 72-96393. $8.50.

Bierman's basic premise is that the city life is the best and concentrates on the changes in attitude which are necessary to reform American or any other cities. Not as difficult as its title might indicate, it is a useful reflection on human ideas.

514. Bookchin, Murray. **The Limits of the City.** New York: Harper & Row, 1973. 147 pp. LC 73-17852. pap. $2.75.

From a sociological perspective, Bookchin tries to delineate an urban process which has operated in history but which has been negated in today's cities. Moreover, Bookchin believes that the future community will go beyond the bounds of present cities. Theoretical, not for beginners.

515. **Boomsville.** National Film Board of Canada/Learning Corporation of America, 1969. 16mm. Color. Sound. 11 min. $130.

An animated account of the growth of cities showing how the land was exploited to create urban centers and ends with the total despoilation of the planet earth and the commencement of the same process on another one. For nearly all audiences.

516. Burgess, Ernest Watson, ed. **The Urban Community: Selected Papers from the Proceedings of the American Sociological Society, 1925.** Westport, Conn.: Greenwood Press, 1972 (originally published in 1926). 268 pp. LC 68-57591. $12.

Burgess was one of the prominent leaders in the Chicago School of Sociology. In this reprint, originally issued by the University of Chicago Press, Burgess collated a group of articles directed at the problems of city life. This pioneering volume belongs in collections on urban sociology or in histories of urban thought.

517. Clapp, James A. **New Towns and Urban Policy.** Port Washington, N.Y.: Kennikat/Dunellan, 1971. 342 pp. LC 78-136245. $12.50, pap. $5.95.

Considers whether or not the "new" town idea is the best way to control growing urbanization. Written from the viewpoint of an urban planner, emphasizes that discipline as well as others in the social sciences. It is balanced but not easy; consequently, it is recommended for larger libraries with already existing collections on urban planning.

518. Conner, Paul W. **Poor Richard's Politicks: Benjamin Franklin and His New American Order.** New York: Oxford University Press, 1965. 285 pp. LC 65-25056. pap. $1.95.

Conner attempts to sort out Franklin's ideas about the desired shape of the American future. Conner says Franklin's praise of rural life was a disguised attack on shopkeeper ethics. For the advanced reader.

519. Corrigan, Anne Woodward. **Learning from British New Towns.** Washington, D.C.: U.S. Department of Labor, Manpower Administration, 1971. 27 pp. free.

A fairly successful attempt to suggest ways in which American city planners and developers can utilize the hard-won insights of British creators of "new" towns. Corrigan believes that the "new" town movement does have merit and that some British experiences can be transplanted.

520. Doxiadis, Konstantinos Apostolou, and Douglass, Truman B. **The New World of Urban Man.** Philadelphia: United Church Press, 1965. 127 pp. LC 65-23113. pap. $1.60.

Doxiadis is an urbanologist and utopian planner who envisages a better world through social planning and physical engineering. Here he gives a hint of that future. Intended for general readers and not for architects or city planners.

521. Doxiadis, Konstantinos Apostolou. **Ekistics: An Introduction to the Science of Human Settlement.** New York: Oxford University Press, 1968. LC 68-11162. $35.

The most important exposition of Doxiadis' ideas. Can only be afforded by large libraries.

522. Forrester, J. W. **Urban Dynamics.** Cambridge, Mass.: MIT Press, 1969. 285 pp. LC 69-19246. $12.50.

Forrester's attempt to work out a systems model for cities is heavily mathematical and therefore is suited to the reader who can cope with this kind of thinking. Only for research libraries.

523. **John Kenneth Galbraith: The Idea of a City.** Chelsea House, 1969. Videotape. 16mm. Super 8. Color. Sound. 28 min. $216 for videotape, $360 for 16mm, Super-8 rent $40 (single showing).

Galbraith, the noted economist, traces the historic transition from the pre-industrial to the industrial city in terms of economic efficiency. He tends to take an organic view of the city, but this does not detract from an essentially stimulating effort. Suitable for sophisticated and advanced students.

524. Goodman, Robert. **After the Planners.** New York: Simon & Schuster, 1971. 231 pp. LC 74-154100. $8.95, pap. $2.95.

Unsympathetic to city planning, Goodman, in this polemical account, points to a number of glaring deficiencies which he claims planning possesses. Popularly written and counterbalances those studies which assume that city planning will end all urban difficulties.

525. Greer, Scott. **The Emerging City: Myth and Reality.** New York: Free Press, 1965. 232 pp. LC 62-11851. $7.95.

Greer predicts the future by projecting from today's metropolis. He analyzes the contemporary urban crisis and the changes occurring in the cities. Stimulating, and recommended for teacher resources and special student projects.

526. Handlin, Oscar, and Burchard, John, eds. **The Historian and the City.** Cambridge, Mass.: MIT Press, 1963. 299 pp. LC 63-18004. $12.50, pap. $2.95.

A noted historian and an architect have collaborated to write on the problems of urban history. Essential as a starting point for those interested in theory and in what historians have done in the past. For advanced readers.

527. Hawley, Amos H. **Human Ecology.** New York: Ronald Press, 1950. 456 pp. LC 50-7591. $8.50.

One of the first books to stimulate interest in human ecology and to apply principles of animal ecology to man's behavior. Relatively difficult.

528. Howard, Ebenezer. **Garden Cities of Tomorrow.** Cambridge, Mass.: MIT Press, 1965. 168 pp. LC 65-10521. pap. $2.45.

Howard was an English visionary at the turn of the century whose work (reprinted) had wide impact on urban planning in England as well as in the United States. A classic that should be in every library with materials on the urban condition.

529. Jackson, John N. **The Urban Future: A Choice Between Alternatives.** London: Allen & Unwin, 1972. 335 pp. LC 72-193884. $13.75.

Presents several scenerios of possible future urban development. Jackson does concede the presence of a number of problems but is hopeful that the future, if rationally approached, can be manipulated. Recommended for those interested or involved in the projection of urban futures.

530. Jacobs, Jane. **The Death and Life of Great American Cities.** New York: Random House, 1961. 458 pp. LC 61-6262. $10, pap. $1.95.

Jacobs is highly critical of urban renewal, and argues for diversity and for the idea of mixed neighborhoods (commercial, residential, etc.). Controversial but significant.

531. Jacobs, Jane. **The Economy of Cities.** New York: Random House, 1969. 268 pp. LC 69-16413. pap. $1.95.

Here the controversial writer on urban affairs lays claim for primacy in civilization to the city. Contains many references to historical cities and, while well written, may be somewhat difficult for students. Ms. Jacobs' ideas, however, are challenging and must be confronted.

532. Kantor, Harvey A. **Designs for the American City: Utopian, Utilitarian, and Useless.** St. Charles, Mo.: Forum Press, 1973. 16 pp. LC 73-81060. pap. $.95.

Kantor's essay claims that the visions of urban designers have not been carried out and that American cities have suffered as a result of this failure. The pamphlet is a sharp critique of city planning as it is now implemented and is a useful introduction to contemporary views on planning.

533. Kennedy, Albert S., and Woods, Robert A. **The Zone of Emergence,** 2nd ed. Cambridge, Mass.: MIT Press, 1969. LC 76-076450. $10, pap. $1.95.

Woods and Kennedy originated the concept to describe the lower-middle and middle-class neighborhoods located just beyond the slums of the central city. This is an analysis on Boston utilizing the model and tracing the problems of a population which, though fairly successful, had little in the way of security and dreaded the possible slide back into lower-class conditions. Suggested for persons with some background in urban theory.

534. Marx, Leo. **The Machine in the Garden.** New York: Oxford University Press, 1964. 392 pp. LC 64-14864. $11.50.

Shows how much our ideas of cities are based upon a view of the good life as a pastoral one. Marx draws heavily from 19th-century literary efforts, though he devotes some space to F. Scott Fitzgerald.

535. Meadows, Paul, and Mizruchi, Ephriam H., eds. **Urbanism, Urbanization and Change: Comparative Perspectives.** Reading, Mass.: Addison-Wesley, 1969. 579 pp. LC 69-11629. $10.95.

Another collection of theoretical essays which attempts to define and classify urban phenomena. Difficult.

536. Meier, R. S. "Game Procedure in the Simulation of Cities," in J. L. Duhl, ed. **The Urban Condition.** New York: Simon & Schuster, 1969. 410 pp. NUC 70-66525.

Discusses the whys and hows of setting up an urban game. An imaginative and innovative person could use Meier's suggestions.

537. Meyerson, Martin, and Banfield, Edward C. **Boston: The Job Ahead.** Cambridge, Mass.: Harvard University Press, 1966. 121 pp. LC 66-14449. $6.

This work of two well-known writers on urban affairs suggests what needs to be done to improve the urban climate in Boston. Since neither of the authors is utopian, the suggestions are not radical. Has wider application than its title suggests.

538. **Toward a National Urban Policy.** Daniel P. Moynihan, ed. New York: Basic Books, 1970. 348 pp. LC 79-103092. $8.95.

Moynihan, an urbanologist with both the Johnson and Nixon administrations, edited this collection of essays on current urban dilemmas as well as contributing two of his own. The volume dwells on urban problems but it also offers a number of alternatives for future urban planning. Helpful for the informed layperson to catch the flavor of current thinking about urban affairs.

539. Mumford, Lewis. **Art and Technics.** New York: Columbia University Press, 1952. 162 pp. LC 52-1930. $10, pap. $1.95.

Here Mumford elucidates his belief that man's greatest creation is his own personality, not his tools. He expresses his basic philosophy, that aesthetics precedes technological development and that imagination predates rationalism. This book, along with the *The Myth of the Machine: I Technics and Human Development* (Harcourt, 1967) *and The Myth of the Machine: II The Pentagon of Power* (New York: Harcourt Brace Jovanovich, 1970), articulates the theoretical base of much of Mumford's thought.

540. Mumford, Lewis. **The Brown Decades: A Study of the Arts in America, 1865–1895,** 2nd rev. ed. New York: Dover, 1955. 266 pp. LC 55-14851. pap. $2.

The relationships between art and architecture in 30 of the last 35 years in the 19th century. This is an elaboration, in a particular period, of Mumford's pioneer study of American architecture, *Sticks and Stones*. It is particularly useful for this period of city development as it does discuss current building theory and practice.

541. Mumford, Lewis. **The City in History: Its Origins, Its Transformations, and Its Prospects.** New York: Harcourt, Brace, and World, 1961. 657 pp. LC 61-7689. $18.50, pap. $4.95.

One of the two major works on urban history by Mumford. The other is *The Culture of Cities*. *The City in History* goes back to prehistoric times to trace the origins of the modern city. Mumford claims the city came from an "urban implosion" which merged settled neolithic and nomadic paleolithic groups and thus the city combined both constructive and destructive forces at its inception. A panoramic view of the whole of urban history that won the National Book Award for nonfiction in 1961. Ought to be in every library.

542. Mumford, Lewis. **The Culture of Cities.** New York: Harcourt, Brace, 1934; New York: Harvest Book, Harcourt Brace Jovanovich, 1970. 586 pp. LC 76-17434. $12.50.

Part of a four-volume effort of Mumford's gathered together under the title and theme "Renewal of Life." Mumford proposed three books, one concerned with technology, another with cities, and the third with human personality. The first was *Technics and Civilization*, the second was *The Culture of Cities*, and the third became two books, *The Condition of Man* (Harcourt, 1944) and *The Conduct of Life* (Harcourt, 1951). In his book on the culture of the cities, Mumford argued that some cities of the past had provided the physical setting for human dignity and cultural advance but that the last 300 years of urban growth had demolished the sense of balance and had resulted in dehumanized cities.

543. Mumford, Lewis. **The Highway and the City.** New York: Harvest Books, Harcourt, Brace, and World, 1963, paperback; New York: Mentor Books, New American Library, 1964, paperback. 246 pp. LC 36-10598. pap. $2.35.

Essays primarily aimed at American and European city planning and development after World War II. Mumford is quite critical of the developers who were less concerned with social needs than for the provision of parking places for automobiles and for rapid exit from the city to the suburb. Mumford's criticism has become more apt as the time goes on, and this volume can be used by those interested in recent urban history as well as those in recent urban planning.

544. **Lewis Mumford on the City.** National Film Board of Canada/Sterling Education Films, 1963–1965. 16mm. b/w. Sound. approx. 30 min. each. Sale $185 each from Sterling; rent $9.25 from Indiana University Audio-Visual Center. The titles in the series are:

The City—Cars or People. Parallels *The Highway and the City* in that it demonstrates the present impasse in urban transportation and then tries to show alternatives to the present system.

The City and the Future. Here Mumford offers a choice between low-grade urban sprawl and new regional cities, and suggests ways to achieve the latter, which he says is the focus of man's highest achievement.

The City—Heaven and Hell. Mumford's theme is the historical background of cities. His theories of city growth and development are presented and explained.

The City and Its Regions. The emphasis on regional planning and development is a thread which runs through Mumford's work. Here he examines the relationship between countryside and city and offers suggestions as to how this relationship can be maintained.

The City as Man's Home. Here Mumford describes the social problems inherent in slums, high-rise housing, and suburbia. Again, he indicates how he thinks better planning and design will raise the standards of low income groups.

The Heart of the City. The last film in Mumford's series shows the dullness and sterility of the central city and advances ways and means of brightening and improving these areas.

545. Mumford, Lewis. **Sticks and Stones: A Study of American Architecture and Culture,** 2nd rev. ed. New York: Dover, 1955. 238 pp. LC 55-14852. pap. $2.

A pioneer survey of American architectural history, *Sticks and Stones* relates the development of cities to other aspects of cultural development. Mumford shows how the "spirit of an age" informed art and architecture, buildings and paintings, literature and life. Important as the jumping-off place for those interested in Mumford and architectural history.

546. Mumford, Lewis. **Technics and Civilization.** New York: Harcourt Brace Jovanovich, 1967. 495 pp. LC 67-160088. pap. $5.25.

Mumford expresses his theory of technological evolution based on three stages of development: eotechnic, paleotechnic, and neotechnic. The last emerged in the 1880s and resulted in such phenomena as urban slums and bombed-out cities. The first of the Renewal series, *Technics and Civilization* best outlines Mumford's theory of the relation of humans to technology and suggests how today's horrors can be overcome.

547. Mumford, Lewis. **The Urban Prospect.** New York: Harcourt, Brace, and World, 1968. 255 pp. LC 68-20631. $7.95, pap. $2.75.

Written during the 1960s, these essays may be considered as later expressions of themes found in *The Highway and the City*. Mumford decries the shortsightedness of builders of public housing who failed to take into account human amenities, and architects such as Le Corbusier and Mies van der Rohe whose emphasis on structural forms denigrated sociability and human values.

548. Newman, Elmer. **Lewis Mumford: A Bibliography, 1914–1970.** New York: Harcourt Brace Jovanovich, 1971. 167 pp. LC 72-16407. $10.

Contains over 120 pages of listings of Mumford's writings. For reference purposes.

549. **New Towns Symposium, Los Angeles, 1972; New Towns: Why and for Whom?** Harvey S. Perloff and Neil C. Sandberg, eds. New York: Praeger, 1973. 250 pp. LC 73-1094. $16.50.

Papers given at a 1972 conference on New Towns at UCLA and sponsored by the American Jewish Committee. The papers are by persons from various disciplines and professions. Not difficult and the general reader will find it a good place to begin for the theory and practice of "new" town development.

550. Schmandt, Henry J., and Bloomberg, Warner. **The Quality of Urban Life.** Urban Affairs Annual Review. Beverly Hills, Cal.: Sage Publications, 1969. 590 pp. LC 69-133009. $22.50, pap. $7.50.

Concentrates upon the definition as well as the conduct of the good life in cities. The essays are by such noted urbanologists as Scott Greer and Hans Blumenfeld, and include thoughts on citizenship, mental health, the arts, the mass media, education, leadership, and management. Like others in the series, this should be in any sizable library.

551. Sennett, Richard. **The Uses of Disorder: Personal Identity and City Life.** New York: Knopf, 1970. 198 pp. LC 71-106628. $5.95. Random House, pap. $1.95.

Another argument for the city. Sennett believes that association with others of like identity develops a personality that has little tolerance of ambiguity. Therefore, city areas ought to be composed of people of mixed incomes and shops of mixed occupancy. Sennett advocates vertical streets with stores, bars, and laundromats on various building levels. To accomplish all this, Sennett would eliminate centralized authority and zoning laws. His work is interesting and provocative and can be recommended for better students.

552. Soleri, Paolo. **The Bridge Between Matter and Spirit Is Matter Becoming Spirit: The Arcology of Paolo Soleri.** Garden City, N.Y.: Doubleday, 1973. 253 pp. LC 72-87501. $2.95.

Soleri coined a new term, arcology (architecture ecology), to describe his work. His essays here discuss efforts to apply his ideas in central Arizona in a structure called Arconsanto. Quite interesting, and valuable to those absorbed in architectural theory.

553. Starr, Roger. **The Living End.** New York: Coward-McCann, 1966. 284 pp. LC 66-10429. $5.95.

Examines the critics of the city and their overly simplistic solutions to its problems. Starr identifies five areas which are the most significant trouble spots and suggests solutions. For better students.

554. Strong, Josiah. **The Twentieth Century City.** History of Urban America. New York: Arno Press, 1970 (originally published in 1898). 186 pp. LC 77-112575. $7.

Strong was an important minister of the social gospel persuasion. In this reprint, Strong voices his concern over the shape of the future American city. Strong believed that cities would continue to grow and recognized that this growth was a product of economic forces endemic in larger societies. Still he feared that the problems of the city might prove too much and, to counteract growing problems, he suggested greater religious concentration upon evangelizing city people. Belongs in libraries which have collections on the idea of the city and impact of this idea on religious thought and institutions.

555. Task Force on Land Use and Urban Growth; The Use of Land: A Citizen's Policy Guide to Urban Growth. William K. Reilly, ed. New York: Crowell, 1973. 318 pp. LC 73-8215. $10, pap. $3.95.

This report takes a middle position on urban growth, arguing that some growth is not only possible but necessary and that this growth can be made compatible with a livable environment. Not difficult; should have a wide circulation.

556. White, Morton, and White, Lucia. The Intellectual Versus the City: From Thomas Jefferson to Frank Lloyd Wright. Cambridge, Mass.: Harvard University Press, 1962. 270 pp. LC 62-17229. $7.50. Mentor, pap. $1.25.

The Whites focus specifically upon antiurban sentiment and rely upon thinkers like Emerson, Henry Adams, and Henry James. While difficult, it is useful in providing a long overview.

Perceptions of the American city are not scarce in the visual and literary arts. The subject of human and natural life in cities has attracted the artist, the photographer, the novelist, and the musician. Nor has this subject been the property of the professional in the area of the creative arts. Everyday citizens form some kind of cognitive map which enables them to navigate through the city with consistent ease and without requiring conscious thought. The creation of this cognitive map is often best understood through the psychology of perception and not through the mechanisms of aesthetic choice.

This section contains books, records, filmstrips, films, and games which show how American cities have been captured in print, in paintings, and in photographs. These materials range from scholarly research on American novelists and readings from serious works to popular insights into the city. This section is more impressionistic than the one on urban design and often contains materials which are more emotionally evocative and less cognitively oriented.

557. Abbott, Bernice. **New York in the Thirties.** New York: Dover, 1973 (originally published in 1939). 97 pp. LC 73-77375. pap. $3.

An unabridged republication of a collection of photographs taken during the 1930s by Bernice Abbott. Contains 97 photographs taken under the auspices of the WPA. Like its pictorial counterpart on rural life sponsored by the FSA, this collection catches both the technological developments of the 1930s as well as memorable social scenes. Good and useful, on several levels.

558. **American Literature—The Westward Movement.** Coronet Instructional Films/Purdue University, 1954. 16mm. Sound. Color and b/w. 11 min. Sale b/w $65, color $130; rent $3.75.

Authors whose views are explored are Washington Irving, Mark Twain, Joaquin Miller, Bess Streeter Aldrich, and Emerson Hough. While not commenting specifically upon city and country, the authors do reveal their feelings on the nature of the West and the possibility of cities there. For both junior and senior high school students.

559. Chase, Ilka. **New York 22: That District of the City Which Lies between Fiftieth and Sixtieth Streets, Fifth Avenue and the East River.** Westport, Conn.: Greenwood Press, 1972 (originally published in 1951). 308 pp. LC 73-112322. $14.75.

Ilka Chase's popular description of a New York district appeared first as a Doubleday book. Chase's style is a pleasant and easy one; the book is chatty, but does convey a sense of a certain type of urban existence. The reprint has more, therefore, than just curiosity value.

560. Cities—The Dream. Cities—The Reality. Filmstrip House, 1971. (The 1970's.) 2 filmstrips (85 fr. and 92 fr.) Color. Sound. $72 with cassettes; $60 with records.

The first part of this set portrays the way cities should be; the second shows what they are. The level is from junior high school through adult. Because of the attempt to meet the requirements of such mixed audiences, it is not particularly sophisticated.

561. The City and the Modern Writer. Guidance Associates, 1971. 2 filmstrips. Color. Sound. 2 discs. $48.50.

The level is junior high and the theme is the image of the city as seen by contemporary authors. The first filmstrip is entitled *Images and Impressions*. The underlying idea is a good one and ties in well with the book resources of a library.

562. The City in American Painting. Allentown, Pa.: Allentown Art Museum, 1973. 41 pp. LC 72-97164. pap. $3.

A catalog of 19th- and 20th-century paintings at the Allentown Art Museum by artists who were inspired by urban themes. Of broad interest, recommended for general as well as specialized libraries.

563. The City in the Modern World. Educational Dimensions Group, 1973. 2 filmstrips (85 fr. each). Color. Sound. 40 min. $49 with cassettes.

A contemporary cities filmstrip set designed for students from junior high through college. Although somewhat elementary, it does illustrate the physical impact of the city quite well.

564. Cook, Ann, Gittell, Marilyn, and Mach, Herb, eds. **City Life, 1865–1900; Views of Urban America.** New York: Praeger, 1973. 292 pp. LC 78-95674. $10.

This collection relies heavily upon visual materials to show the growth of American cities in the post-Civil War decades. Included are such items as maps, posters, drawings, and newspaper photographs. Recommended for those libraries which lack other kinds of visual materials and that have persons interested in the shape and design of the American city.

565. Cook, David Miller. **The Small Town in American Literature.** New York: Dodd, Mead, 1969. 253 pp. LC 69-18469. pap. $4.95.

General discussion of treatment of small towns in novels. Definitive for reference purposes.

566. Cowan, Michael H. City of the West: Emerson, America, and Urban Metaphor. New Haven, Conn: Yale University Press, 1967. 284 pp. LC 67-24492. $7.50.

Necessary resource for delineating the metaphor of the city. Wider in scope than the subtitle indicates.

567. The Crowd. Gades Films International/Learning Corporation of America. 16mm. b/w. Sound. 18 min. Sale $130, rent $10.

A film with no dialogue that focuses on crowds of all descriptions, human mostly, but also animal and cellular. Its impact is visual and psychological, making it profitable for most audiences.

568. Dos Passos, John. U.S.A.: Selection from the "42nd Parallel." Caedmon Records, 1968. 3 discs $20.94; 3 cassettes $23.85. John Dos Passos, Ed Begley, Rip Torn, and George Gizzard, narrators.

Excerpts are from the novel which concerns American life in the 20th century and includes much material on urban styles. Selections include some from the "Camera's Eye" and biographical excerpts. Recommended for adults.

569. Dunlap, George A. The City in the American Novel, 1789-1900. New York: Russell and Russell, 1965 (originally published in 1934). 187 pp. LC 65-17889. $10.

This reprint correctly points out that the first American novel was written with an urban background. Dunlap has limited his book more than the title would indicate, as it covers only eastern cities.

570. Dyos, H.J., and Wolff, Michael, eds. The Victorian City: Images and Realities. 2 vols. Boston: Routledge, 1973. LC 73-76088. $46.50 per vol., $85 set.

A huge two-volume set with a high price. The size and price are results of many contributors and numerous illustrations. The title should be acquired, if only for reference purposes.

571. Ellison, Ralph. Invisible Man. New York: Random House, 1952. 439 pp. LC 52-5159. $7.50. Signet, pap. $1.95.

Ellison's superb novel attempts to recreate the experience of the Black man in America. Can be used for Black images of the city.

572. Gelfant, Blanche H. The American City Novel, 1900-1940. Norman, Okla.: University of Oklahoma Press, 1954. 289 pp. LC 54-5986. $4.95.

Gelfant applies sociological insights to such writers as Dreiser and Dos Passos. Nicely analyzes writers of the period.

573. Ghost Towns of the Great Divide. Classroom Film Distributors, 1951. 16mm. Color. Sound. 13 min. Sale $150, rent $10.

While this film of Leadville, Colorado, treats a town that no longer exists in its gold-rush-days glory it is good in showing aspirations of the town as seen through its opera house and hotel. The furnishings and general decor ought to interest viewers.

574. Gill, Don, and Bonnett, Penelope. **Nature in the Urban Landscape: A Study of City Ecosystems.** Baltimore: York Press, 1973. 209 pp. LC 73-76409. $12.

An excursion into the biology of urban areas. Gill and Bonnet show how much life exists in the natural areas of the city as well as how to encourage the further growth of such life. Although of primary interest to biologists, it also should attract the notice of architects, city planners, and developers. As such, it should be purchased by all urban libraries.

575. The Green City. Stuart Finley, 1963. 16mm. Color. Sound. 23 min. Sale $200, rent $7.50.

International Film Festival first prize winner in 1963, it describes the destruction of green spaces by city development. An excellent, aesthetically pleasing film that students will enjoy.

576. Hansen, Gladys, ed. **San Francisco, The Bay and Its Cities,** 3rd ed. New York: Hastings House, 1973. $12.50.

This is the third edition and second revision of the Federal Writers' Project guide to San Francisco. The original was published during the depression. This edition is up to date, using material from the 1970 census. An excellent reference for libraries since it can be used as a guide book as well as a research tool. Illustrations will appeal to the general reader.

577. Hawes, Josiah Johnson. **The Legacy of Josiah Johnson Hawes: 19th Century Photographs of Boston,** edited and with an introduction by Rachel Johnson Hawes. Barre, Mass.: Barre Publishers, 1972. 131 pp. LC 72-83295. $12.50.

Readers who are interested in the appearance of the city will welcome this collection of photographs of Boston. Those involved in architectural design or city planning can use the collection with profit, but it is also suited to the general public as it catches the flavor of the 19th-century city.

578. How to Look at a City. National Educational Television/Indiana University Audio-Visual Center, 1964. (*Metropolis—Creator or Destroyer.*) 16 mm. b/w. Sound. 28½ min. Sale $75, rent $6.75.

Eugene Raskin, noted architect and author, discusses the standards used by architects and city planners to judge the quality of city neighborhoods. These standards include human scale, density, and variety. Not an easy film, but essential to courses on the city.

579. Hunstein, Don. **New York, A Book of Photographs,** rev. ed. London: Spring Books, 1962. LC 64-9731/CD.

Revised edition of an older classic. The skyline of New York has changed, but the buildings in this book are still significant. For general as well as for more specialized collections.

580. Kazin: **The Writer and the City.** Chelsea House, 1969. 16 mm and videotape. Color. Sound. 28 min. Sale $360 for film, $216 for videotape, rent $40 (film only).

The city as an aesthetic force in literature from Whitman and Melville to Norman Mailer. For more sophisticated students, but well worth the effort for any interested person. Particularly good for an approach which attempts to combine literature and history; it offers much on images of the city.

581. Kieran, John. **A Natural History of New York City**, rev. and abridged ed. Garden City, N.Y.: Published for the American Museum of Natural History by Natural History Press, 1971. 309 pp. LC 70-13909. $6.25.

A mine of information on the animals and birds which have lived or do live in New York City and on the author's experience with them. Kieran is a journalist so the book is well written and is a source of pleasure to the ordinary reader.

582. King, Moses. **King's Handbook of New York City, 1893**, 2nd ed. New York: B. Blom, 1973 (originally published in 1893). LC 72-87641. $28.50.

A huge volume with profuse illustrations of New York City buildings. Of interest to those concerned with architecture, urban design, and urban history. Recommended for libraries which are in the process of or already have extensive collections in these areas.

583. Kirschner, Don S. **City and Country: Rural Responses to Urbanization in the 1920's.** Westport, Conn.: Greenwood Press, 1970. 279 pp. LC 78-95502. $12.50.

Chiefly a study of rural attitudes regarding the city, not just of the process of urbanization. Limited in coverage, it can help those who wish to know the kinds of reactions a nation of cities engendered.

584. Kouwenhoven, John A. **Made in America: The Arts in Modern Civilization.** New York: Norton, 1967. 259 pp. NUC 67-100516. pap. $2.95.

Illustrated and suitable for more mature high school students. Kouwenhoven weaves technological development and design together in an engaging way. Valuable for its discussion of the balloon-frame house and cast-iron fronts. *Made in America* ought to help round out students' general education.

585. Leisure in the Cities. New York Times, 1970. 1 filmstrip (66 fr.) Color. Sound. 1 disc. $9.

Intended for schools, and illustrates the variety of recreational opportunities which a large city can afford. More appropriate to those areas unacquainted with urban life.

586. Living in the Cities. New York Times, 1970. 1 filmstrip (73 fr.) Color. Sound. 1 disc. $9.

The variety of life-styles possible for urban residents is the subject matter. Recommended for those libraries in areas uninformed about this aspect of urban communities.

587. Lynch, Kevin. **The Image of the City.** Cambridge, Mass.: MIT Press, 1960. 194 pp. LC 60-7632. $8.50, pap. $2.95.

A must for a theoretical approach to urban form. Touching on theories of perception, Lynch documents the images of specific cities in the United States. A slim volume for advanced students.

588. Man and His Environment. Hester and Associates. 12 Super—8mm film loop cartridges. Color. Silent. Sale $22.50 each.

A series with the following titles: *The Inner City I, The Inner City II, Suburbia, A Portrait of a Small Town, Faces in the City, City at Work, City at Play, Moving City, Where I Live, Signs of the City, Times of the City, The Fair.* Because of the character of the film loops, the significant feature is the visual one. The aim is to catch an impression of social activity, not to teach any necessary lessons. Given this goal, the film loops seem to have met it.

589. Mark Twain's America. NBC-TV/McGraw-Hill, 1960. 16mm. b/w. Sound. 54 min. Sale $275.

Originally an NBC Project 20 production, this film uses photographs, prints, and engravings to portray Twain's view of America. The time span covers most of the 19th century and the movie helps to focus on the literary imagination. For junior and senior high school students.

590. Masters, Edgar Lee. Spoon River Anthology. Caedmon Records. 1 disc. 56 min. $6.98. Cassette $7.95. Julie Harris, narrator.

Life as it was lived in a small Illinois town and as was represented by figures in a graveyard is the topic of these poems (epitaphs) by Masters. Catches the flavor of a different kind of urban experience.

591. Maurice, Arthur Bartlett. New York in Fiction. Port Washington, N.Y.: Ira J. Friedman, 1969 (originally published in 1899). LC 68-28930. $6.

Donnal V. Smith has provided a new introduction to an old book. Maurice patterned his book after Thackery's *London*, using as a format portions of imaginative works along with pictures of the area. Maurice knew many 19th-century authors and these friendships provided insights into their works. Also has value for its illustrations of a vanished, or rapidly vanishing, city.

592. Millionaires of Poverty Gulch. National Educational Television/Indiana University Audio-Visual Center, 1965. 16mm. b/w. Sound. 30 min. Rent $6.75.

Cripple Creek, Colorado, as a typical gold mining community in the West. Suitable for junior and senior high school students.

593. The Miracle Builders. Classroom Film Distributors/Indiana University, 1954. 16mm. Color. Sound. 13 min. Rent $7.

The theme is the architectural and engineering genius that went into building Baalbek in Lebanon, the church of San Sophia in Istanbul, and the fortress of Sacsahuaman in the Peruvian Andes. Valuable for its cross-cultural comparisons. Probably best suited for senior high school students, but useful in lower grades as well.

594. The Mural on Our Street. Henry Street Settlement/Contemporary Films, 1964. 16mm. Sound. Color. 18 min. Sale $175. Judith Crist, narrator.

Shows how the members of the Henry Street settlement house made a ceramic tile mural. Can be understood by high school students, and is an interesting introduction to the operation of a settlement house in our time.

595. Nairn, Ian. **The American Landscape: A Critical View.** New York: Random House, 1965. 152 pp. LC 64-11982. $7.95.

Nairn takes a hard look at American cities based upon his travels in this country from 1940 to 1960. He has sharp criticisms about architecture and the lack of planning. Highly recommended for interested readers.

596. New York Historical Society. **Old New York in Early Photographs, 1853 –1901.** Mary Black, ed. New York: Dover, 1973. 228 pp. LC 72-90527. $6.

191 photographs taken from the New York Historical Society and running from 1853 to 1901. Black has selected the photographs and has written an introduction and commentary for the text. Inexpensive, and highly recommended for libraries which need illustrated material.

597. The Persistent Seed. National Film Board of Canada, 1963. 16 mm. Color. Sound. 14 min. Sale $150.

A poetic treatment of how nature persists despite man's attempts to alter and shape it. The camera views shrubs and grass growing in very unlikely places, and in so doing comments on the values of modern society. The optimism here may be a useful antidote to the pessimism found in most films on air pollution. Also useful in suggesting images of the city, the major one being the country in the city.

598. Strauss, Anselm L., ed. **The American City: A Sourcebook of Urban Imagery.** Chicago: Aldine, 1968. 530 pp. LC 67-17610. $12.95.

Readings paralleling Strauss' *Images* . . . .

599. Strauss, Anselm L., ed. **Images of the American City.** New York: Free Press of Glencoe, 1961. LC 60-10904. $7.95.

Strauss' books are an attempt to catalog images of the city. His sources are mainly the reactions of individuals to the cities of their times; he does not rely on imaginative literature.

600. Street Musique. National Film Board of Canada/Learning Corporation of America, 1973. 16mm. Color. Sound. 9 min. Sale $145, rent $15.

This award-winning film at the National Educational Film Festival in 1973 is an animated one done by Ryan Larkin. It is abstract and shows the reaction of the author to a band of street musicians. Funny, and will appeal to older children and adults.

601. Syrinx/Cityscape. National Film Board of Canada/Learning Corporation of America, 1970. 16mm. b/w. Sound. 3 min. Sale $95, rent $10.

Two parts, both relying on visual impressions done through the medium of charcoal drawings. The first part tells the story of the god Pan and is accompanied by Debussy's music for the solo flute. The second part shows shifting images of the city. Ryan Larkin created the film, which has won International Film Festival awards in New York, San Francisco, Canada, and Ethiopia.

602. Tager, Jack, and Goist, Park Dixon, eds. **The Urban Vision.** Homewood, Ill.: Dorsey, 1970. 310 pp. LC 70-118191. pap. $4.95.

Tager and Goist have collected a group of articles centering around the shape the American city should take. They include the Burnham Plan for Chicago and the ideas of city planners and theorists like the sociologists Robert E. Park and Louis Wirth and the planners Clarence S. Stein and Lewis Mumford. Primarily about the American city in the 20th century and contains only a little about early eras, it is a good book to start those readers out who are interested in the history of the modern city and city planning.

603. Terkel, Studs. **Division Street: America.** New York: Pantheon, 1967. 381 pp. LC 66-10415. $7.95. Avon, pap. $2.25.

Studs Terkel's forte is interviewing people. Here he looks at his city, Chicago, through the eyes of many persons of varying ethnic backgrounds. Eminently readable and can be assigned to senior high school students.

604. Terkel, Studs. **Hard Times; The Story of the Depression in the Voices of Those Who Lived.** Caedmon Records, 1971. 2 discs or cassettes. $13 for discs, $15.90 for cassettes.

In his pioneering effort in oral history, Studs Terkel recorded actual conversations with inhabitants of Chicago who reflected on their experiences in the depression of the 1930s. Terkel used these interviews as a foundation for his book of the same name. Suitable for general audiences.

605. Trachtenberg, Alan. **Brooklyn Bridge: Myth and Symbol.** New York: Oxford University Press, 1965. 182 pp. LC 65-17431. $7.50.

By concentrating on one structure, Trachtenberg has shown how technology and values intermix and how the construction of a bridge can be taken to characterize a society. Provocative; for better students.

606. Trachtenberg, Alan, Neill, Peter, and Bunnell, Peter C., eds. **The City: American Experience.** New York: Oxford University Press, 1971. 620 pp. LC 76-146043. pap. $6.50.

This reader was intended for college level classes in urban studies, but it has a broader appeal than this. Containing photographs, poetry, excerpts from novels and short stories, as well as scholarly articles, the anthology is sensitively done and ought to be attractive to the general reader.

607. Tunnard, Christopher. **The City of Man.** New York: Scribner, 1953. 424 pp. LC 53-11226. $5.95.

Tunnard describes the periods of city design in this book, which is easy to read.

608. Tunnard, Christopher. **The Modern American City.** Princeton, N.J.: Van Nostrand, 1968. 191 pp. LC 68-2085. pap. $3.25.

A mixture of narrative and documents that can be managed by the average reader. It treats of recent city design but goes to the background of American cities.

609. Tunnard, Christopher, and Reed, Henry H. **American Skyline: The Growth and Form of Our Cities and Towns.** Boston: Houghton Mifflin, 1955. 302 pp. LC 55-6553. Mentor, pap. $1.25.

A design history of American cities organized in a manner that may be useful as a counterweight to conventional organization of political history. For advanced students.

610. The Urban Experience and Folk Tradition. American Folklore Society Bibliographical and Special Series. Americo Paredes and Ellen I. Stekert, eds. Austin, Tex.: University of Texas Press, 1971. 207 pp. LC 72-157253. $6.50.

An attempt to trace the remnants of rural culture in a city setting. The essayists include scholars from disciplines other than folklore, although that is the major emphasis. Helpful for those libraries with special interest in rural migration to cities.

611. Walking. National Film Board of Canada/Learning Corporation of America, 1970. 16mm. Color. Sound. 5 min. Sale $120, rent $15.

Another Ryan Larkin film. The topic is people walking and the views are of urban pedestrians done in line drawings, color wash, and watercolor sketches. Suitable for all levels; younger audiences will like its rock music score.

612. Walt Whitman's Western Journey. Line Films, 1965. 16mm. Color. Sound. 15 min. Sale $150.

Whitman took a western trip in 1879, going as far as the Rockies. In this re-creation of his trip, Whitman's attitudes toward the town and country alike can be found. Suitable for junior and senior high school students.

613. Walt Whitman's World. Walter P. Lewisohn/Coronet Films, 1966. (Cultural History.) 16mm. b/w and color. Sound. 14 min. Rental available from Indiana University. $6.75 color, $4.80 b/w.

Lewisohn uses Whitman's manuscripts and hospital notes in juxtaposition with pictures of the scenes he was describing. A good portrayal of the cities in Whitman's experience. Meant for senior high school students but suitable also for lower grades.

614. Washington Irving's World. Walter P. Lewisohn/Coronet Films, 1966. (Cultural History.) 16mm. Sound. b/w and color. 11 min. Rental available from Indiana University: $4.75 color, $3.15 b/w.

Employs the same techniques as in *Walt Whitman's World*; some paintings and prints also appear. Clearly, Irving is less consciously antiurban than were his contemporaries. For junior and senior high school students.

615. Washington University, St. Louis. Institute for Urban and Regional Studies. **Urban Life and Form**; Werner Z. Hirsch, ed. 248 pp. LC 63-10967. $7.50.

Papers presented at the faculty seminar on foundations of urban life and form (1961–1962) sponsored by the Institute for Urban and Region Studies, Washington University. This collection centers upon the design element in urban life and on the connection between form and planning.

616. Watson, Patrick. **Fasanella's City: The Paintings of Ralph Fasanella with the Story of His Life and Art.** New York: Knopf, 1973. 148 pp. LC 73-7269. $15. Ballantine, pap. $4.95.

Fasanella is a primitive artist whose subject is New York City and whose perspective is that of a worker within the city. He gives an inside, aesthetic view of the metropolis which should appeal to the general reader as well as to the specialist in art.

617. Weimer, David R., ed. **City and Country in America.** New York: Appleton Century Crofts, 1962. 399 pp. LC 62-12332. pap. $5.25.

Documents on visual elements emphasizing the distinction between urban and rural landscapes.

618. Whitman, Walt. **Crossing Brooklyn Ferry and Other Poems.** Caedmon Records, 1969. $6.98 for disc, $7.95 for cassette. Ed Begley, narrator.

Whitman's poetry gives an aesthetic sense of the city, and this recording will be attractive to more mature students and adults.

619. Whyte, William H. **The Last Landscape.** Garden City, N.Y.: Doubleday, 1968. 376 pp. LC 67-15350. $7.95, pap. $2.95.

Whyte is concerned with improving the quality of urban life in America, and he suggests ways in which this may be done. Whyte favors the reform and reconstruction of present cities rather than having people move into new suburbs or rural developments. Well written and in no way technical.

620. Winslow, Ola Elizabeth. **Meetinghouse Hill 1630–1783.** New York: Macmillan, 1952. 344 pp. LC 52-11102. pap. $2.95.

Social history of New England churches down to the successful termination of the Revolution. For the design student's special project.

621. Wright, Richard. **Native Son.** New York: Harper, 1969. 392 pp. LC 79-86654. $8.95, pap. $1.25.

Native Son has become a classic. Based on Wright's own experience in Chicago, it tells the story of Bigger Thomas, a Black boy who grew up in the ghetto and went wrong. It can be used in English as well as history classes for the sense of Black urban life.

622. Wright, Richard. **Native Son.** Caedmon Records. 2 discs, 2 cassettes. $13.96 for discs, $15 for cassettes. James Earl Jones, narrator.

A condensation of Wright's novel, telling much of the futility and dehumanization of city life in the 1930s.

By its very nature, the profession of architecture in the United States has been practiced with most noticeable results in cities, in the construction of both public and private buildings. Indeed, skyscrapers—the epitome of American urban design—seem to be the result of the conjunction of architects and insurance companies. While the architect is concerned with city planning and an image of the city, his primary loyalty is to his client, and the pressures on his building design are more often derived from financial motives than from aesthetic ones. On the other hand, the creation of specific urban structures have had a significant impact upon the cities in which they were built. The skyscraper tradition in Chicago is perpetuated by the Sears and the John Hancock buildings, and the Empire State building remains the logo of New York City.

This section contains general histories of American architecture as well as histories of the architecture in particular regions or historical epochs. It also has representative works on the American aesthetic and the mesh of the American character with American buildings. In addition, there are biographies of noted American architects and European architects with an American impact. Critics of these designers may also be found; these critics propose their own solutions to the question of how building design can make the city more attractive to its human inhabitants.

623. Andrews, Wayne. **Architecture, Ambition and Americans.** New York: Harper & Row, 1955. 315 pp. LC 55-8014. Free Press, pap. $3.45.

Andrews, a well-known architectural historian, tries to show how architecture and social pretensions interact. His account is comprehensive, profusely illustrated, and well written.

624. Andrews, Wayne. **Architecture in Chicago and Mid-America.** New York: Harper & Row, 1968. 188 pp. LC 68-23511. Icon Editions, pap. $4.95.

The architecture of selected Midwestern cities. Andrews' taste is good; his comments, enlightened. Highly recommended.

625. Andrews, Wayne. **Architecture in New England: A Photographic History.** Brattleboro, Vt.: Stephen Greene Press, 1973. 202 pp. LC 72-91797. $16.95.

A composite pictorial illustrating rural and urban structures in the Northeast. The volume is of general interest and will appeal to photography buffs as well as professional architects.

626. Andrews, Wayne. **Architecture in New York: A Photographic History.** New York: Harper & Row, 1964. LC 70-81933. $20.

A solid selection of pictures on architectural features of New York City. Expensive, but has considerable potential.

627. Bach, Ira J. **Chicago on Foot: An Architectural Walking Tour,** 2nd ed. Chicago: J. P. O'Hara, 1973. LC 69-20278. $8.95, pap. $6.95.

Bach's work contains over 30 walking tours in the city of Chicago. Should be shelved as a reference book for those who plan trips to the Windy City. Also should be available to those libraries with a clientele including architects.

628. Bacon, Edmund N. **Design of Cities,** rev. ed. New York: Viking Press, 1974. 336 pp. LC 73-185988. $20.

The evolution of city design from Greece to the present day, emphasizing form, function, and their interrelation. A useful reference, but too expensive for smaller libraries.

629. Bourne, Larry S., ed. **Internal Structure of the City: Readings on Space and Environment.** New York: Oxford University Press, 1971. 528 pp. LC 73-135977. pap. $5.95.

Although primarily a text for city designers, its utility goes beyond that. Reasonably well-informed laymen also can profit from reading its articles.

630. Burchard, John, and Bush-Brown, Albert. **The Architecture of America: A Social and Cultural History.** Boston: Little, Brown, 1961. 549 pp. LC 61-5736. $16.50, pap. $4.95.

Official history of architecture authorized by the American Institute of Architects; nonetheless this is a valuable work. An abridged version is available in paperback.

631. Condit, Carl W. **Chicago, 1910–29: Building, Planning and Urban Technology.** Chicago: University of Chicago Press, 1973. 354 pp. LC 74-155457. $12.50.

The well-known historian of urban design concerns himself with the changing urban environment of Chicago in a restricted period of time but a very significant one in terms of construction.

632. Condit, Carl W. **Chicago, 1930–70: Building, Planning, and Urban Technology.** Chicago: University of Chicago Press, 1974. 351 pp. LC 73-79996. $12.50.

The second of a two-volume work on Chicago's architecture and planning in the 20th century. Condit argues that, despite the outstanding technology and the creative architectural forms, Chicago has failed to create even a minimally acceptable living environment for many of its residents. Highly recommended as a statement of the relation, or lack of it, of urban design to urban life.

633. Condit, Carl W. **The Chicago School of Architecture.** Chicago: University of Chicago Press, 1964. 238 pp. LC 64-13287. $12.50, pap. $5.95.

Condit recounts here the history of such architects as Sullivan and Frank Lloyd Wright. Interesting and valuable for understanding the pioneers of urban skyscrapers.

634. Condit, Carl W. The Rise of the Skyscraper. Chicago: University of Chicago Press, 1952. 235 pp. LC 52-6468. O.P.

Condit's study is the standard work on the history of the steel-framed skyscraper. Interesting, and can be read with profit by better students.

635. Cook, John Wesley, and Klatz, Henrich. Conversations with Architects: Philip Johnson, Kevin Roche, Paul Rudolph, Bertrand Goldberg, Morris Lapidus, Louis Kahn, Charles Moore, Robert Venturi, and Denise Scott Brown. New York: Praeger, 1973. 272 pp. LC 72-85972. $17.50.

In addition to Cook's conversations, there is a significant introduction by Vincent Scully. The architects interviewed discuss their ideas and their works; the format is such that both the informed layman and the expert in the field will benefit from reading about these people who contributed so much to the urban design scene.

636. Cowan, Peter, et al. The Office: A Facet of Urban Growth. New York: American Elsevier, 1969. 280 pp. LC 69-18137. $12.50.

This is an American edition of an English book which contains a foreword by Lord Llewelyn-Davies. The subject is appropriate and significant for those interested in architecture and in urban development. Recommended for specialized libraries.

637. Crosby, Theodore. Architecture: City Sense. New York: Reinholt, 1965. 95 pp. LC 65-14036. pap. $2.45. O.P.

Crosby examines cities in the United States and England with an eye to developments since 1945. A personal view.

638. Fitch, James Marston. American Building: The Historical Forces that Shaped It, 2nd ed. 2 vols. Boston: Houghton Mifflin, 1972. LC 65-10689. $12.50 set. Schocken, pap. $4.95.

In his standard work on architectural history, Fitch is not technical in approach and the result is a highly readable account of the development of American architecture. Can serve as an excellent starting point for a survey of building and should be in all libraries with architectural collections.

639. Fitch, James Marston. Architecture and the Aesthetics of Plenty. New York: Columbia University Press, 1961. 304 pp. LC 61-8510. $10.

Fitch discusses American architecture in terms of what is American about it. He claims that abundance leads to vulgarity.

640. Garvan, Anthony N. B. Architecture and Town Planning in Colonial Connecticut. New Haven, Conn.: Yale University Press, 1951. 166 pp. LC 51-14684. O.P.

A specialized study of Connecticut that sees English and American influences at work there. A reference work for teachers or students.

641. Giedion, Sigfried. **Space, Time and Architecture**, 5th ed. Cambridge, Mass.: Harvard University Press, 1962. 897 pp. LC 67-17310. $25.

A standard work in architectural history and design. Should be included as a reference work for students in art, design, and history.

642. Hamlin, Talbot. **Benjamin Henry Latrobe.** New York: Oxford University Press, 1955. 633 pp. LC 55-8117. $15.

Hamlin's biography is the definitive work on Latrobe and includes the work Latrobe did in rebuilding Washington, D.C., after the War of 1812. Ironically, Latrobe and his son, Henry, were both victims of yellow fever in New Orleans, where they were building a water system similar to Philadelphia's, designed to eliminate the disease. This biography might be assigned to students interested in architecture or early attempts at urban water systems.

643. Hines, Thomas S. **Burnham of Chicago, Architect and Planner.** New York: Oxford University Press, 1974. 445 pp. LC 74-79625. $19.50.

Daniel Burnham was a pioneering architect in Chicago at the end of the 19th century and the beginning of the 20th. This most recent biography details his work in Chicago, Cleveland, and Washington, D.C. Essential for those involved in the history of city planning, urban design, and architecture.

644. Hoffmann, Donald. **The Architecture of John Wellborn Root.** Johns Hopkins Studies in Nineteenth-Century Architecture. Baltimore: Johns Hopkins University Press, 1973. 263 pp. LC 72-4008. $13.50.

The work of the *Kansas City Star* art critic. Root was a notable architect who designed such buildings as the Rookery and the Monadnoch in Chicago and the Board of Trade in Kansas City. Should appeal to those interested in the history of architecture or of the two mentioned cities.

645. Jencks, Charles. **Le Corbusier and the Tragic View of Architecture.** Cambridge, Mass.: Harvard University Press, 1973. 198 pp. LC 73-83422. $13.95.

A dispassionate biography of Le Corbusier. Jencks depicts Le Corbusier's architecture as a product of a Nietzchean view of man with an implicit moral base. Jencks suggests Le Corbusier might have changed his ideas had he lived longer but admits that his city design has contributed to wrong urban renewal efforts. Recommended for the informed amateur as well as the practicing architect.

646. Jencks, Charles. **Modern Movements in Architecture.** Garden City, N.Y.: Doubleday, 1973. 432 pp. LC 72-86674. $10. Anchor, pap. $4.95.

Jencks traces the significant architects who have contributed to the modernism movement in the 20th century. He criticizes the movement and separates it into its component parts. This is an epitaph for the end of an architectural era and deserves to be read by all those with interest in recent architectural development.

647. Kite, Elizabeth S., ed. **L'Enfant and Washington 1791–1792. Published and Unpublished Documents Brought Together for the First Time.** New York: Arno Press, 1970 (originally published in 1929). 182 pp. LC 79-112554. $8.

Letters and papers of L'Enfant, Washington, and Jefferson concerning plans for the construction of Washington, D.C. The documents show both the genius of L'Enfant and his political weaknesses, but make quite clear his contribution to the present shape of the city on the Potomac. Of most interest to libraries with collections on the physical aspects of city planning.

648. Kurtz, Stephen A. **Wasteland: Building the American Dream.** New York: Praeger, 1973. 125 pp. LC 73-6972. $7.95, pap $3.95.

Kurtz attacks popular taste in architecture and the architects who produce Levittowns and high-rises. He believes that modern urban architecture reflects a system which is in drastic need of revision. This radical critique will appeal to those convinced of America's many problems.

649. Morrison, Hugh Sinclair. **Louis Sullivan, Prophet of Modern Architecture.** Westport, Conn.: Greenwood Press, 1971 (originally published in 1935). 391 pp. LC 78-139141. $17.25. Norton, pap. $4.50.

Morrison's biography of Sullivan, the great Chicago architect, is an old one. It still is a good look at the life and works of a man who had considerable impact upon the shape of American cities and is recommended for collections on urban architecture.

650. Mumford, Lewis, ed. **Roots of Contemporary American Architecture: A Series of Thirty-Seven Essays Dating from the Mid-Nineteenth Century to the Present.** New York: Dover, 1972. 452 pp. LC 75-171490. pap. $4.50.

Mumford has included a representative group of writers on American architecture for this collection. His expertise in the area makes this volume a valuable one which is recommended for inclusion in sections on architecture.

651. Olmsted, Frederick Law. **Civilizing American Cities: A Selection of Frederick Law Olmsted's Writings on City Landscapes.** S. B. Sutton, ed. Cambridge, Mass.: MIT Press, 1971. 310 pp. NUC 81916. $12.50.

A companion volume to Fein's *Landscape into Cityscape* which deals primarily with New York City. Sutton has put together a collection that is broader, encompassing other cities than just New York. Necessary for those interested in the beginning of American city design in the 19th century.

652. Olmsted, Frederick Law. **Landscape into Cityscape: Frederick Law Olmsted's Plans for a Greater New York City.** Albert Fein, ed. Ithaca, N.Y.: Cornell University Press, 1967. 490 pp. LC 67-13045. $17.50.

Olmsted was a pioneering American landscape architect who designed Central Park in New York City, Prospect Park in Brooklyn, and Jackson Park in Chicago along with a number of others. He also planned suburbs and the Columbian Exposition of 1893. Essential for those libraries concerned with the history of American planning.

653. Olmsted, Frederick Law. **Public Parks and the Enlargement of Towns.** New York: Arno Press, 1970 (originally published in 1870). 39 pp. LC 76-112564. $6.

This pamphlet is a reprint of a lecture Olmsted gave to the American Social Science Association in 1870 and contains a plea for comprehensive planning. Should find a place in libraries interested in building a collection on urban design.

654. Pierson, William Harvey. American Buildings and Their Architects: Academic and Progressive Ideals at the Turn of the Twentieth Century. Garden City, N.Y.: Doubleday, 1972. LC 79-84361. $15.

Pierson's works on the history of American architecture are basic. This volume concerns the development of such pioneer American architects as Louis Sullivan and Frank Lloyd Wright.

655. Pierson, William Harvey. American Buildings and Their Architects: The Colonial and Neo-Classical Styles. Garden City, N.Y.: Doubleday, 1970. LC 79-84361. $12.50.

The history of American architecture down to the Civil War. Concerns the transplanting and transformation of European building ideas and techniques.

656. Pierson, William Harvey. American Buildings and Their Architects: The Impact of European Modernism in the Mid-Twentieth Century. Garden City, N.Y.: Doubleday, 1972. LC 79-84361. $15.

Traces the impact of the ideas of such prominent European architects as Marcel Breur and Ludwig Mies van der Rohe.

657. Redstone, Louis G. New Dimensions in Shopping Centers and Stores. New York: McGraw-Hill, 1973. 323 pp. LC 73-4021. $19.95.

Architectural study of the suburban phenomenon, shopping centers. Redstone is primarily interested in such centers from the standpoint of design. While the book has limited appeal, for those who are engaged in building or designing centers, it is quite essential.

658. Reiff, Daniel Drake. Washington Architecture 1791–1861: Problems in Development. Washington, D.C.: U.S. Commission of Fine Arts, 1971. 161 pp. LC 72-602603. $3.50.

Available from the Superintendent of Documents, this is a useful addition to literature about the building of the Capitol City. It is recommended for those libraries which already have a good architectural section and which are interested in architectural history.

659. The Rise of an American Architecture [by] Henry Riessel Hitchcock [and others]. New York: Praeger, 1970. 241 pp. LC 70-116442. $10, pap. $4.95.

Catalog written to accompany an exhibition sponsored by the Metropolitan Museum of Art and the National Trust for Historic Preservation. The exhibition emphasized primarily the architectural achievements in America from 1815 to 1915. Kaufmann wrote the introduction and the project texts; there are also essays by four other authors—Henry Russell Hitchcock, Winston Weisman, Vincent Scully, and Albert Fein. The book and exhibition are valuable contributions to architectural history.

660. Roper, Laura Wood. **FLO.** Baltimore: Johns Hopkins University Press, 1974. 555 pp. LC 73-8125. $15.

An excellent biography of Frederick Law Olmsted that ought to interest not only specialists in urban and park design but also enlightened people.

661. Rudofsky, Bernard. **Architecture Without Architects.** Garden City, N.Y.: Museum of Modern Art, distributed by Doubleday, 1972. LC 64-8755. pap. $4.95.

Although an architect, Rudofsky is not convinced that professional training is necessarily the best guide to the building art. Instead, he opts for "communal architecture" which takes into account the needs of a community and its physical location. Unconventional with considerable appeal.

662. Rudofsky, Bernard. **Streets for People: A Primer for Americans.** Garden City, N.Y.: Doubleday, 1969. 351 pp. LC 76-78735. $14.95, pap. $5.95.

Rudofsky attacks the grid, which he sees as typical of the American city plan and which he claims was set in 1811. He feels the grid reflects a belief that people are secondary to the city and hence a kind of antiurbanism. For possible ways to make streets usable for people he uses illustrations from Perugia, Osaka, Milan, Alcudia, and other cities. A good reference work for comparing city layouts; the ideas may be used for discussion material.

663. Scully, Vincent. **American Architecture and Urbanism.** New York: Praeger, 1969. 275 pp. LC 70-76793. $18.50, pap. $5.95.

Scully, who teaches at Yale, considers the concept of urbanism in American architectural history. He evaluates architects who have contributed to the urban experience and ties the whole package together neatly. Essential for anyone interested in the American design of cities.

664. Siegel, Arthur, ed. **Chicago's Famous Buildings; A Photographic Guide to the City's Architectural Landmarks and Other Notable Buildings,** 2nd ed. Chicago: University of Chicago Press, 1969. 272 pp. LC 69-15367. $6.95, pap. $3.25.

One of the best picture collections on the architectural heritage of Chicago. Not difficult, and can be understood by the general reader as well as the beginning architectural student. Should be purchased by libraries with an interest in urban architecture.

665. Spreiregen, Paul D. **Urban Design: The Architecture of Towns and Cities.** New York: McGraw-Hill, 1965. 243 pp. LC 65-25520. $17.50.

A history of urban design which emphasizes principles and contains sketches of what Spreiregen considers to be good city design.

666. Stone, Harris. **Workbook of An Unsuccessful Architect.** New York: Monthly Review Press, 1973. 192 pp. LC 73-8052. $8.95, pap. $3.45.

Stone, formerly a staff member of the urban renewal program at New Haven, Connecticut, a program that failed, recounts his experiences there. This is difficult to read since it is not set in type but reproduces Stone's handwriting. For libraries with extensive collections.

667. Twombly, Robert C. **Frank Lloyd Wright: An Interpretive Biography.**
New York: Harper & Row, 1974. 373 pp. LC 72-9248. $10.95, pap. $3.95.
Twombly's is the latest and the best biography of the famed American architect. He emphasizes Wright's human qualities and treats his work as a function of his psychological needs. Ought to be purchased by libraries of all kinds, both for urban studies and for its biographical qualities.

668. Von Eckhardt, Wolf. **A Place to Live.** New York: Delacorte, 1967.
430 pp. LC 67-20653. $9.95. Dell, pap. $2.65.
Von Eckhardt is an architecture critic for the *Washington Post* and writes for the *Saturday Review*. In focusing on architecture, he criticizes a number of buildings for not meeting the needs of the citizen of the city. Recommended for design-oriented students.

669. Walker, John Albert. **Glossary of Art, Architecture, and Design Since
1945.** Hamden, Conn.: Linnet Books, 1973. 240 pp. LC 73-3339. $10.50.
A basic reference work for every library. Walker has taken the terms he uses from artists and critics who have either coined or used them.

670. Wilson, William H. **The City Beautiful Movement in Kansas City.**
Columbia, Mo.: University of Missouri Press, 1964. 171 pp. LC 64-17648.
$5.
Wilson's study of Kansas City shows how the city was changed by conscious architectural design. Recommended for special collections.

671. Wright, Frank Lloyd. **The Living City.** New York: Horizon Press, 1958.
222 pp. LC 58-13550. $12.50. New American Library, pap. $2.95.
Wright's thoughts on urban design. Conceived in the 1930s, Broadacre city (the living city of the title) tried to demolish the line between city and country. Although never put into practice, Wright's city ideas are still necessary to study.

American city planning began its modern phase in the 20th century with the Chicago plan. At the same time that cities were creating planning departments to rebuild and alter existing physical features and to predict social and economic needs, they were also passing zoning ordinances aimed at freezing land use into existing homogeneous patterns. The first assumed growth while the second impeded growth. Both, however, contained the implicit faith that the American city had to be managed and controlled and that a policy of salutory neglect no longer worked. Whether that faith was justified remains to be seen.

This section contains materials on both planning and land use regulations, some critical and some laudatory. There are historical treatments of the forces which led to planning as well as philosophical expositions of the principles underlying good planning. Also included are planning guides and case studies of planned communities, some still existing and others dead. Finally, this section has many films and games on planning and on land use which aid in conceptualizing both the aims and the problems inherent in these areas.

672. Alpern, Robert. **Pratt Guide to Planning and Renewal for New Yorkers**, rev. ed. New York: Quadrangle, 1973. LC 72-94651. $15.
Revision of a 1965 work which serves as a directory of agencies involved in urban planning in New York City and as a blueprint for citizens to use in attempting to obtain services. While specifically about New York City, it does provide insights for the researcher into the nature of the planning process in cities today.

673. Altshuler, Alan. **The City Planning Process**. Ithaca, N.Y.: Cornell University Press, 1965. 466 pp. LC 65-25498. $14.50, pap. $4.95.
Altshuler examines the decisions made in Minneapolis-St. Paul and recounts the pressures placed upon the planners by verbal sections of the community. A good source for those interested in the kinds of forces which impinge upon professionals as they try to work for better urban situations.

674. Anderson, Martin. **The Federal Bulldozer: A Critical Analysis of Urban Renewal, 1949–1962**. New York: McGraw-Hill, 1967. 272 pp. LC 68-74284. pap. $2.45.
The most critical book on urban renewal, it stimulated much controversy. Indispensable for an in-depth study of the topic. Recommended for units on urban renewal.

675. Babcock, Richard F. **The Zoning Game: Municipal Practices and Policies.** Madison, Wis.: University of Wisconsin Press, 1966. 202 pp. LC 66-22864. $7.50, pap. $3.50.

Babcock examines the actual operation of zoning in cities and demonstrates how often policies are set aside because of pressures from politicians, developers, and others with an interest in securing variants. A needed antidote to those books which consider planning only in the abstract.

676. Barnett, Jonathan. **Urban Design as Public Policy.** New York: Architectural Record Books, 1974. 200 pp. LC 73-88222. $15.

Head of the New York Planning Commission's Urban Design Group, Barnett suggests ways in which his New York experience can be utilized in other cities. Included in his discussion is the use of such techniques as special zoning, landmark preservation, joint development by private and public sponsors, and rejuvenation of old buildings and areas. Architects and city planners will need this as a special reference tool, but it is unlikely to have widespread general appeal.

677. Bellush, Jewel, and Hausknecht, Murray, eds. **Urban Renewal: People, Politics, and Planning.** Garden City, N.Y.: Doubleday, 1967. 542 pp. LC 67-10410. pap. $2.45.

The editors of this collection have tried to put together a balanced selection, pro and con, of opinions of the failures and successes of urban renewal from the standpoint of the persons planning and carrying out the renewal as well as from the standpoint of those directly affected. Recommended for those libraries who have already acquired other basic sources on urban renewal.

678. Bergman, Edward M. **Eliminating Exclusionary Zoning.** Cambridge, Mass.: Ballinger, 1974. 307 pp. LC 73-18252. $13.50.

Designed primarily for planners, this represents an attempt to develop a performance standard for zoning which better serves community needs. Recommended for libraries which have, or are planning, collections on the theory and practice of zoning.

679. Bor, Walter. **The Making of Cities.** New York: Barnes & Noble, 1972. 256 pp. LC 72-183680. $16.50.

Bor, who has worked as a city planner in Great Britain and in the United States, wrote this account for a lay audience. He includes case studies illustrated by plans as well as photographs. A good introduction to the field of planning, also containing much material for advanced students.

680. Bosselman, Fred P., and Collies, David. **The Quiet Revolution in Land Use Control.** Washington, D.C.: U.S. Government Printing Office, 1971. 327 pp. LC 70-616368.

This is the report of the Council on Environmental Quality which takes as its subject the present status of laws and codes on land use. The document is necessary for libraries which cater to planners or to people who develop zoning policies.

681. Breese, Gerald William, and Whiteman, Dorothe Ed., eds. **An Approach to Urban Planning.** Westport, Conn.: Greenwood Press, 1969 (originally published in 1953). 147 pp. LC 73-90474. $9.

First published by the Princeton University Press, this reprint represents quite typically the thinking on urban planning of 20 years ago and serves as a useful resource for libraries on the history of urban planning.

682. Brooks, Richard Oliver. **New Towns and Communal Values: A Case Study of Columbia, Maryland.** New York: Praeger, 1974. 229 pp. LC 73-553. $16.50.

A study of a recently planned community, Columbia, Maryland, near Washington, D.C. The community has had only limited success and is now made up of largely upper-middle-class families. Should be purchased by libraries with a clientele interested in the creation of new towns.

683. Buder, Stanley. **Pullman: An Experiment in Industrial Order and Community Planning, 1880–1930.** Urban Life in America. New York: Oxford University Press, 1967. 263 pp. LC 67-25456. pap. $2.95.

Pullman was a suburban development planned by the sleeping car company; it collapsed in 1894 after labor-management difficulties. The community then became another suburban area. Recommended as an example of a unique development in industrial cities. For those with an interest in company towns.

684. Burnham, Daniel H., Jr., and Kingery, Robert. **Planning the Region of Chicago.** Chicago: Lakeside Press/Donnelley & Sons, 1956. 191 pp. LC 56-58177.

Daniel H. Burnham, Jr., is the son of the man who was in large measure responsible for the present physical shape of Chicago with his 1909 plan. Traces the growth of planning in Chicago down to the time of publication and, as such, is of value to planners and urban historians.

685. Cities of the Future. CBS-21st Century Series/Contemporary Films, 1967. 16mm. Color. Sound. 25 min. Rent $11. Walter Cronkite, narrator.

A cartoon sequence on the growth of cities begins this film and can be used as quick introduction to that topic. The main thrust, however, is that planning will solve the problems of the future metropolis. Despite this questionable thesis, it is worth seeing and using.

686. Cities for Warm Bodies. Center for the Study of Democratic Institutions. 1 cassette. 57 min.

Discussion of the effects of planning in the past as well as an evaluation of the futuristic projections of today's planners. The discussants are critical of what they perceive to be the overemphasis upon technology at the expense of human values. Interesting and stimulating.

687. City Classification Handbook: Methods and Applications. J. L. Berry, ed. New York: Wiley-Interscience, 1972. 394 pp. LC 71-171911. $23.

Useful reference for planners as well as those engaged in more theoretical efforts. Suggestions for a scheme for categorizing cities that ought to find a place in many large libraries.

688. City of Chicago. Department of Development and Planning. **The Comprehensive Plan of Chicago.** Chicago: City of Chicago. Department of Development and Planning, 1966. 117 pp. 68-42521.

The latest plan drafted for Chicago. It relies upon the policies plan approach which combines the goals of seven systems of planning elements and the overall structure of Chicago. It replaced the Development Plan for the central area of Chicago done in 1958 and represents the culmination of the planning process. Of use to planners and historians of planning.

689. Claire, William H., ed. **Handbook on Urban Planning.** New York: Van Nostrand Reinhold, 1973. 393 pp. LC 73-2574. $19.95.

A collection of essays written by five persons who are experts in city planning, city engineering, and urban geography. Explains how to collect and analyze data, how to use the data to develop plans, and how to put plans in operation through such devices as zoning and urban renewal. While written and priced for professional planners, the average reader can also profit from it.

690. Clawson, Marion, and Hall, Peter. **Planning and Urban Growth: An Anglo-American Comparison.** Baltimore: published for Resources for the Future by Johns Hopkins University Press, 1973. 300 pp. LC 72-12364. $12.50.

The authors take an area from the United States—the Northeast metropolitan corridor—and one from Great Britain—the megalopolitan triangle—and compare experiences in planning, in urbanization, and land use. The study was underwritten by research foundations and is a sophisticated one suitable for professional planners and urbanists.

691. Commercial Club of Chicago. **Plan of Chicago by Daniel H. Burnham and Edward H. Bennett.** Charles Moore, ed. New York: De Capo Press, 1970. 164 pp. LC 71-75303. $37.50.

Reprinting of the 1909 plan for Chicago, the pioneer effort which served to create much of the interest in planning which has characterized 20th-century American society. Should be available to those involved in the planning process or interested in research on the history of planning.

692. Community Land Use Game (CLUG), rev. ed., G. Feldt, designer. 1972. Ithaca, N.Y.: Systems Gaming Associates. $125, $4.95 each additional manual, $4 miscellaneous paper.

This land-use game tries to replicate the experience of an urban analyst as he determines the best possible land use. The game is expensive; it can be obtained with an optional computer program using an IBM 1130. It also takes considerable time to play, requiring from 5 to 10 one-hour rounds. From 3 to 30 persons can play. A sophisticated game best suited to larger institutions.

693. Cullingworth, J. B. **The Problems of an Urban Society.** 3 vols. Buffalo, N.Y.: University of Toronto Press, 1973. LC 73-79291. set $31.50.

Focuses on planning. The first volume concerns the social framework of planning; the second, the social content of planning; and the third, planning for change. The author believes that political solutions are more significant than professional planning ones and that the key to urban problems is a sensitive belief in social justice. An advanced work.

694. Delafons, John. **Land-Use Controls in the United States,** 2nd ed. Cambridge, Mass.: MIT Press, 1970. 203 pp. LC 76-92781. $10.

This is the second edition of a text widely used in graduate courses in urban planning. It takes a developmental approach, showing how what Delafons calls the "prairie philosophy" of the planners came into being. He compares American planning with that in England and concludes that planners in the latter society do better. Indispensable for those interested in planning.

695. Erber, Ernest, ed. **Urban Planning in Transition.** New York: Grossman, 1970. 323 pp. LC 77-86110. $15, pap. $4.95.

Problems faced by urban planners in the 1960s. The authors are sympathetic to planning, and, in general, are convinced that improvements in the planning process will help diminish urban problems. Useful, as it reveals the temper of the contemporary planning profession.

696. Firey, Walter. **Land Use in Central Boston.** New York: Greenwood Press, 1968 (originally published in 1947). 367 pp. LC 68-23288. $16.25.

In this pioneering, detailed analysis of Boston, Firey proved that urban land value was a function of community sentiment as well as a matter of location, thus rebutting ecological claims. Advanced students might dip into Firey for his insights into the role of cemeteries and historical landmarks in a city.

697. Friedmann, John. **Retracking America: A Theory of Societal Planning.** Garden City, N.Y.: Doubleday, 1973. 289 pp. LC 72-89308.

Friedmann teaches urban planning and is the director of the Ford Foundation's Urban and Regional Planning Program. This is a plea for a system of planning which the author calls transactive. This planning would include inputs from all segments of society and would be educative as well as functioning as a blueprint for a future society.

698. Gans, Herbert J. **People and Plans; Essays on Urban Problems and Solutions.** New York: Basic Books, 1968. 395 pp. LC 68-54134. $10.75, pap. $5.75.

Gans pleads for better planning to take into account human needs. For informed readers.

699. Haller, William. **The Puritan Frontier: Town Planning in New England Colonial Development, 1630–1660.** New York: Columbia University Press, 1951. 119 pp. LC 51-11284. $10.

Puritan views of town development are presented in this sophisticated book. Probably for research projects only.

700. **Inner City Planning.** Creative Studies/Macmillan, 1971. $16.80, classroom kit. $6.99, player's manuals for 10 players. $.30 each additional manual.

This simulation game, available in pocket form, is designed to help conceptualize the problem of a blighted area—"James Park" in "Port City." Specially concerned with urban renewal, the game can be played by 20 to 40 players who form six groups with a stake in urban renewal in "Port City." The data are taken from experiences in Boston. Suitable for high school students as well as adults.

701. Kaitz, Edward M., and Hyman, Herbert Harvey. **Urban Planning for Social Welfare: A Model Cities Approach.** New York: Praeger, 1970. 241 pp. LC 69-19333. $13.50.

Kaitz and Hyman were consultants to the Human Resources Administration of New York City. They are concerned here with the experience of the Model Cities program in New York. The major difficulty emphasized is the problem of informing and working with area residents. For special collections only.

702. Linowes, R. Robert, and Allensworth, Don T. **The Politics of Land Use: Planning, Zoning, and the Private Developer.** New York: Praeger, 1973. 166 pp. LC 73-8176. $13.50.

This is a short analysis of the problems faced by real estate developers in coping with the complexities of land use regulation. The authors believe that mixed land use should be the goal of planners and that the mechanisms of control should be simplified. Can be read with profit by the average reader, and should be acquired by most libraries.

703. Lovejoy, Derek, ed. **Land Use and Landscape Planning Techniques.** New York: Barnes & Noble, 1973. 308 pp. LC 74-157862. $35.

A how-to-do-it anthology aimed at local and regional planners. Includes both theory and application brought together in a concluding section which contains several case studies. Expensive, and is probably suitable only for those specialized libraries which planners need.

704. Lubove, Roy. **Community Planning in the 1920's.** Pittsburgh: University of Pittsburgh Press, 1963. 155 pp. LC 64-12492. pap. $2.25.

Lubove traces the history of the Regional Planning Association of America, one of the original groups interested in planning in the 20th century.

705. MacKaye, Benton. **The New Exploration: A Philosophy of Regional Planning.** Urbana, Ill.: University of Illinois Press, 1962 (originally published in 1928). 243 pp. LC 62-17510. pap. $1.75.

MacKaye was a leader in the Regional Planning Association of America. He expresses quite well his theories of how regions should be developed. Useful for informed readers.

706. Makielski, S. J., Jr. **The Politics of Zoning: The New York Experience.** New York, 1966. 241 pp. LC 65-25662. $12.50.

The first attempt to evaluate the planning process in one city, and it is a successful one. Makielski covers the years from 1911 to 1938, but does not bring the experience up to date. Because of its unique coverage, it is essential for those interested in the practice as well as the theory of urban planning.

707. Merlin, Pierre. **New Towns: Regional Planning and Development.** New York: Barnes & Noble, 1971. 276 pp. LC 70-875632. $17.25, pap. $9.75.

A comparative study of "new" towns as they have been conceived in Great Britain, Denmark, Sweden, Finland, the Netherlands, France, as well as the United States. Merlin employed material gathered from the study to construct a plan for the Paris region. Most appropriate for urban geographers and planners.

708. **Modernizing Urban Land Policy.** Marion Clawson, ed. Baltimore: Johns Hopkins University Press, 1973. 248 pp. LC 72-12365. $11.

Essays pointing out present errors in land use policies and suggesting improvement which can be made. The topic is timely, but the book is not easy. Still, it is a needed reference for urban planners and those involved with zoning and other land regulation.

709. Moses, Robert. **The City Planner: Robert Moses Describes the Crisis of Today's Cities.** Center for Cassette Studies. 1 cassette. 29 min. $12.95.

Robert Moses is a controversial figure in city planning, both because of his admitted achievements in redesigning New York City and because of his authoritarian methods of obtaining changes in urban features. This audiotape contains Moses' evaluation of the problems of American cities based upon his many years of experience. An intellectually stimulating tape, one well worth having.

710. **New Town.** Harwell Associates, 1971. $12–$75. (Price depends upon which variation the customer orders: $12 for 4 players, $16 Kit I for 10 players, $28 Kit II for 20 players, $75 professional planner's kit, 4 teams.)

New Town is a simulation game which can be played by individuals from the junior high level up. The theme is the impact of human decision as well as technology on community development in new areas. The game takes 4 to 10 players—with the more expensive options, more players can be accommodated—and can be completed in one to three hours.

711. **One Dimension . . . Two Dimension . . . Three Dimension . . . Four!** Hearst Metrotone News/National Audiovisual Center, 1967. 16mm. Color. Sound. 15 min. $60. Rod Serling, narrator.

This film was produced for the Department of Housing and Urban Development. The subject is the need for planning in American cities, illustrated by the planning experiences of Chicago and Norfolk. In addition, the film suggests the shape of the future. Sophisticated, but useful.

712. **Planning and Cities.** New York: Braziller.

This series, published in both paperback and cloth, is historical in nature and reflects upon the development of city planning. Two representative titles are Norma Evenson's *Le Corbusier: The Machine and the Grand Design* (1969, $5.95, pap. $2.95) and Francoise Choay's *The Modern City: Planning in the Nineteenth Century* (1969, $5.95, pap. $2.95) translated by Marguerite Hugo and George Collins.

713. **Planning and Cities in the 19th Century.** George R. Collins, ed. New York: Braziller, 1968. $7.95, pap. $3.95.

This series, written by historians who are interested in city planning and architecture, is invaluable for students and teachers. One of its most appealing features is the lavish use of visual materials. Fully half of each book is composed of maps, photographs, drawings, and plans. The text may be too difficult for average students; nonetheless, this series is necessary for school libraries with some emphasis on planning.

714. **Plans**. Project SIMILE, 1965–1966. Sample kit $3, 25-student kit $35, 35-student kit $50.

Participants take the roles of various interest groups in this game. The object is to secure maximum advantage for your own group. While it can be used at lower levels, it is most appropriate for senior high school students.

715. Reps, John W. **The Making of Urban America: A History of City Planning in the United States.** Princeton, N.J.: Princeton University Press, 1965. 574 pp. LC 63-23424. $37.50.

Rich in graphic material, this is the most complete, full-scale study of planning yet published. The author begins with the European background of the subject and continues to 1910. Ought to be available in school libraries as a resource, and could be used profitably by students who are visually and design oriented.

716. Reps, John W. **Town Planning in Frontier America.** Princeton, N.J.: Princeton University Press, 1969. 473 pp. LC 68-20877. $16.50, pap. $3.95.

An abridgment of Reps' larger book and more specifically oriented to American city origins.

717. **The Rise of New Towns.** National Educational Television/Indiana University, 1966. (America's Crises.) 16mm. b/w. 60 min. Sound. Rent $9.25.

Describes the development of totally planned communities, such as Foster City and Irvine, California. Planners, government officials, and others discuss the implications of the "new" town movement.

718. **Robert Moses.** NBC/Encyclopaedia Britannica Films, 1960. (The Wilson Series.) 16mm. b/w. Sound. 30 min. Sale $175, rent $15.50.

Robert Moses is interviewed by Gilmore Clark, designer of the court and gardens of the United Nations. Moses describes his planning ideas. Recommended for senior high school students.

719. Robinson, Charles M. **Modern Civic Art.** New York: Arno Press, 1970 (originally published in 1918). 381 pp. LC 79-112570. $18.

A landmark title. Robinson, an early proponent of city planning and of the teaching of planning in universities, had an exaggerated idea of what planning could accomplish. Like some other progressives, he believed that changes in physical environment would result in permanent social improvement.

720. Scott, Mel. **American City Planning.** Berkeley, Cal.: University of California Press, 1969. 747 pp. LC 70-84533. $25, pap. $7.95.

Commissioned to celebrate the 50th anniversary of the American Institute of Planners, this is a valuable historical study which traces the beginnings of urban planning through interviews with early planners and through careful scrutiny of documentary evidence. Essential for an understanding of the growth of the planning profession.

721. Sitte. Simile II/Social Studies School Service 1969. $35 for classroom set for 25 players, $50 for classroom set for 35 players, sample set $3.

Sitte is a game designed for students from junior high school through college. It may be played by as few as 15 players or as many as 35, divided into five teams. The total playing time is from two to four hours. The game centers upon the interaction of interest groups in both city planning and municipal government and does provide information on how both processes occur.

722. The Social Impact of Urban Design. Chicago: Center for Policy Study, University of Chicago Press, 1966. 75 pp. LC 72-27060. $3.95.

Primarily a consideration of Chicago and the effects plans for Chicago have had on the city. Because of its limited nature, belongs mainly in specialized libraries.

723. Stein, Clarence. Toward New Towns for America. Cambridge, Mass.: MIT Press, 1966. 263 pp. LC 66-6296/CD. $12.50, pap. $3.95.

Stein was an architect-turned-planner who was one of the founders of the Regional Planning Association of America in 1923. Here he recounts some of the early 20th century experiments in "new" town development in the United States. Essential for those interested in the "new" town idea.

724. Toll, Seymour. Zoned American. New York: Grossman, 1969. 370 pp. LC 75-88544. $13.95.

Toll's book is not a difficult one and well worth reading by the nonexpert. It treats urban planning as well as zoning and describes the dynamics of city growth.

725. Town Planning. National Film Board of Canada/International Film Bureau, University of Illinois, 1959. 16mm. b/w. 15 min. Rent $4.10.

This older film shows what properly zoned business, industrial, and residential areas should look like, and indicates how in a nontechnical fashion a city may be replanned.

726. Tracts. Instructional Simulations/Didactic Systems, 1969. $39.

This simulation game involves the conflict of interest groups when confronted with decisions on urban land use. It is designed for junior high school students through adults who divide into four teams of from 3 to 10 players each. The game takes from two to four hours to play and does provide an excellent illustration of the elements involved in zoning decisions.

727. Urban Action: Planning for Change. Boston: Ginn, 1971. $260.

Multimedia presentation aimed at intermediate and high school students; its theme is how city planning should operate. The technique is an effective one which utilizes several media to provide a significant sensory impression.

728. Urban Planning—A Contrast Between the American Approach and the European Approach. Pacifica Tape Library, 1971. Audiotape reel. 53 min. $10.50.

From a broadcast by Pacifica radio. Informative, and discusses the major differences between the premises of American and European planners as well as the kinds of problems each encounters. The discussion is best understood by persons with some background in urban planning.

729. Urban Redevelopment. New York: Popular Science Audio Visuals, 1970. 1 filmstrip (44 fr.). Color.

A filmstrip with captions aimed at the junior and senior high school levels. The theme is the problem which urban redevelopment seeks to remedy and the difficulties which such attempts encounter.

730. Walker, Robert A. The Planning Function in Urban Government. Chicago: University of Chicago Press, 1950. 410 pp. LC 50-10651. O.P.

The historical growth of planning in the United States and the relationship between planning and governmental functions.

731. Warner, Sam Bass, Jr., ed. Planning for a Nation of Cities. Cambridge, Mass.: MIT Press, 1966. 310 pp. LC 66-21355. $10, pap. $2.95.

Articles oriented around the theme of urban America. Specialized, but a good teacher resource.

732. Weiler, Conrad. Philadelphia: Neighborhood, Authority, and the Urban Crisis. New York: Praeger, 1974. 218 pp. LC 73-16899. $12.50.

Weiler's study involves the composition of areas in Philadelphia and the control of these areas as well as the reaction to this control. Should interest urban planners and other individuals attempting to solve urban problems.

733. Whittick, Arnold, ed. Encyclopedia of Urban Planning. New York: McGraw-Hill, 1974. 1,218 pp. LC 73-19757. $29.50.

First work of its kind and, as such, is a valuable reference tool. The volume is a combination biographical dictionary (noted architects, urban planners and reformers, writers on city themes) and an encyclopedia which defines terms and ideas. The main body consists of over 400 articles contributed by 70 leading persons in the field of urban planning. Should be in every large library.

734. Zucker, Paul. New Architecture and City Planning. Freeport, N.Y.: Books for Libraries, 1971 (originally published in 1944). 694 pp. LC 76-128337. $31.75.

Reprint of a symposium which was held near the end of World War II. Significant in that it shows what kind of thinking was considered the most proper at that time. Should be ordered by those libraries which have a need for older views of the American city planning process.

One of the roots of American sociology lies deep in the city. The Chicago School of Sociology used the city as a living laboratory for the study of social relations. Dividing Chicago into various zones—the Gold Coast, the ghetto, etc.—Chicago sociologists attempted to extract the various elements which contributed to making those sections what they were. As the discipline developed, however, the city or even the section appeared to be too large or too diffuse to be studied in the meticulous ways that sociologists desired. Hence, the field of view of urban sociology narrowed from the city to the small group and the interaction of individuals in that group. Despite the narrowing, some sociologists perpetuated the tradition of the city as the center of intellectual attention.

This section contains works in urban sociology which are both classical and contemporary. There are samples of the work of the Chicago sociologists as well as those of modern scholars such as Leo Schnore. Some of the works are theoretical while others deal with such topics as Black streetcorner men and mobile home parks. In addition, there are studies which use the historical past and attempt to reconstruct the social networks existent then.

736. Abrams, Charles. **The City Is the Frontier.** New York: Harper & Row, 1965. 394 pp. LC 64-25145. pap. $1.95.

Abrams, an urban sociologist, analyzes urban problems, particularly those connected with housing and urban renewal. He has an excellent historical perspective as well as a keen insight into the problems. For reference.

737. Adams, Bert N. **Kinship in an Urban Setting.** Chicago, Markham, 1968. 228 pp. LC 68-20258. $6, pap. $2.95.

Using the techniques of a social anthropologist, Adams examines how kinship networks operate in cities. Specialized, this will be most attractive to scholars interested in the social ties that hold people together in urban areas.

738. **Alienation and Mass Society.** Associated Press/Scott Education Division, 1972. 2 filmstrips (189 fr.). Color. Sound. 2 discs. 15 min. each. $39 with discs or cassettes.

The setting and the indicated causes of the individual alienation are urban ones. Strong on the psychic impact of cities on their human inhabitants.

739. Bahr, Howard M. **Skid Row: An Introduction to Disaffiliation.** New York: Oxford University Press, 1973. LC 73-82660. $6.95, pap. $3.95.

Bahr treats of the Bowery and its derelicts. He reviews the literature on the topic and adds some thoughts of his own. His account is not excessively sociological despite its title and should enjoy fairly wide circulation.

740. Barker, Roger Garlock, and Schoggen, Phil. **Qualities of Community Life.** San Francisco: Jossey-Bass, 1973. 562 pp. LC 72-13601. $35.

The authors studied a small town in England and one in the American Midwest over a 10-year period. They emphasized the way persons acted in a community setting in Europe and in one in America. The book is sociological in emphasis and, because of this and its length, will probably not have wide appeal. For libraries with significant collections in urban sociology.

741. Beshers, James M. **Urban Social Structure.** New York: Free Press, 1962. 207 pp. LC 62-11844. $6.50.

Statistical study of the structures of social groups in cities and towns. Advanced; for scholars only.

742. Bott, Elizabeth. **Family and Social Network: Roles, Norms, and External Relationships in Ordinary Urban Families,** 2nd ed. New York: Free Press, 1972. LC 71-161235. pap. $3.95.

A standard work in urban sociology which describes the lives of persons in ordinary city families in terms of their values, their contacts with other people, their jobs, and their successes or failures. Recommended for libraries as an insightful but not overly technical book.

743. Cressey, Paul Goalby. **The Taxi-Dance Hall; A Sociological Study in Commercialized Recreation and City Life.** New York: AMS Press, 1972 (originally published in 1932). 300 pp. LC 77-180706. $8.50.

One of a series on Chicago influenced by the Chicago School of Sociology, this reprint shows how the element of social disorganization engaged the attention of that school and how these scholars somehow were most attracted to the sensational. Deserves a place on shelves in collections on the history of sociological thought as well as on the history of Chicago.

744. **Delivery Systems for Model Cities: New Concepts in Serving the Urban Community.** Eddie N. Williams, ed. Chicago: University of Chicago Press, 1969. 111 pp. LC 75-29150. pap. $1.75.

Despite its title's sociological jargon, this collection is not difficult. The concerns of the essayists are with improving the quality of urban life and with reducing the size and scope of urban problems. Best suited to the specialized reader, however.

745. Eldredge, H. Wentworth, ed. **Taming Megalopolis.** 2 vols. Vol. I: **What Is and What Could Be.** Vol. II: **How to Manage an Urbanized World.** Garden City, N.Y.: Doubleday, 1967. 1,166 pp. LC 67-9839. $9.25 each, pap. vol. I $2.50, vol. II $3.50.

The editor of these two volumes teaches sociology at Dartmouth and served as head of Dartmouth's City Planning and Urban Studies Program. He has put together essays from a number of disciplines—architecture, city planning, sociology, political science, and government—on both design of cities and theories of urban development. Recommended for readers with more than surface acquaintance with urban studies.

746. Gans, Herbert J. **The Urban Villagers.** New York: Free Press, 1962. 367 pp. LC 62-15362. $8.95, pap. $2.95.

Gans, a sociologist, argues that the Italians in Boston view their area as a village with definite physical and cultural features. The thesis is provocative. Can be used by moderately sophisticated readers.

747. Gutman, Robert, and Popence, David, eds. **Neighborhood, City, and Metropolis: An Integrated Reader in Urban Sociology.** New York: Random House, 1970. 942 pp. LC 77-115420. $11.95.

A good collection further enhanced by an analysis, in the introduction, of the present state of urban sociology. Recommended for libraries which lack depth in collections on urban sociology.

748. Halebsky, Sandor, ed. **The Sociology of the City.** New York: Scribner, 1973. 696 pp. LC 72-1906. $10.95.

A collection of recent essays showing how sociologists attempt to study the city. It is aimed at readers who have some foundation in the discipline, and hence is suited to larger libraries with more scholarly demands.

749. Hauser, Philip M. **The Study of Urbanization.** Philip M. Hauser and Leo F. Schnore, eds. New York: Wiley, 1965. 554 pp. LC 65-24223. $13.50.

Schnore teams here with Philip M. Hauser, a University of Chicago sociologist, to look at the process of urbanization from the standpoint of five academic disciplines: history, geography, political science, sociology, and economics. The essays are not easy but, like Schnore's other works, contain valuable theoretical and bibliographical materials which can be used for further reading and for developing projects.

750. Johnson, Sheila K. **Idle Haven; Community Building Among the Working Class Retired.** Berkeley, Cal.: University of California Press, 1971. 208 pp. LC 72-145786. $8.95.

Little has been written about mobile parks and the social interaction in these communities. Johnson remedies this lack with her study of working-class retired persons who live in mobile homes. Offers insights into the reasons why people move into mobile homes and what their concepts are of themselves and of their surroundings.

751. Liebow, Elliot. **Tally's Corner: A Study of Negro Streetcorner Men.** Boston: Little, Brown, 1967. 260 pp. LC 67-18106. $6.95, pap. $2.75.

Liebow is a sociologist who studied Black men who congregated at a particular streetcorner in Washington, D.C. He worked from the inside as a kind of participant-observer and showed the frustration and anger of these part-time laboring men, as well as the defenses they erected to protect their none too strong egos. Demonstrates the social cost of poverty to these Black men and their families in a very vivid way.

752. Lofland, Lyn H. **A World of Strangers: Order and Action in Urban Public Space.** New York: Basic Books, 1973. 223 pp. LC 73-81199. $9.50.

Lofland's book is rather unconventional, based on historical and sociological data on how people behave in public space and how they try to avoid and escape from it. She is particularly interested in how individuals come to terms with strangers with whom they share urban spaces. Of wide interest—to city planners, architects, urban historians, and the general reader.

753. McKenzie, Roderick Duncan. **The Neighborhood: A Study of Local Life in the City of Columbus, Ohio.** New York: Arno Press, 1970 (originally published in 1923). LC 71-112560. $9.

McKenzie was a member of the Chicago School of Sociology who directed his attention to Columbus, Ohio. McKenzie concluded that the downtown neighborhood which he studied intensively was quite unstable and disorganized. He decided that the saloon and the political boss filled a void in the lives of persons in these poor neighborhoods and that the boss rule of Columbus could not be ended unless better communities were forthcoming. This reprint is suitable either as an example of urban reform ideology or as an example of historical sociology.

754. Martindale, Don, and Hanson, R. Galen. **Small Town and the Nation: The Conflict of Local and Translocal Forces.** Westport, Conn.: Greenwood Press, 1969. 211 pp. LC 79-90793. $11.50, pap. $2.95.

Images the residents of the small town named Benson have of themselves and of the town in which they live. These persons tend to cluster at two ends of the spectrum, one which says keep the town as it is, while the other wants to bring the town up to national levels. Of scholarly interest to sociologists and will have limited general appeal.

755. Park, Robert E., and Burgess, Ernest W. **The City.** Heritage of Sociology. Chicago: University of Chicago Press, 1967. 239 pp. LC 66-23694. $7.50, pap. $2.45.

The series includes writings of those who were most seminal in the development of sociological ideas. This volume details the views of two such pioneers who helped give the Chicago School of Sociology its tremendous reputation. Basic to any library on urban affairs.

756. Pessen, Edward. **Riches, Class, and Power Before the Civil War.** Lexington, Mass.: D. C. Heath, 1973. LC 72-12460. $8.95.

Pessen's study is more limited than the title would indicate since he draws his data from the rich in New York, Boston, Philadelphia, and Brooklyn. Useful to the urban and social historian since it does tell much about the American upper class. Also has attraction for the nonspecialist.

757. Rose, Arnold M., ed. **Human Behavior and Social Process: An Interactionist Approach.** Boston: Houghton Mifflin, 1962. 680 pp. LC 62-93. $11.50.

Herbert J. Gans's chapter entitled "Urbanism and Suburbanism as Ways of Life: A Re-evaluation of Definitions" questions Wirth's definition of the city and also attacks the belief that ecology is a key to looking at the city. Gans does not believe that the city and the suburbs are different entities nor that they offer different ways of life.

758. Schnore, Leo F. **Class and Race in Cities and Suburbs.** Chicago: Markham, 1972. 106 pp. LC 72-82192. $6.95. Rand, pap. $2.75.

Schnore is a veteran sociologist with an abiding interest in demographic problems. In this volume, Schnore discusses recent developments which have tended to make both the city and the suburb more economically and socially homogeneous. While it will not probably achieve wide circulation, it is a good one to have on the shelf.

759. Schnore, Leo F. **Social Science and the City: A Survey of Urban Research.** New York: Praeger, 1968. 335 pp. LC 68-26898. pap. $4.95.

Another of Schnore's works which is pertinent because of its theoretical and bibliographical material. Not for the average student.

760. Schnore, Leo F., and Fagin, Henry. **Urban Research and Policy Planning.** Urban Affairs Annual Review. Beverly Hills, Cal.: Sage Publications, 1967. 640 pp. NUC 68-8131. $22.50, pap. $7.50.

The most theoretical of the eight volumes in the series yet published. In this initial volume, specialists from economics, geography, sociology, history, political science, urban planning, and design discuss the possibilities of their disciplines in urban analysis and indicate what directions new research should take. Every library of any size should have the annual reviews as reference works.

761. Schnore, Leo R. **The Urban Scene: Human Ecology and Demography.** New York: Free Press, 1965. 374 pp. LC 65-13067. $8.95.

A sophisticated treatment of ecology and demography, suitable only for those familiar with the statistical and sociological vocabulary.

762. Sennett, Richard, ed. **Classic Essays on Cultural Cities.** Englewood Cliffs, N.J.: Prentice-Hall, 1969. 233 pp. LC 71-77533. pap. $6.

Sennett has collected essays on city culture by such well-known sociologists, historians, and anthropologists as Max Weber, George Simmel, Robert Park, Louis Wirth, Milton Singer, Oswald Spengler, and Robert Redfield. These essays date from 1900 to the 1940s and include the German originators of sociology and the Chicago School of Sociology. The essays are not easy and, while the collection should be available as a theoretical base for urban sociology, it probably will not have wide circulation.

763. **Sense and Struggle of the City.** Paul S. Amidon, 1971. 3 audiotapes. Reel or cassettes. $32.75.

There are five titles in this series: "Control and the City," "Cosmopolitan Aspects of the City," "Creativity and the City," "Culture and the City," and "The Origin of the City." The level is high school and college, and the subject matter is the potential and reality of American cities. Discussing social change, violence, and distribution of power, the series conveys a sense of city problems and of the opportunity cities afford.

764. Shevky, Eshreh, and Williams, Marilyn. **The Social Areas of Los Angeles, Analysis and Typology.** Westport, Conn.: Greenwood Press, 1972 (originally published in 1949). 172 pp. LC 72-138186. $16.75.

Scholarly. The authors use a sophisticated technique, social area analysis, to dissect various neighborhoods in Los Angeles. Belongs in research libraries with sections on theories of urban study or on urban sociology.

765. Sobin, Dennis P. **Dynamics of Community Change; The Case of Long Island's Declining "Gold Coast."** New York: Friedman, 1968. 205 pp. LC 68-8249. $6.

Sobin's is a case study of the Gold Coast on Long Island's northeastern shore which is now in the process of decline. It is a fascinating account of the growth and subsequent decline of a suburban community. While most suited to scholars, it can also attract the educated layman.

766. Suttles, Gerald D. **The Social Construction of Communities.** Chicago: University of Chicago Press, 1972. 278 pp. LC 74-177310. $9.50, pap. $2.95.

Suttles examines the sociology of community life. Aimed at a scholarly audience and thus attracting few general readers, it is an important book for libraries with sections on urban sociology.

767. Suttles, Gerald D. **The Social Order of the Slum: Ethnicity and Territory in the Inner City.** Chicago: University of Chicago Press, 1968. 243 pp. LC 68-26762. $8.95, pap. $2.95.

Suttles looks into the structure of urban ghettoes with an eye as to how residents conceive of themselves and their neighbors. The book does shed light on the development of slums although it suffers from an esoteric vocabulary.

768. Wirth, Louis. **On Cities and Social Life.** Heritage of Sociology. Chicago: University of Chicago Press, 1964. 350 pp. LC 64-24970. $12, pap. $2.95.

Wirth was a pioneering student of urbanization in the University of Chicago sociology department. A classic in the field and still useful for the student of urban development.

769. Withers, Carl. **Plainville, U.S.A.** Westport, Conn.: Greenwood Press, 1971 (originally published in 1945). 238 pp. LC 72-141271. $12.25.

Classic sociological study of a small American town in the mid-1940s. As such, reveals much of the physical characteristics of the town as well as the attitudes of the residents. Hardly difficult, ought to interest the general reader as well as the specialist in urban sociology.

770. Young, James Sterling. **The Washington Community, 1800–1828.** New York: Columbia University Press, 1966. 307 pp. LC 66-14080. $13.50. Harcourt Brace Javonovich, pap. $2.95.

Sociological study that has implications for both urban historians and urban sociologists. Essentially about how the legislative and executive members in Washington interact both formally and informally. The study is statistical; Young uses the Rice Index of Cohesion so that persons unacquainted with this index will find it heavy going. The quality of the work is high enough so this is a necessary title for libraries which have more than a beginning collection in urban studies.

Urban Geography

Recently, geographers have shown much interest in urban affairs; they have felt that urban geography was an entree to the high school curriculum and that spatial analysis of cities provided important insights into urban growth and re-construction. In addition, they have become mathematically oriented and are heavily engaged in model building, using computer assistance to work out the details of their models. The discipline is an expanding one which has and is borrowing ideas from other disciplines as well as elaborating those of its own.

This section contains a sampling of what the field of urban geography covers. It includes materials on how geography can contribute to an understanding of power conflicts in the city, to a theory of ghetto development and a more sophisticated analysis of what a ghetto is, to a history of city growth, to a better knowledge of what makes areas of the city adequate and others inade-quate, and to how immigrants to America settled into cities. While the macro-theory of the 19th century no longer is the main preoccupation of geographers, they do possess several generalizations about urban growth in the past and pro-jections in the future which are of use to other disciplines and to the educated layperson.

771. Berry, Brian J. L. **Geography of Market Centers and Retail Distribution.** Englewood Cliffs, N.J.: Prentice-Hall, 1967. 146 pp. LC 67-13355. pap. $3.15.

By using the tool of economic analysis, Berry tries to make some sense out of why certain cities take on the economic characteristics they have. Of most interest to geographers but will appeal to some economists as well.

772. Broek, Jan O. M. **Geography, Its Scope and Spirit.** Columbus, Ohio: Merrill, 1965. 116 pp. LC 65-21171. $4.95, pap. $2.50.

Contains definitions and terms used in geography profession; useful for teaching scope of the field.

773. **The City and Its Region.** National Film Board of Canada/Sterling Educa-tional Films, 1964. (City Series.) 16mm. b/w. Sound. 29 min. Rent $7.50.

Mumford examines the relation between city and countryside and explains how balance can be maintained.

774. Cox, Kevin R. **Conflict, Power and Politics in the City: A Geographic View.** New York: McGraw-Hill, 1973. 133 pp. LC 72-6644. $5.95, pap. $3.95.

A brief elaboration of the theory of spatial cause of urban conflict. Cox argues that part of the cause of urban conflict is locational inequalities. Not for the uninitiated nor for those who seek a social solution for urban problems.

775. Geography in an Urban Age, Unit I: Geography of Cities. Association of American Geographers/Macmillan, 1968. $306.

A multimedia project containing maps of Seattle, models, and aerial views for photointerpretation. A highly useful tool for conceptualization despite some of its more facile generalizations.

776. Geography in an Urban Age, Unit III: Cultural Geography. Association of American Geographers/Macmillan, 1968. $22 per student.

A high school geography project which includes five integral activities: 1. "Different Ideas about Cattle," a 16-fr. filmstrip and additional student reading; 2. "Lesson from Sports," a student reading with map exercises; 3. "Expansion of Islam," a student reading with map exercises; 4. "Canada, a Regional Question," reading and map exercises; 5. "Cultural Change: a Trend Toward Uniformity," a 16-fr. filmstrip and student reading. The project also includes two optional activities: "Games Illustrating the Spread of Ideas," which includes three games involving entire group of students and additional reading; and "The Long Road," a 16-page reading.

777. Geography of the Ghetto: Perceptions, Problems and Alternatives. Harold M. Rose, ed. De Kalb, Ill.: Northern Illinois University, 1972. 273 pp. LC 72-1388. $15.

Put together by geographer Rose, this collection deals largely with the numbers of people within urban limits. The articles are timely and provide insight into different ways of looking at the ghetto.

778. Gottman, Jean. Megalopolis: The Urbanized Northeastern Seaboard of the United States. Cambridge, Mass.: MIT Press, 1964. 810 pp. NUC 65-43986. $10, pap. $4.95.

Gottman, a French geographer and professor at the University of Paris, popularized the Greek word megalopolis in this book which was commissioned by the Twentieth Century Fund. An important book; recommended.

779. Hall, Peter. The World Cities. World University Library. New York: McGraw-Hill, 1966. 236 pp. LC 64-66181. $4.95, pap. $2.45.

Hall, an English economic geographer, discusses seven major metropolitan areas of the world—London, Moscow, New York, Paris, Tokyo, and the Randstad and Rhine-Ruhr (two complexes of cities in Holland and Germany). The book puts the American city in a world perspective and is suitable for the advanced student. It is visually attractive with many colored schematics and black-and-white photographs of cities and areas of cities.

780. Jones, Emrys. Towns and Cities. New York: Oxford University Press, 1966. 152 pp. LC 66-8567. pap. $1.95.

A short, well-written, and interesting history, suitable for the general reader. Written by an English geographer, it treats both preindustrial and modern cities and urbanization as well as social problems.

781. Landforms and Man. McGraw-Hill Films, 1964. (World Geography.) 1 filmstrip (36 fr.). Color.

One of eight in the series. The emphasis is on man's response to natural conditions—his ability to adapt himself and his tools. Appropriate for junior and senior high school students.

782. Let's Tour Megalopolis. Milliken. Color. Transparencies. $6.95.

A rather simple set of transparencies on a variety of urban topics. The titles are "Agricultural Activities," "Cultural and Recreational Activities," "Economic Problems," "Government Structure," "Health and Community Services Problems," "Industrial Activities," "The Megalopolis of Tomorrow," "Multi-urbia," "Physical-Political Map of Megalopolis," "Transportation Problems," "Urban Growth Problems," and "Water Problems." The set might be of use to beginners who are starting to think in terms of large urban agglomerates.

783. Megalopolis—Cradle of the Future. Encyclopaedia Britannica Films, 1962. 16mm. Color and b/w. Sound. 22 min. Color $265, b/w $135.

Life and problems in the urbanized Northeast seaboard from Boston to Washington, D.C., support a plea for better planning and organization of American cities. It is based upon Jean Gottmann's book *Megalopolis*.

784. Middle Atlantic Seaboard Region, the Great Cities—Megalopolis. A.C.I. Productions/McGraw Hill Films, 1963. (United States Geography Social Studies.) 35mm. Color and b/w. 17 min. Color $180, b/w $90.

Problems of the urbanized seaboard region from Boston to Washington, D.C. Shows the industrial city and the results engendered by sprawl and suburban development. For junior and senior high school students.

785. Morrill, Richard, and Woldenberg, Ernest. The Geography of Poverty in the United States. New York: McGraw-Hill, 1971. 148 pp. LC 72-178931. $5.95, pap. $3.95.

While not specifically confined to urban topics, nonetheless it is useful for purposes of comparison. It shows statistically and graphically the locations of poor families and individuals within the United States, which makes possible a comparison of city with country as well as a comparison of city with city.

786. Murphy, Raymond E. The American City: An Urban Geography, 2nd ed. New York: McGraw-Hill, 1974. 556 pp. LC 65-24894. $12.95, pap. $3.95.

Standard college textbook in urban geography. Does not use complicated statistical methods, though it does use some mathematical devices. Murphy's work is helpful because of its wealth of definitions and summaries of research. Excellent bibliography.

787. Parkins, Almon. The Historical Geography of Detroit. Port Washington, N.Y.: Kennikat, 1970 (originally published in 1918). 356 pp. LC 77-118422. $12.75.

Originally published by the Michigan Historical Commission, this is the classic study of the development and physical expansion of the Motor City. Recommended for libraries with materials on the geography of cities.

788. **Population Patterns in the United States.** Coronet Instructional Films. 16mm. Color and b/w. Sound. 11 min. Color $120, b/w $60.

Discusses the patterns of settlement which were obvious at the beginning of the decade of the sixties, including data on life span, infant mortality, immigration trends, as well as movements to the city and from East to West. Basic for the average person.

789. Pred, Allan R. **The Spatial Dynamics of U.S. Urban-Industrial Growth, 1800–1914: Interpretive and Theoretical Essays.** Regional Studies. Cambridge, Mass.: MIT Press, 1966. 225 pp. LC 66-26016. $11.

Quite sophisticated, as Pred takes a design viewpoint. Valuable for a reader with a strong background.

790. Pred, Allan R. **Urban Growth and the Circulation of Information: The United States System of Cities, 1790–1840.** Cambridge, Mass.: Harvard University Press, 1973. 348 pp. LC 73-76384. $15.

Pred is a geographer who uses mathematical models to determine the rapidity and extent of information flow between cities prior to the establishment of a telegraph network. He uses data about newspaper circulation, the transportation of goods, the United States mail, and the travel of private individuals. Complicated and of use only to the specialist in communication theory and urban geography. Recommended mainly for research libraries.

791. Rose, Harold. **The Black Ghetto; A Spatial Behavorial Perspective.** New York: McGraw-Hill, 1972. LC 70-179713. $5.95, pap. $3.95.

Rose looks at the spatial dimensions of the living areas of Blacks in American cities. The major thrust is demography with numbers as a base. Especially useful for reference work as it does provide many pertinent statistics.

792. Smith, David M. **The Geography of Social Well-Being in the United States; An Introduction to Territorial Social Indicators.** New York: McGraw-Hill, 1973. 144 pp. LC 72-6605. $4.95, pap. $3.95.

Companion piece to Richard Morrill and Ernest Woldenberg's *The Geography of Poverty in the United States* in that it shows where the amenities of life considered to be the best are located while the latter shows where they are worst. Heavily laced with statistics, making it more a reference work than a book to be read for pleasure.

793. Taylor, John L., and Maddison, Richard N. "A Land Use Gaming Simulation," **Urban Affairs Quarterly,** III (June, 1968), 37–51.

Taylor and Maddison have created a game which, while sophisticated and British, could be adapted for advanced American students.

794. **Village, Town, and City.** McGraw-Hill Films, 1964. (World Geography.) 1 filmstrip (36 fr.). Color.

Concentrates on dwelling in groups. For the average student.

795. Ward, David. **Cities and Immigrants: A Geography of Change in Nineteenth Century America.** New York: Oxford University Press, 1971. 164 pp. LC 74-124612. $6.75, pap. $3.50.

Ward's is the most successful attempt to date to use geographical concepts to study the American urban past. His study encompasses the years from 1790 to 1920 and touches on physical mobility, social geography, and land use patterns. It is highly recommended for use by urban geographers, historians, planners, and theorists. It belongs in every library.

796. Wilson, Albert Geoffrey. **Urban and Regional Models in Geography and Planning.** New York: Wiley, 1974. 418 pp. LC 73-8200. $24.50, pap. $12.50.

Wilson, a professor of Urban and Regional Geography at the University of Leeds, was trained as a mathematician. Consequently, the book is quite abstruse and can only be comprehended by the mathematically sophisticated. There is no attempt to apply the models; rather the emphasis is on model building. For specialists only.

797. Yeates, Maurice, and Garner, Barry. **North American Cities.** New York: Harper & Row, 1971. 536 pp. LC 72-148449. $14.95.

Textbook in urban geography which emphasizes the shape of modern cities in the northern hemisphere of America. The book says little about historical development or the cultural present, but is a useful overview of physical features. Recommended for libraries which have limited collections and which need basic books on geographical forms.

Urban History

Although historians had tried to come to terms with the American urban experience from the late 19th century on, the discipline of urban history emerged as a subspecies of history only after World War II. Urban history is still somewhat fuzzy and unfocused; as practiced by some historians, it is social history in an urban setting. Other historians regard the discipline as a study of demographic change over periods of time while still others emphasize the impact of technology upon the shape and development of the city. Other historians have written histories of the growth of municipal services or the evolution of police systems. All have found a place under the rubric of urban history.

The materials in this section are varied, ranging from general surveys of American urban development to accounts of the growth of particular types of towns such as company towns or New England towns. They also include data on urban religious and political movements and the contribution of the people of the cities to already established institutions. Attention is paid to different rates of urbanization in various sections of the country. In addition, there are materials on the kind of life lived in towns and cities in a number of historical epochs. Also included are studies of social and physical mobility in 19th-century American cities, the subject of the new urban history.

798. Abell, Aaron. **The Urban Impact on American Protestantism.** Hamden, Conn.: Archon, 1962 (originally published in 1943). 275 pp. LC 62-5420 rev. $8.50.

Abell's history is general, but it does describe the beginnings of the Social Gospel movement. For reference.

799. Allen, James B. **The Company Town in the American West.** Norman, Okla.: University of Oklahoma Press, 1966. 205 pp. LC 66-13420. $7.95.

Allen studies various lumbering and mining companies which built towns for their employees. He also evaluates the results, including the Ludlow massacre. Can be utilized for an in-depth study of this phase of urban development.

800. American History 400: A Slide System. Harcourt Brace Jovanovich, 1968–1971. Cartridge H, *Industrialization of the United States.* 80 2 X 2 slides. Color. $60.

Part of an American history series which may be purchased separately. Focuses on U.S. industrialization. Several of the slides concern demographic trends while others concern urbanization. The pictures are well selected.

801. Anderson, Nels. **The Industrial Urban Community: Historical and Comparative Perspectives.** New York: Appleton Century Crofts, 1971. 438 pp. LC 71-131432. $12.50.

The growth and development of the industrial city in the 19th and 20th centuries. Recommended for libraries with urban history collections.

802. Boorstin, Daniel J. **The Americans: The National Experience.** New York: Random House, 1965. 517 pp. LC 65-17440. $12.50, pap. $3.45.

The section on Boosterism is a good antidote to the antiurban thought found in *The Intellectual Versus the City*. While Boorstin's account is sophisticated, better students can profit from it.

803. Brown, Richard D. **Revolutionary Politics in Massachusetts: The Boston Committee of Correspondence and the Towns, 1772-1774.** Cambridge, Mass.: Harvard University Press, 1970. 282 pp. LC 71-119072. $10.

Brown shows how the urban milieu fostered the growth of revolutionary sentiments and how the urban network facilitated the work of revolutionary committees. He indicates how much the Revolution was a product of urban centers in New England. Primarily for scholars.

804. Brownell, Blaine A. **The Urban South in the Twentieth Century.** Forums in History. St. Charles, Mo.: Forum Press, 1974. 38 pp. LC 73-81060. $.95.

In this essay Brownell argues that cities in the South have not deviated significantly from the pattern of growth of cities in the North in recent times and, hence, have incurred most of the urbanization problems of other American cities. A useful introduction to urbanization in the South, outlining as it does the recent research on the topic.

805. Calkins, Earnest Elmo. **They Broke the Prairie; Being Some Account of the Settlement of the Upper Mississippi Valley by Religious and Educational Pioneers, Told in Terms of One City; Galesburg, and of One College; Knox.** Westport, Conn.: Greenwood Press, 1971 (originally published in 1937). 451 pp. LC 75-138103. $17.50.

History of a small Illinois town which had a large infusion of Presbyterians. These settlers created a community and what became an excellent liberal arts college. This reprint is more than an institutional history; it is the history of how one town was built. Should interest urban historians as well as historians of education.

806. Callow, Alexander B., Jr., ed. **American Urban History; An Interpretive Reader with Comments.** New York: Oxford University Press, 1969. 674 pp. pap. LC 75-75599. $5.95.

An excellent collection of interpretive articles. Organized chronologically, it contains a number of theoretical as well as factual essays.

807. **The Changing City.** Coronet Films, 1963. Color. Sound. 16 mm. Rental available from University of Illinois. $6.50.

Essentially a look at how cities grow and what affect this growth has on their inhabitants, including the implications of land use and urban renewal. For all high school students.

808. Chapman, Edward M. **New England Village Life.** New York: B. Blom, 1971 (originally published in 1937). 232 pp. LC 73-174367. $10.75.

This reprint was written by an author from southern Connecticut who based it upon a daily record kept for 75 years by his ancestors. The towns involved are Lyme and Saybrook, and the materials center upon economic activity, social life, and educational growth. Easy to read, and also has research possibilities for the urban historian.

809. The City in U.S. History. Popular Science Audio-Visuals/Denoyer-Geppert, 1969. 1 filmstrip (42 fr.). Color. Captioned. $7.50.

Designed for students from the high school level through college. Because of its shortness and because of the heterogeneous audience for which it is intended, the filmstrip is neither a detailed nor sophisticated survey of the subject, but it does provide a useful introduction to the topic.

810. City of Gold. National Film Board of Canada/McGraw-Hill Films, 1957. 16mm. b/w. Sound. 23 min. Rent $6.

While this movie is composed primarily of photographs of the Klondike Gold Rush and its impact on Alaska, it does help one understand the critical location of Seattle in the 1890s. Aimed at the junior and senior high school levels.

811. Clinch, Thomas A. **Urban Populism and Free Silver in Montana: A Narrative of Ideology in Political Action.** Missoula, Mont.: University of Montana Press, 1970. 190 pp. LC 77-14198. $5.95.

Most historical surveys ignore the urban dimension of populism and, as a result, the role of trade unions and other reformist groups in the cities is largely unknown. Clinch tries to remedy this lack of knowledge, at least in the urban centers of Montana. He argues that urban radicalism was an integral part of the whole populist movement.

812. Colonial Cities, 1700–1750. Popular Science Audio-Visuals/Denoyer-Geppert, 1968. 1 filmstrip (43 fr.). Color. $7.50.

Elementary; recommended only as a simple visual experience.

813. Cross, Robert D., ed. **The Church and the City, 1865–1910.** Indianapolis, Ind.: Bobbs-Merrill, 1967. 359 pp. LC 66-17273. $7.50, pap. $3.75.

Cross has put together a collection of documents about the impact of the city on the church during the period of rapid urbanization after the Civil War. These documents provide interesting insights into the conceptions of individuals in the period. Cross has an introduction to this collection which successfully provides a framework for understanding varying responses to the challenges of the city.

814. Danckaerts, Jasper, and Sluyter, Peter. **Journal of a Voyage to New York, and Tour in Several of the American Colonies in 1679-80.** Henry C. Murphy, trans. and ed. Ann Arbor, Mich.: University Microfilms, 1966 (originally published in 1867). 440 pp. LC 66-24084. $20.80.

Danckaerts was a Dutchman who traveled to New York after it had become an English possession but while it still had many Dutch citizens. He also visited Albany, New York, as well as the colonies in New England and the colony of

Maryland. An excellent reference for the history of colonial New York City; should be useful for research libraries.

815. Dawn of a New Era—America Enters the Twentieth Century. S-L Film Productions, 1966. 16mm. b/w. Sound. 20 min. Sale $115, rent $15.

The period 1897–1905 is the focus of this film, which utilizes cuts from films of the era and shows some of its notable people—inventors, political leaders, and entertainers. Gives the flavor of the times and offers some first-hand views of cities. Suitable for senior high school students.

816. Dorsett, Lyle W. The Early American City. St. Charles, Mo.: Forum Press, 1973. 16 pp. LC 73-81060. $.95.

Dorsett discusses how the compact city of preindustrial America was transformed by large-scale industry and immigration. The short essay can be helpful as an introduction to the history of the American city.

817. Dykstra, Robert. The Cattle Towns. New York: Knopf, 1968. 286 pp. LC 68-12677. $10. Atheneum, pap. $3.95.

One of the first attempts to cut through the romantic haze surrounding the Kansas cattle towns and to introduce some behavorial criteria into the study.

818. Emergence of a Nation, 1800–1817. NBC/Time-Life Films, 1968. (Exploring: The Story of America.) 16mm. Color. Sound. 24 min. $300.

The main events of the period. There is some reference to cities, although the concentration is elsewhere.

819. Ershkowitz, Herbert. The People of the Jacksonian City. St. Charles, Mo.: Forum Press, 1973. LC 73-81060. $.95.

There has been considerable study recently of violence in American cities in the 1830s and this essay provides a brief synthesis of the scholarship on the topic. Although intended for courses in college, the pamphlet can be used as an introduction for laypeople.

820. Fur Trappers Westward. Arthur Barr Productions, 1953. 16mm. Color and b/w. Sound. 31 min. Color $300, b/w $160.

Fur trapping, including the exploration of California, trading with the Indians, and the rendezvous. Useful as an example of perpetuating the romantic myth. It can be used on several levels, elementary and advanced.

821. Glaab, Charles N., ed. The American City: A Documentary History. Homewood, Ill.: Dorsey Press, 1963. 478 pp. LC 63-19883. pap. $6.15.

This collection of documents on the city in America is quite strong on the 19th century, as is Glaab's text. Could serve as a primary source for class research.

822. Glaab, Charles N., and Brown, Theodore A. A History of Urban America. New York: Macmillan, 1967. 328 pp. LC 67-15198. $6.95, pap. $4.95.

Central to this book is that "From the beginning, the tensions and impulses of America's cities have given direction to the growth of the nation." Especially strong on the 19th century, this general survey is informative and interpretive, and is arranged topically. It does not go beyond World War II.

823. Goetzmann, William H. **Exploration and Empire; The Explorer and the Scientist in the Winning of the American West.** New York: Knopf, 1966. 656 pp. LC 65-11123. $12.50. Random House, pap. $3.95.

This award-winning book on the West puts the mountain man in his proper historical perspective and is vital for the study of that phenomenon. Ought to be a reference work for students and teachers.

824. Green, Constance McLaughlin. **American Cities in the Growth of the Nation.** New York: John De Graff, 1957. 258 pp. LC 57-12021. Harper, pap. $2.25.

These are Mrs. Green's Commonwealth Fund lectures in history at University College, London, in 1951. For the student interested in the biography of specific cities in the Midwest, this book is more valuable than her *Rise of Urban America*.

825. Green, Constance McLaughlin. **The Rise of Urban America.** New York: Harper & Row, 1965. 208 pp. LC 65-14681. $6.95.

A good general survey, not particularly interpretive. Suitable for the upper-level high school student.

826. Haeger, John D. **From Commonwealth to Commerce: The Pre-Industrial City in America.** St. Charles, Mo.: Forum Press, 1973. LC 73-81060. $.95.

A short history of the transition from the Puritan village to the commercial city in America. It indicates what factors promoted this change as well as what the social costs were. The level of the essay is for the undergraduate college student, but it can be used by the general reader to gain an overview of early American urban history.

827. Hegel, Richard. **Nineteenth-Century Historians of New Haven.** Hamden, Conn.: Archon Books, 1973. 105 pp. LC 70-181318. $6.

An esoteric book of reference use to historiographers and to regional libraries.

828. Hewitt, Abram Stevens. **Selected Writings.** Allen Nevins, ed. New York: Kennikat, 1965 (originally published in 1937). 414 pp. LC 64-24462. $12.50.

Hewitt was a prominent New York industrialist in the latter half of the 19th century who was instrumental in helping to defeat the Tweed Ring. Provides a valuable research source for libraries which have a need for primary materials.

829. Hoffman, Charles F. **A Winter in the West; By a New-Yorker.** 2 vols. Ann Arbor, Mich.: University Microfilms, 1966 (originally published in 1835). LC 66-26345. set $14.95.

Hoffman made his way to Chicago via Pittsburgh, Cleveland, and Detroit. On his return journey, he visited Wisconsin, Minnesota, Missouri, Kentucky, and Virginia. The main thrust, however, is a vigorous defense of Chicago and other Western cities against the calumnies of foreign observers. Specialized; best suited to research libraries.

830. Hone, Philip. **Diary of Philip Hone, 1828–1851.** Rise of Urban America. 2 vols. in 1. Allan Nevins, ed. New York: Arno Press, 1970 (originally published in 1927). LC 77-112559. $34.

A necessary volume for anyone interested in the history of New York City before the Civil War. Hone was a successful businessman in New York who also served as mayor. He was at home with the notables of his day, including Webster, Clay, Washington Irving, Cooper, and Emerson. His diary is an excellent resource for urban historians.

831. Ingraham, Joseph Holt. **The South-West; By a Yankee.** 2 vols. Ann Arbor, Mich.: University Microfilms, 1966 (originally published in 1835). LC 66-26346. set $12.95.

Ingraham was a native of Portland, Maine, and hence qualified as a Yankee. He went to Mississippi in 1830 to teach in a college. The two volumes, however, are about New Orleans and Natchez, respectively. Ingraham is sympathetic to the South and does not denigrate southern cities. Recommended for research libraries.

832. Innocent Years, 1901–1914. NBC/McGraw-Hill Films, 1965. 16mm. b/w. Sound. 48 min. $250.

While the name seems a misnomer, this Project 20 film shows the significant events of the era, including immigration, industrialization, and the growth of cities. Helpful, and highly recommended for high school students and above.

833. Jackson, Kenneth T., and Schultz, Stanley K., eds. **Cities in American History.** New York: Knopf, 1972. 508 pp. LC 72-160265. $12.50, pap. $6.25.

This collection contains original as well as reprinted essays. It is the kind of book which a library ought to have if its budget for urban history is low, since it provides so many starting places for study.

834. Knights, Peter R. **The Plain People of Boston, 1830–1860: A Study in City Growth.** New York: Oxford University Press, 1971. 204 pp. LC 74-159647. $7.95, pap. $2.50.

Knights is a young scholar whose research reflects the interest in social mobility of the new urban history. What he attempts is a study of geographical mobility through the use of demographic techniques. His book is technical, but it does show the goals and methods of those historians who are informed by sociology.

835. McKelvey, Blake. **The City in American History.** Historical Problems: Studies and Documents. New York: Barnes & Noble, 1969. 229 pp. LC 79-452038. $8.50.

A survey of city growth through analysis of primary sources, the collection is an excellent one which ought to be in a basic library of urban history.

836. McKelvey, Blake. **The Emergence of Metropolitan America: 1915–1966.** New Brunswick, N.J.: Rutgers—the State University Press, 1968. 311 pp. LC 68-18695. $10.

The most detailed study of this period of urbanization in the United States. A valuable reference source because of its detail and extensive bibliography.

837. McKelvey, Blake. **The Urbanization of America, 1860–1915.** New Brunswick, N.J.: Rutgers—the State University Press, 1963. 370 pp. LC 62-21248. $10.

This is the first volume of McKelvey's two-volume study of American city growth. It examines the development of cities and towns as well as the economic conditions which contributed to this development. One of the first to deal with pre-World War I urban forces in America. While there is some description of the city as a social organism, the main thrust is factual and bibliographic.

838. Mann, Arthur, Harris, Neil, and Warner, Sam Bass, Jr. **History and the Role of the City in American Life.** Indiana Historical Society Lectures, 1971–1972. Indianapolis, Ind.: Indiana Historical Society, 1972. 65 pp. LC 73-161979. $1.50.

There are three essays in this book: Arthur Mann, "The City as a Melting Pot;" Neil Harris, "Four Stages of Cultural Growth;" and Sam Bass Warner, Jr., "An Urban Historian's Agenda for the Profession."

839. Mohl, Raymond A., and Richardson, James F. **The Urban Experience: Themes in American History.** Belmont, Cal.: Wadsworth, 1973. 265 pp. LC 72-97322. pap. $5.95.

Readings designed to be used in urban history courses. Topically arranged and consists of original essays by younger urban historians. Recommended for those libraries with few books in urban history.

840. Mohl, Raymond A., and Betten, Neil, eds. **Urban America in Historical Perspective.** New York: Weybright & Talley, 1970. 426 pp. LC 70-99002. $8.50.

Chapter 3 in this anthology has two sections on working-class and immigrant conditions in the city before the Civil War. For research projects.

841. Mowry, George E. **The Urban Nation: 1920–1960.** New York: Hill & Wang, 1965. 278 pp. LC 65-17423. $5.95, pap. $1.95.

Mowry traces the impact of mass production, mass consumption, and urbanization during this period, and discusses the effect of foreign affairs on the domestic scene. There is little theoretical discussion of the problems of urbanization and urban development.

842. Nadeau, Remi A. **City-Makers: The Story of Southern California's First Boom, 1868–76,** 3rd ed. rev. Los Angeles: Trans-Angelo Books, 1965. 168 pp. LC 74-165799. $8.95.

A good study showing how an area can take off into rapid urbanization. For projects on Los Angeles and other southern California cities.

843. Nash, Gerald D. **The American West in the Twentieth Century: A Short History of an Urban Oasis.** Englewood Cliffs, N.J.: Prentice-Hall, 1973. 312 pp. LC 72-11880. $9.95, pap. $4.95.

A history of the West which claims that the experimentation done in western cities toward a pluralistic, multiracial, and ethnic society has shown the direction the rest of American society will take. Scholarly but well written, and should appeal to a wide audience. Highly recommended.

844. New York State. University Films/McGraw-Hill, 1965. 8 filmstrips. Color. $8.50 each, $60 set.

This set has three filmstrips suitable for a course emphasizing urban history:

Colonial New York (36 fr.)
New York's Communities (42 fr.)
New York City: Fabulous Metropolis (44 fr.)

While New York is not a typical state nor New York City a typical city, they are important examples.

845. Overton, Richard C. Burlington West: A Colonization History of the Burlington Railroad. New York: Russell and Russell, 1967 (originally published in 1941). LC 66-24744. $15.

Overton takes the case of a particular railroad, the Burlington, and considers how it colonized towns through Iowa and Nebraska and westward. For special projects.

846. Pomeroy, Earl. The Pacific Slope; A History of California, Oregon, Washington, Idaho, Utah, and Nevada. Seattle: University of Washington Press, 1965. 403 pp. LC 65-11128. $12.50, pap. $3.95.

The definitive history of that part of the West beyond the last range of mountains. Well written and can be understood by the average reader.

847. The Real West. NBC-TV/McGraw-Hill, 1961. 16mm. b/w. Sound. 54 min. Sale $275. Gary Cooper, narrator.

This Project 20 film shows social and economic development in the West from 1849 to 1900. While the major thrust is to debunk the myth of the gunfighter and to show the conquest of the Plains Indians, the film also shows town development, particularly in mining camps. It is most fruitful for high school students.

848. Richardson, James F., ed. The American City; Historical Studies. Waltham, Mass.: Xerox College Publishing, 1972. 407 pp. LC 70-161682. Wiley, pap. $5.95.

Richardson's reader is one of several that recently have been put together for the use of college classes in urban history. It is competently done and is suited for college or high school libraries.

849. Rutman, Darrett. Husbandmen of Plymouth: Farms and Villages in the Old Colony, 1620–1692. Boston: Published for Plymouth Plantation by Beacon Press, 1967. 100 pp. LC 67-25868. $5.95.

Study of town formation in the Plymouth area in great detail. Rutman is interested in social history and traces life-styles in rural and village life. Useful for further readings and study.

850. Schlesinger, Arthur M., Sr. **The Rise of The City: 1878–1898.** A History of American Life. Chicago: Quadrangle, 1971 (originally published in 1933). 494 pp. LC 78-29656. $8.95. Watts, pap. $3.45.

This pioneer effort in the field of urban history still has value if one has access to the other 13 books in the series edited by Schlesinger and Dixon Ryan Fox. Using the idea of city growth as his theme, Schlesinger had few urban studies to guide him in his work and hence is somewhat more general than McKelvey's.

851. Smith, Page. **As a City Upon a Hill.** New York: Knopf, 1966. 332 pp. LC 66-19400. $7.95. MIT Press, pap. $3.95.

The first chapter sets out Smith's theme, that New England towns provided a "covenanted community" as a model for small-town America. This community represented a sense of unity and emphasized conformity. It affected small-town growth throughout the United States as New England model towns spread to the West. These towns, according to Smith, exercised a pernicious effect upon democratic attitudes and were strongholds of conservatism. The ideas lend themselves to inquiry and can be used for senior high school students.

852. Smith, Wilson, ed. **Cities of Our Past and Present.** New York: Wiley, 1964. 292 pp. LC 64-15001. $7.50, pap. $4.95.

Another useful collection of documents, Smith's has more material on contemporary problems than does Glaab's *The American City: A Documentary History*.

853. Starbuck, James C. **The Use and Abuse of the American City.** St. Charles, Mo.: Forum Press, 1973. 16 pp. LC 73-81060. $.95.

Starbuck defends the performance of the contemporary American city by comparing the problems of these cities with those of past cities. The short essay is an interesting antidote to the usual cry of doom about the gloomy fate of American cities.

854. Sutter, Ruth. **Towns and Downtowns in Early America.** St. Charles, Mo.: Forum Press, 1973. 16 pp. LC 73-81060. $.95.

The kinds of town development in pioneer America. Sutter claims that the types of towns which evolved depended upon both the tradition of the community and the tradition of physical construction. The essay is a brief introduction to the origins of towns in America which was designed for use in undergraduate college classes.

855. Thernstrom, Stephan. **The Other Bostonians: Poverty and Progress in the American Metropolis, 1880–1970.** Cambridge, Mass.: Harvard University Press, 1973. 345 pp. LC 73-77469. $12.

Typical of recent urban history in that it is statistically oriented and is quite concerned with population mobility. Thernstrom uses data from census reports, tax records, city directories, and other sources to derive his conclusion that there was considerable population mobility in Boston. Not easy, as it presupposes considerable background in the field.

856. Thernstrom, Stephan. **Poverty and Progress: Social Mobility in a Nineteenth-Century City.** Cambridge, Mass.: Harvard University Press, 1964. 286 pp. LC 64-21793. $10. Atheneum, pap. $2.95.

Thernstrom's study of Newburyport is mainly concerned with social mobility, but the mobility of workers sheds much light on industrialization and suburbanization, for the major goal and achievement of workers was the ownership of a home. For better readers.

857. Toward the Gilded Age—Inventions and Big Business. NBC/Graphic Curriculum., 1968. (Story of America.) 16mm. Color. Sound. 25 min. Rent $11.

The impact of electrification, the telegraph and telephone, and the elevator. The film fits in well with books on this period of time and can be used for junior and senior high school students.

858. United States History, 2. Hammond, 1969. Color. 32 transparencies. $234.24 set, $7.96 each.

These transparencies can be used in lecture and discussion groups. The two titles in the series which are appropriate are "Modern Urban Problems" and "U.S.—Growth of Industry and Cities." The level is junior and senior high school.

859. Urban Centers and Historical Background. Society for Visual Education, 1970. 1 filmstrip (50 fr.). Color. 17 min. 1 disc. $9.

Designed for junior and senior high school students. The topic is urban history and the approach is to describe the growth of selected cities. Starting point for those with little background.

860. Wade, Richard C. The Urban Frontier: Pioneer Life in Early Pittsburgh, Cincinnati, Lexington, Louisville, and St. Louis. Chicago: University of Chicago Press, 1964. 360 pp. LC NUC 65-9946. pap. $2.45.

Essential to the study of the symbiotic relation of the city to the frontier. Contains much factual as well as interpretive material and can be understood by senior high school students.

861. Wade, Richard C., Wilder, Howard B., and Wade, Louise C. A History of the United States. Boston: Houghton Mifflin, 1966. 880 pp. LC 66-5680.

This textbook was written by an urban historian and thus concentrates heavily on urban history. Recommended for collections of textbooks.

862. Wakstein, Allen, ed. The Urbanization of America: An Historical Anthology. Boston: Houghton Mifflin, 1970. 502 pp. LC 72-19438. $7.50.

A collection of interpretive essays of the same high quality as Callow's. The organization is also similar to Callow's. Should be useful to the teacher and the advanced student.

863. Waring, George E., Jr. Report on the Social Statistics of Cities: Part I— The New England and the Middle States. Part II—The Southern and the Western States. Rise of Urban America. 2 vols. New York: Arno Press, 1970 (originally published in 1886 and 1887). LC 74-112577. set $130.

Based upon the census data of 1880, the set contains detailed descriptions of over 200 American cities. Also included are histories of major cities written by well-known authors; one of these is George W. Cable's history of New Orleans. The data contained in these reports deserve to be in all research libraries with any interest in urban history and urban development.

864. Wertenbaker, Thomas J. **The Golden Age of Colonial Culture,** 2nd ed. Ithaca, N.Y.: Cornell University Press, 1942. 171 pp. NUC 69-47362. pap. $1.95.

Wertenbaker puts together his vast knowledge of colonial social history, including some material on urban history. A good reference work.

865. **Westward Movement Series.** Encyclopaedia Britannica, 1962. 16mm. Color. Sound.

This film contains information on the backgrounds and destinations of settlers. While not directly oriented to cities, it does include information about their growth. For elementary through high school students.

    Settlement of the Mississippi Valley. 16 min. Sale $220, rent $11.
    Settlers of the Old Northwest. 15 min. Sale $220, rent $11.

Similar treatment of the early development of this area.

866. Wheeler, Kenneth W. **To Wear a City's Crown: The Beginnings of Urban Growth in Texas, 1836–1865.** Cambridge, Mass.: Harvard University Press, 1968. 222 pp. LC 68-28698. $10.

Considering four Texas cities—Galveston, Houston, Austin, and San Antonio— Wheeler concludes that this last urban frontier of the Old South served the same function in Texas that Cincinnati, Louisville, Lexington, and St. Louis did in the Midwest. For informed readers.

867. Wiebe, Robert H. **The Search for Order, 1877–1920.** New York: Hill & Wang, 1967. 333 pp. LC 66-27609. $5.75, pap. $2.25.

Wiebe's theme is that the decentralized small-town community which typified the American scene in 1877 was supplanted by a new order which was the product of an urban middle class. This class wanted a rational, secular, bureaucratic society to go along with industrialization and urbanization. Useful and provocative on the impact of the industrial city.

868. **William Penn and the Quakers—The Pennsylvania Colony.** Coronet Instructional Films, 1959. 16mm. Color. Sound. 11 min. Rent $3.15.

While concentrating mainly on the issue of religious freedom, this film also discusses Philadelphia. It can be used in junior and senior high school classes.

869. Wolle, Muriel V. S. **The Bonanza Trail: Ghost Towns and Mining Camps of the West.** Bloomington, Ind.: Indiana University Press, 1953. 510 pp. O.P. LC 53-10019. Swallow, pap. $9.95.

An excellent study of how towns in the West were founded, grew, and were abandoned. For special projects.

870. Zuckerman, Michael. **Peaceable Kingdoms: New England Towns in the Eighteenth Century.** New York: Knopf, 1970. 329 pp. LC 72-98646. $7.95.

Not too much attention has been devoted to 18th-century American cities. Zuckerman remedies this with his study of communities in New England. His findings suggest that these communities did impose considerable constraint upon their members and did emphasize conformity. Somewhat specialized, and would probably be best suited to the history buff.

Urban Economics

American cities, perhaps even more than cities in other places, have been the product of economic forces. Commitments to economic growth and private gain have combined to shape both the size and extension of cities. City promoters, whether private individuals or corporations, believed themselves to be in competition with other cities and used all the advertising techniques later to be associated with the automobile industry. Once cities began to grow, these promoters acted to maximize growth. Nor did economic forces contribute only to the origin and early development of cities. The problems of central cities in the post-World War II years were in large measure economic. Declining tax bases, increased demand for increasingly expensive services, spiraling costs for land, and tax laws which helped to make ghetto property profitable—all accelerated the decay of American urban centers.

This section attempts to include information on all of these factors. It includes books on economic rivalry between cities and between central cities and suburbs. It has materials on the problems of obtaining sufficient municipal revenues and on the kinds of policies needed to make American cities both more livable and less economically sick. The impact of land prices on city shape and problems is considered as are the economic advantages and disadvantages of urban renewal. The economic forces which created and sustained urban ghettoes are examined. The histories of several industrial towns are included in order to provide case studies of the dynamics of growth. The economic costs of pollution and congestion are contained in this section, as well as a look at the working conditions and the developing unionism of workers in the city, both in private and in public employment.

871. Belcher, Wyatt W. **The Economic Rivalry Between St. Louis and Chicago, 1850–1880.** New York: Columbia University Press, 1947. LC A47-6082. $12.50.
The rivalry involved alternate methods of transportation as well as competition for industry and railroads. For scholars and reference only.

872. Berry, Brian J. L. **Growth Centers in the American Urban System.** 2 vols. Cambridge, Mass.: Ballinger, 1973. LC 73-10362. vol. I $9.50, vol. II $19.50.
Volume I in this set outlines both the methodology of the study and its results; the second volume contains the data used to derive the results. Berry bases his work on the concept of commuting regions which surround large urban centers. He identifies the urban centers in the United States, sets them in the framework

of an urban hierarchy, and then tries to assess their growth in the 1960s and 1970s. An important reference work and should be on the shelf of every library with any pretensions about urban affairs.

873. Boulding, Kenneth. **Principles of Economic Policy.** Englewood Cliffs, N.J.: Prentice-Hall, 1958. 440 pp. LC 58-7320. $10.95.

Boulding is one of the most imaginative of the present generation of economists who can speak to a general public.

874. Chinitz, Benjamin, ed. **City and Suburb: The Economics of Metropolitan Growth.** Englewood Cliffs, N.J.: Prentice-Hall, 1965. 181 pp. LC 64-23569. pap. $1.95.

Chinitz's collection contains essays on why recent urban development has taken the form it has. The problems of keeping a broad tax base in the center city are detailed as are the difficulties with economically homogeneous areas in the suburbs. Suggested for smaller libraries which lack adequate coverage of the economic basis of American city form.

875. Cooper, James R., and Guntermann, Karl L., eds. **Real Estate and Urban Land Analysis.** Lexington, Mass.: Lexington Books, 1974. 732 pp. LC 73-10397. $27.50.

Emphasizes the urban setting where real estate decisions are made which influence city growth and physical shape. While most suited to economists and real estate theorists, it can be understood by educated laypersons.

876. Costonis, John J. **Space Adrift: Landmark Preservation and the Marketplace.** Urbana, Ill.: University of Illinois Press and National Trust for Historic Preservation, 1974. illus. LC 73-5405. $10.

Costonis proposes a land development rights bank whose capital comes from the sale of air rights for skyscraper development over landmark structures. Builders would buy these air rights and the proceeds would be used to keep up the landmarks. Costonis is a law professor who has specialized in urban planning and in land development law, which makes him an expert. Wide appeal and highly recommended.

877. Crecine, John P., ed. **Financing the Metropolis: Public Policy in Urban Economics.** Urban Affairs Annual Review. Beverly Hills, Cal.: Sage Publications, 1970. 640 pp. NUC 70-88334. $22.50, pap. $7.50.

Topic is economics and the question is how to get the greatest benefit from the limited available resources. The essays include, but are not limited to, the topics of taxation, urban renewal, welfare and other services, budgeting, and the costs of segregation and poverty. Like the rest of the series, this is a necessary volume for libraries with an involvement in urban affairs.

878. Curran, Donald J. **Metropolitan Financing: The Milwaukee Experience, 1920–1970.** Madison, Wis.: University of Wisconsin Press, 1973. 166 pp. LC 72-7984. $11.50.

Curran's study of what happened in Milwaukee in 50 years confirms the truism that many of the economic difficulties of the contemporary city stem from fragmentation into small governmental entities. Curran sees no end to inequalities between these entities; if anything, these inequalities are growing. Should be included in libraries with an interest in urban history, urban economics, and public finance.

879. Curry, Leonard P. Rail Routes South: Louisville's Fight for the Southern Market, 1865-1872. Lexington, Ky.: University of Kentucky Press, 1969. 150 pp. LC 68-55046. $5.95.

Curry details the competition between Cincinnati and Louisville after the Civil War to monopolize the Southern trade. Interesting and significant in that it extends the usual survey of urban rivalry to the period after the Civil War.

880. Delineating the Area. Iowa State University Film Production Unit, 1962. 16mm. Color. Sound. 28 min. Sale $250, rent $8.

Discusses the problem of competing units attempting to obtain industries for their towns. Instead of piecemeal competition, this film argues for a development concept based on a unit consisting of a central city, its satellite towns, and surrounding rural areas. This is particularly appropriate for those students in rural or small-town areas which are struggling to survive and grow.

881. Economic Decision Games. Science Research Associates and Didactic Systems. Series of 8 games $12, $1.87 each, $2 A Guide to Teaching.

Two of the games—"The Community" and "Scarcity and Allocation"—can be used in a course on urban development. All of the games are good for developing economic concepts.

882. Evans, Alan W. The Economics of Residential Location. New York: St. Martin's Press, 1973. 281 pp. LC 73-88176. $15.95.

Evans attempts a comparative analysis of the economic factors which influence the location of households in both the United States and Great Britain. His findings seem commonplace in that he demonstrates that persons like to live near their work and near to others of the same social class. He does show how this process operates in cities and his book is useful for this documentation.

883. Focus on America—The Northeast Region. Society for Visual Education, 1971. 6 filmstrips. Color. Sound. $54 with records, $60.50 with cassettes.

The level is junior and senior high school. The first filmstrip is "Machiasport, Maine: A Case Study" (90 fr.), a study of a small regional port. The second is "The Merrimac River Valley: A Case Study" (79 fr.), a look at the industrial development in this area. The third is "The Boston Area: A Case Study" (71 fr.), a study of greater Boston and the problems of a heavily populated older urban center. The fourth is "The Pittsburgh Area: A Case Study" (63 fr.), which does the same for Pittsburgh as the third does for Boston. The fifth is "The Chesapeake Bay Area: A Case Study" (84 fr.), which turns to this region for a look at its economic and demographic characteristics. The last is "The East Coast Megalopolis" (84 fr.), which covers the urbanized region from Boston to Washington, D.C. Well done and highly recommended.

884. Fusfeld, Daniel R. The Basic Economics of the Urban Racial Crisis. New York: Holt, Rinehart and Winston, 1973. 122 pp. LC 73-184. Hill & Wang, pap. $3.50.

Fusfeld takes a pessimistic look at the economic problems of the ghetto, utilizing the techniques of input-output analysis, and concludes that these problems will not be solved unless a racial crisis occurs. The author designed the book for college students with backgrounds in economics, but others familiar with the economic terms can benefit from it.

885. Galbraith, John Kenneth. **Economics and the Art of Controversy.** New Brunswick, N.J.: Rutgers—the State University Press, 1955. 105 pp. LC 55-6103. pap. $1.25.

Galbraith writes extremely well. This paperback may be used to advantage by advanced students.

886. Gavett, Thomas W. **Development of the Labor Movement in Milwaukee.** Madison, Wis.: University of Wisconsin Press, 1965. 256 pp. LC 65-13501.

One of a number of studies on the urban influence on labor movements. Milwaukee is a special case with its tradition of Socialist mayors and with its large population of Germans but, nonetheless, the history of unionization and political action in that city does shed light upon the problems of workers in American cities.

887. Harris, Curtis C. **The Urban Economics, 1985.: A Multiregional, Multiindustry Forecasting Model.** Lexington, Mass.: Lexington Books, 1973. 230 pp. LC 73-6593. $13.50.

A sophisticated account which applies mathematical models to forecast urban development. Harris utilizes an input-output model for his basic theoretical tool and tries to show the impact of federal spending on various regions. Will have a limited audience because of its difficulty but, for those who are competent to understand it, it is recommended.

888. Hawley, Willis D., and Rogers, David. **Improving the Quality of Urban Management.** Urban Affairs Annual Review. Beverly Hills, Cal.: Sage Publications, 1974. 639 pp. LC 72-98108. $22.50.

Focuses on the improvement of the delivery of urban services. The articles consider the questions of how to make information available faster, whether to decentralize, what lessons can be derived from the private sector, and how management can be made more sophisticated. Like its predecessors, should be purchased by libraries of some size.

889. Heilbroner, Robert L. **The Making of Economic Society.** Englewood Cliffs, N.J.: Prentice-Hall, 1962. LC 62-16453. pap. $4.25.

Heilbroner's writings are clear, well reasoned, and based on historical perspective.

890. Holleb, Doris B. **Social and Economic Information for Urban Planning.** 2 vols. Chicago: Center for Urban Studies, University of Chicago Press, 1969. LC 75-600765. pap. $3.50, $4.50.

Necessary for those engaged in practicing city planning. It provides insights into what kinds of data are significant for the planner and how these data can be obtained. Should be available in libraries as a reference work.

891. Horton, Raymond D. **Municipal Labor Relations in New York City: Lessons of the Lindsay-Wagner Years.** New York: Praeger, 1973. 168 pp. LC 79-176879. $15.

Not for beginners. Necessary for specialists in municipal unions and the problems of city government workers, and should be acquired by libraries serving these patrons.

892. Hoyt, Homer. **One Hundred Years of Land Values in Chicago: The Relationship of the Growth of Chicago to the Rise in Its Land Values. 1830–1933.** New York: Arno Press, 1970 (originally published in 1933). 519 pp. LC 74-112550. $21.

Classic study of the interrelationships between external growth of a society and the internal growth of a city. Hoyt shows how land values varied with the building of canals and railroads, with the fire, with the advent of the skyscraper, and the coming of mass transit. Ought to be in every library with any pretension on urban affairs.

893. Hurd, Richard M. **Principles of City Land Values.** New York: Arno Press, 1970 (originally published in 1924). 159 pp. LC 78-112551. $8.

Hurd was manager of the Mortgage Department of U.S. Mortgage and Trust Co. and thus could easily obtain information on land and building valuation as well as on rental prices and mortgage indebtedness. Using local histories, Hurd was able to reconstruct the structure of 50 cities and then to relate this structure to land values. Hurd was one of the first to correlate land values and land usage. His classic study deserves inclusion in sections on urban economics.

894. Ingram, Gregory K., Kain, John F., and Ginn, J. Royce. **The Detroit Prototype of the NBER Urban Simulation Model.** New York: National Bureau of Economic Research, distributed by Columbia University Press, 1972. 233 pp. LC 72-75806. $12.50.

The use of simulation in order to predict future trends has become increasingly common. This model is, as the name suggests, one based on Detroit. The model is probably best suited to more specialized libraries and would not be appropriate for general ones.

895. Jaher, Frederick C., ed. **The Age of Industrialism in America.** New York: Free Press, 1968. LC 68-14107. $9.95.

A collection of essays that combines history, economics, and political science. They cover the period from 1870 to 1940 and are on such diverse topics as changing social structures and cultural values, urban elites in Denver and San Francisco, and a comparison of the World's Fairs of 1876, 1893, and 1933. The above-average reader will be interested.

896. Kirkland, Edward C. **Industry Comes of Age: Business, Labor, and Public Policy, 1860–1897.** New York: Holt, Rinehart and Winston, 1961. 445 pp. LC 61-9816. O.P. Quadrangle, pap. $2.95.

Specialized, and should be assigned only to those interested in and competent to understand economic development. Kirkland considers the impact of cities on economic growth and the extent to which cities were a product of that growth.

897. Knight, Robert. Industrial Relations in the San Francisco Bay Area, 1900 –1918. Berkeley, Cal.: University of California Press, 1960. 463 pp. LC 59-15332. $15.

San Francisco retains the facade of a continental, urbane community but behind the facade are many stresses and conflicts. Knight discusses a critical period in San Francisco's development from 1900 to the end of World War I. This study belongs with those of other cities at this period and at this stage of urban development.

898. Land Use. Educational Ventures. Available from producer and Social Studies Service. $7.95.

Land Use is a simulation game geared to the vocabulary and the interests of junior and senior high school students. It can be played alone or by as many as 30 players for a minimum of two hours. The game involves the conflict in values between environmentalists who desire to keep the land in a natural state and developers who wish to make money from commercial growth. The game has a topical subject and should be attractive to persons from 12 to 18 years of age.

899. Livingood, James W. The Philadelphia-Baltimore Trade Rivalry. New York: Arno Press, 1970 (originally published in 1947). 195 pp. LC 70-112557. $10.

During the first half of the 19th century, Baltimore grew faster than Philadelphia. This book suggests reasons why.

900. Man and the Cities—Economics of the City. BFA Educational Media, 1972. 6 filmstrips. Color. $78 with records, $90 with cassettes.

The level is intermediate or junior high, and the focus is on the specialization of labor that occurs in an urban area. The titles are "Cities Are Run by People" (53 fr.), "A City Needs Goods" (58 fr.), "A City Needs Services" (73 fr.), "Economics of Change" (60 fr.), "The Life Cycle of the City" (51 fr.), and "Specialization and Mass Production" (54 fr.). While the intent of the series is primarily to inculcate economic principles, it accomplishes this in an urban context.

901. Martin, Robert L. The City Moves West: Economic and Industrial Growth in Central West Texas. Austin, Tex.: University of Texas Press, 1969. 190 pp. LC 72-89807. $7.50.

Martin recounts the impact of oil development on city growth in the central west part of Texas. For specialists in the economic determinants of city growth.

902. Meltsner, Arnold. The Politics of City Revenue. Berkeley, Cal.: University of California Press, 1971. LC 71-129610. $10.

A case study of how the government of Oakland, California, raises money to run the city. It shows how political pressures close access to some sources of money and open access to others. Specialized, appealing to the expert more than the layperson.

903. Messner, Stephen D. **A Benefit-Cost Analysis of Urban Redevelopment: A Case Study of the Indianapolis Program.** Bloomington, Ind.: Bureau of Business Research, Indiana University, 1967. 115 pp. LC 74-625051. pap. $4.

Reflects the attitude of researchers in the 1960s on the possibility of redoing American cities. It is done from a frame of reference which is oriented to economic principles. Has merit because of its microanalysis of one urban community.

904. Meyers, Edward M., and Musial, John J. **Urban Incentive Tax Credits: A Self-Correcting Strategy to Rebuild Central Cities.** New York: Praeger, 1974. 140 pp. LC 74-743. $13.50.

Wilbur R. Thompson has an introduction which proposes to renew inner city areas by the judicious manipulation of tax credits. The authors argue that the present tax system tends to reinforce the decay of central cities. Sophisticated; best suited to individuals with some background in economics.

905. Miller, Nathan. **The Enterprise of a Free People: Aspects of Economic Development in New York State During the Canal Period, 1792–1838.** Ithaca, N.Y.: Cornell University Press, 1962. 293 pp. LC 62-8487. $9.50.

The growth of state bureaucracy and its impact on city development.

906. Newell, Barbara Warne. **Chicago and the Labor Movement: Metropolitan Unionism in the 1930's.** Urbana, Ill.: University of Illinois Press, 1961. 288 pp. LC 60-11661. $6.

There are relatively few books on the attempts of municipal workers to unionize. This is an exception, as Newell shows the kind of strategy used both by proponents and opponents of a unionized municipal labor force. Of value to those who wish to understand the background of recent labor developments as well as the history of Chicago politics.

907. Niemi, Albert W., Jr. **State and Regional Patterns in American Manufacturing, 1860–1900.** Westport, Conn.: Greenwood Press, 1974. 209 pp. LC 73-13289. $11.

An essay in economic history employing a statistical approach to determine how industries dispersed after the Civil War and how the total pattern of the American industrial system changed. It is a specialized study which does show in graphic form the growth of industrial communities and the economic reasons for such growth.

908. **Packingtown, U.S.A.** University of Illinois Motion Picture Service, 1969. 16mm. b/w. Sound. 32 min. Rent $6.90.

Re-creation of the strike against the meatpackers in Chicago in 1904. The film is sympathetic to the cause of labor. It does show the kinds of conditions workers had to face at the turn of the century.

909. Parker, Margaret Terrell. **Lowell: A Study of Industrial Development.** Port Washington, N.Y.: Kennikat, 1970 (originally published in 1940). 238 pp. LC 73-118421. $12.50.

Parker essayed an historical geography of the industrial town of Lowell, Massachusetts, at the moment of economic decline. Can be used as a city biography as well as an example of an early attempt at urban geography.

910. Perry, Louis B., and Perry, Richard S. **A History of the Los Angeles Labor Movement, 1911–1941.** Berkeley, Cal.: University of California Press, 1963. 622 pp. LC 63-20884. $15.

The Perrys have taken a significant slice from the history of unionization in Los Angeles, but this slice is a vital one encompassing as it does the problems engendered by wartime pressures from 1917 to 1918 and those created by the depression of the 1930s. The book ends with World War II and does not come to grips with the challenges that conflict posed. However, the principle of labor organization had been at least partially established by that date.

911. Pratt, Edward Erving. **Industrial Causes of Congestion of Population in New York City.** New York: AMS Press, 1968 (originally published in 1911). 259 pp. NUC 70-52508. $12.50.

Reflects the concern which early 20th-century observers of the city had about the concentration of people into small areas. Congestion was, to them, one of the major urban problems. Of primary use for urban historians, but has a secondary audience in demographers.

912. **Property Taxes, Housing, and the Cities.** George E. Peterson, et al. Lexington, Mass.: D. C. Heath, 1973. 203 pp. LC 73-11673. $12.50.

Reissue of a report of the staff of Arthur D. Little, Inc., printed by the Government Printing Office as *A Study of Property Taxes and Urban Blight.* The report consists primarily of a critique of responses to questionnaires given by real estate developers, property owners, and governmental officials in ten cities. The data derived contain few surprises; tax policy helps create blight. Libraries with sections on urban problems, housing, or tax policy need this book.

913. **The Quality of the Urban Environment, Essays on "New Resources in an Urban Age."** Harvey S. Perloff, ed. Washington, D.C.: Resources for the Future, distributed by Johns Hopkins University Press, 1969. 332 pp. LC 69-16858. pap. $6.50.

The editor of this collection of essays on both the overall economic system and that of cities assumes much knowledge on the part of the reader. Essays treat of city location and growth and the factors which have led to prosperity and to poverty. Recommended for those who are relatively sophisticated in economic analysis.

914. **Region.** Envirometrics/Washington Center for Metropolitan Studies. Manual $3.

In a growing urban area, the players in this game are confronted with the need to make economic and political choices to solve the problems of the present and to assure future growth. For senior high school students.

915. Sellers, Leila. **Charleston Business on the Eve of the American Revolution.** History of Urban America. New York: Arno Press, 1970 (originally published in 1934). 259 pp. LC 72-112571. $10.

Charleston was the largest and most economically significant city in the South prior to the Revolution, and Sellers shows the implications of Charleston's primacy for the forthcoming war. Sellers argues that the British, by their political and economic policies, alienated persons who had supported them. Recommended for its cross-sectional view of an urban community in the South in the 18th century.

916. Sonenblum, Sidney, Conley, Bryan C., Kramer, Charles, with Meredith Slobod Crist, Roger Augur, and Moshe Shelkar. **Program Budgeting for Urban Health and Welfare Services; With Special References to Los Angeles.** New York: Praeger, 1974. 229 pp. LC 73-13052. $15.

Published in cooperation with the Institute of Government on Public Affairs at UCLA, this highly technical book is oriented to the Los Angeles budget and is so specialized that only libraries with a close working connection with city governments will want to buy it.

917. Spero, Sterling D., and Capozzola, John M. **The Urban Community and Its Unionized Bureaucracies; Pressure Politics in Local Government Labor Relations.** Port Washington, N.Y.: Kennikat/Dunellen, 1973. 361 pp. LC 72-86221. $12.50, pap. $5.95.

Spero and Capozzola are specialists in the area of public administration, and this study of the rise of labor unions among governmental employees reflects that specialty. The authors are not unsympathetic to public labor unions but they do indicate some of the problems that these unions create. They also analyze the reasons for the growth of unions. Specialized, but essential for individuals considering recent economic developments in the city.

918. Stead, William H. **Natural Resource Use in Our Economy,** rev. ed. Study and Teaching Aids by George L. Fersh. New York: Conservation and Resource-Use Education Project, Joint Council on Economic Education, 1960. 88 pp. LC 60-4429.

This short pamphlet is simple enough for average students. The concepts used here are necessary for a foundation of economic knowledge.

919. Stecker, Margaret Loomis. **Intercity Differences in Cost of Living in March, 1935, 59 Cities.** New York: Da Capo Press, 1971 (originally published in 1937). LC 79-165689. $13.50.

Of interest primarily to urban economists who want to do studies which involve a time dimension and to historians of the Depression.

920. Stimson, Grace Heilman. **Rise of the Labor Movement in Los Angeles.** Berkeley, Cal.: University of California Press, 1955. 529 pp. LC 55-5928. $11.50.

Another case study of a labor movement in an American city, this time on the West Coast. This southern California city had special elements in its growth which helped to complicate its labor problems. These elements include the sprawl of the city and its diverse ethnic elements—Mexican and Chinese. This book, along with those concerning other cities, could compose a shelf which would cover the urban origins of organized labor.

921. Thomas, Brinley. **Migration and Urban Development; Reappraisal of British and American Long Cycles.** London, Methuen, 1972. 259 pp. LC 72-196113. $14.50, pap. $6.75.

Comparative study of English and American institutions which takes into account internal as well as external migration. Thomas uses such variables as home investments and consumption, balance of payments, productivity, and output. The basic theoretical principle is the "Kuznets cycle." Not for beginners or those with a weak grasp of economic theory.

922. Thompson, Wilbur R. **A Preface to Urban Economics.** Baltimore: Published for Resources for the Future by Johns Hopkins University Press, 1965. 413 pp. LC 65-19537. $9, pap. $3.95.

Despite its title, this volume is not for the uninitiated. It does consider urban growth based upon interurban, extraurban, and employment analysis. A good theoretical place to begin if the reader has a solid economics base.

923. U.S. Office of Advisor on Negro Affairs. **The Urban Negro Worker in the United States, 1925–1936; An Analysis of the Training, Types, and Conditions of Employment and the Earnings of 200,000 Skilled and White-Collar Negro Workers.** 2 vols. in 1. Westport, Conn.: Negro Universities Press, 1970 (originally published in 1938–1939). 127 pp. LC 79-82095. $23.

Federally sponsored study of the economic condition of urban Blacks in the last half of the 1920s and the first half of the 1930s. Contains much valuable data for the researcher in the area of urban Black economics. As such, it should be on the shelves of research libraries.

924. Vatter, Harold G., and Palm, Thomas, eds. **The Economics of Black America.** New York: Harcourt Brace Jovanovich, 1972. LC 72-180997. pap. $3.50.

Essays by Gunnar Myrdal, Kenneth E. Boulding, Whitney M. Young, Jr., James Tobin, and others, both Black and white. The subjects range from a definition of Black economics to the role of the Black consumer. Intended as supplementary reading in college courses in economics and is suggested only for small libraries which have few books in Black economic problems, particularly in the city.

925. **Why We Have Taxes: The Town That Had No Policeman.** Learning Corporation of America, 1970. 16mm. Color. Sound. 7 min. Sale $125, rent $12.

An animated color film on an elementary level which tries to teach the basic ideas about the provision of police services. It would be suitable for children ages 5 to 8.

926. Wingo, Lowdon, Jr., and Perloff, Harvey, eds. **Issues in Urban Economics.** Baltimore: Johns Hopkins University Press, 1968. LC 68-15454. $15, pap. $5.

The result of eight years of work by the Committee on Urban Economics of Resources for the Future, this report attempts to delineate the important problems in urban economics. For advanced students, but also a useful reference tool for the teacher.

927. Wolff, Anthony. **Unreal Estate: The Lowdown on Land Hustling.** San Francisco: Sierra Club, 1974. 290 pp. LC 72-89544. $7.95.

Cites land speculators who push recreational lands usually located far from any urban amenities. Wolff shows how these speculators operate, who bankrolls them, and how they are able to escape the law. Of general interest and popularly written.

The governing of American cities has always been a matter of concern for scholars; from the creation of professional societies, considerable time has been devoted to the rule, or misrule, of the city. The threat which many Americans saw in the post-Civil War city was in part composed of the loss of political power to machines or bosses, both of whom were utilizing the votes of immigrants who had come to these cities. The low level of municipal morality concerned reformers of the Progressive era and much of the rhetoric of the 20th century involved the problems of governing increasingly fragmented metropolises.

This section includes general surveys of the trials and tribulations of urban government in America. It contains discussions of the lack of power of some groups of citizens, as well as the concentration of power in the hands of others. It has biographies of successful and unsuccessful mayors, and of successful and unsuccessful experiments in urban government. There are theories of political decision making—the pluralism thesis of Dahl and the federalism thesis popularized by Elezar. The focus of the section is on the process of getting things done in the metropolis and on why the system fails to work as well as it might. There is considerable attention to the problems of the latecomers to the American city and their efforts to achieve full participation in the system of government.

928. Adrian, Charles R., and Press, Charles. **Governing Urban America**, 4th ed. New York: McGraw-Hill, 1972. 135 pp. LC 78-174608. $11.95.

Standard college text covering the structure of government, the legal bases of the city, urban functions, and problems of health and welfare. Recommended only for small libraries which have little material on the urban political process.

929. Agger, Robert E., Goldrich, Daniel, and Swanson, Bert E. **The Rulers and the Ruled: Political Power and Impotence in American Communities.** New York: Wiley, 1964. 784 pp. LC 64-17131. $12.50.

The authors studied decision making in four communities between 1945 and 1961 in an effort to discover how political decisions were made and who made them.

930. **American Civics.** Harcourt Brace Jovanovich, 1967. Color. Transparencies. $90.

Transparencies for use in junior and senior high school situations. The titles that are related to cities are "The City—Problems and Solutions," "Forms of City

Government," and "How Community Serves Its Citizens." The first has five overlays, the second has three, and the last has one.

931. Aron, Joan B. The Quest for Regional Cooperation: A Study of the New Metropolitan Regional Council. Berkeley, Cal.: University of California Press, 1969. 225 pp. LC 69-16738.

Aron's study concerns the largest metropolitan agency in the United States, the New York Metropolitan Regional Council. She shows how regional planning operates in practice and how decisions are reached to put policies into effect. It is particularly helpful to those who have some background in municipal government and who want a model.

932. Banfield, Edward C. The Unheavenly City Revisited; The Nature and Future of Our Urban Crisis. Boston: Little Brown, 1970. 358 pp. LC 77-105564. $8.95, pap. $4.25.

Banfield, who headed President Nixon's task force on Model Cities, argues that urban society is not deteriorating, that we are not losing the war on poverty. He recommends that we abolish the minimum wage, reduce the school-leaving age to 14, and institutionalize the incompetent poor. These conservative proposals are calculated to shock, as are his other ideas. Should be read to counterbalance those pessimists who cry the doom of the city.

933. Banfield, Edward C., and Wilson, James Q. City Politics. Cambridge, Mass.: Harvard University Press, 1963. 363 pp. LC 63-19134. $10. Vintage, pap. $1.95.

A product of the Joint Center for Urban Studies, this report is a useful discussion of political life in cities.

934. Beard, Charles A. American City Government: A Survey of Newer Tendencies. Rise of Urban America. New York: Arno Press, 1970 (originally published in 1912). 420 pp. LC 70-112522. $18.

An early survey of progressive municipal legislation. Beard analyzes the move to civil service lists, to the commission form of government, to municipal ownership of utilities, and to legislation attempting to improve tenement houses. Not only useful to urban historians, but also significant for those interested in urban government.

935. Bollens, John C., and Geyer, Grant B. Yorty: Politics of a Constant Candidate. Pacific Palisades, Cal.: Palisades Publishers, 1973. 245 pp. LC 72-95289. $6.95.

Yorty was mayor of Los Angeles from 1961 to 1973 and lost in that last year to a Black candidate. Yorty began as a liberal Democrat in the New Deal mold and ended as a conservative one, attacking communists and becoming a hawk on the Vietnam War. Useful in showing political pressures and currents in American life as illustrated in Los Angeles.

936. Bollens, John C., and Schmandt, Henry J. The Metropolis: Its People, Politics, and Economic Life, 2nd ed. New York: Harper & Row, 1970. 488 pp. LC 77-96227. $11.75, pap. $6.95.

Interdisciplinary approach to decision making. While only suitable for advanced students, this volume ought to be helpful for understanding the interweaving of factors in urban development.

937. Burgess, Margaret Elaine. **Negro Leadership in a Southern City.** New Haven, Conn.: College and University Press, 1964. 231 pp. NUC 70-113027. pap. $2.25.

Case study of how Black political figures were able to achieve some of their desired goals in an urban setting in the South. Specialized; more suited for research libraries than for general ones.

938. The Cities Game, rev. ed. CRM Consumer Division/Psychology Today Games, 1970. $7.

Relatively simple game treating the political process in an urban context which can be played by students on the junior high level. It is an expandable game, utilizing anywhere from 4 to 40 players in four teams and taking from one to three hours to complete. Good for illustrating basic concepts in political science.

939. City and State. New York Times, Office of Educational Activities, 1965. 1 filmstrip (53 fr.). b/w. $6.

The subject is the press of problems on local and state governments. Aimed at junior and senior high school students.

940. Community Decision Games. Educational Ventures/Social Studies School Service. 4 games, $4.95 each.

As the titles suggest, the focus of these games (Budget & Taxes, New Highway, New Schools, and Open Space) is on political decisions with economic consequences. The level is junior high through college, and the game requires six teams, composed of from 6 to 36 players. The game necessitates three rounds of play of one-hour duration. The topics are controversial, although the ones involving new highways and schools seem more dated than the other two.

941. Crick, Bernard. **The American Science of Politics; Its Origins and Conditions.** Berkeley, Cal.: University of California Press, 1959. 252 pp. LC 59-3487 rev. $6.75.

Although 16 years old, a useful summary of the general field.

942. Dahl, Robert A. **Who Governs? Democracy and Power in an American City.** New Haven, Conn.: Yale University Press, 1961. 355 pp. LC 61-16913. $17.50, pap. $3.95.

In this highly regarded study of New Haven by an eminent political scientist, there is contained a theory of community power. Dahl argues that no elite ruled New Haven but that political decisions were made by coalitions brought forth by specific issues. Power then fluctuated from group to group and from issue to issue. This classic study belongs in every library which contains works on urban politics.

943. David, Stephen M., and Peterson, Paul E., eds. **Urban Politics and Public Policy: The City in Crisis.** New York: Praeger, 1973. 337 pp. LC 72-75693. $10, pap. $3.95.

The editors of this collection are experts in political science and they emphasize crucial problems in governing American cities. They identify the problem as one of too many competing political units and include selections to that effect. The other articles reinforce the editors' belief that our urban crisis is a severe one. Recommended for libraries which do not already possess material in urban government.

944. Elezar, Daniel J. **Cities of the Prairie: The Metropolitan Frontier and American Politics.** New York: Basic Books, 1970. 514 pp. LC 76-94297. $15.

Elezar, a political scientist, compares a number of Midwestern American cities. He concludes that corruption is a function of an "individualistic political culture" where politics is regarded as just another business. He also categorizes municipal governments into "representative oligarchies" and "organized polyarchies," both of which are elites. The former is, however, less open than the latter. While the study is scholarly, it can hold a reader with little background knowledge.

945. Elezar, Daniel J. **Federalism and the Community.** Pittsburgh: University of Pittsburgh Institute of Local Government, University of Pittsburgh Press, 1968. 14 pp. LC 78-5658. O.P.

Elezar's contributions to the Wherret Lecture Series on Local Government. Elezar denies that either local elites or pluralistic coalitions control events, arguing instead that key issues in the community are more frequently the product of decisions made on the state and federal levels.

946. Federickson, George H., and O'Leary, Linda Schuter. **Power, Public Opinion, and Policy in a Metropolitan Community: A Case Study of Syracuse, New York.** New York: Praeger, 1973. LC 72-90665. $15.

A study of Syracuse which maintains that there is considerable rapport between governed and government in that city. The authors' findings indicate that the majority of the citizens of the community agree with the pattern of governmental expenditure and that city officials are listened to by state and federal ones. The report is a specialized one which belongs in a section on community decision making.

947. **Fun City.** David Seader, designer. MITRE Corp. Also available from ERIC Document Reproduction Service. $13.16 hard copy, $.65 microfiche.

This simulation game is suitable for high school students or adults and involves a total of seven players. The amount of time needed to complete the game varies according to the way it is played. The game centers on a struggle for power in a large city; participants assume power bases and develop goals. While not the most sophisticated game, it does offer a sense of involvement to the players.

948. The Golden Door. Dynamic Films/Brandon Films, 1963. (Structure and Function of American Government.) 16mm. 15 min. Sale $150.

Analyzes the nature and causes of antialien sentiment which results in anticity attitudes and in legislation to restrict immigration. For better students.

949. Gordon, Diana R. **City Limits: Barriers to Change in Urban Government.** New York: Charterhouse, 1973. LC 73-79959. $7.95.

An analysis of New York City government containing six case studies of problems and the decisions made to handle these problems. Gordon's thesis is that the bureaucracy is as much a barrier to as a help in solving problems and that the keys to success in the area are the internal policies of the bureaucracy and the character of the people in control. Though scholarly, this is not difficult and should have considerable circulation. Recommended for general library acquisition.

950. Government in a Free Society, Book One. Chicago: Rand McNally, 1968. Color. Transparencies.

These are transparencies designed to accompany a textbook in political science. The titles in this set which apply to urban government are "America Becomes an Urban Nation" and "Growth of American Cities." Can be used independently of the text as focal points for discussion or to illustrate lectures.

951. Greenberg, Edward S., Milner, Neal, and Olson D. eds. **Black Politics.** New York: Holt Rinehart and Winston, 1971. LC 71-142828. pap. $5.

Theoretical and descriptive essays creating an overview of Black politics. While there is material on the rural South, the major thrust is on the urban North.

952. Greer, Scott. **The Urbane View: Life and Politics in Metropolitan America.** New York: Oxford University Press, 1972. LC 63-22206. $9.50, pap. $2.95.

Scott Greer has been one of the political scientists most actively involved in urban studies. His work is stimulating and well written, thoughtful, and rewarding.

953. Hahn, Harlan, ed. **People and Politics in Urban Society.** Urban Affairs Annual Review. Beverly Hills, Cal.: Sage Publications, 1972. 640 pp. LC 72-77744. $20.

The theme is the possibility of revitalization of political processes in the city. There are case studies on the 1968 elections on a rapid transit issue in Atlanta, on the barrio, on school board decisions, and on a Black mayoral candidate. This particular collection places less emphasis upon other Western countries, although there is an article on urban policy in the United States as compared to Canada. The book and the series are a must for libraries with any collection on urban affairs.

954. Hayes, Edward C. **Power Structure and Urban Policy: Who Rules in Oakland?** Policy Impact and Political Change in America. New York: McGraw-Hill, 1972. LC 79-31868. $6.50, pap. $3.95.

The business community exercises the most control in Oakland by constant pressure on the political institutions of the city, and even social welfare programs are frustrated by this community. Sophisticated; most suitable to political scientists.

955. Hickey, Neil, and Edwin, Ed. **Adam Clayton Powell and the Politics of Race.** New York: Fleet Publishing Corp., 1965. 308 pp. LC 65-16313. O.P.

How Congressman Powell attracted voters of his district in New York City. It is recommended for libraries with an interest in Black and urban politics.

956. Holloway, Harry. **The Politics of the Southern Negro: From Exclusion to Big City Organization.** New York: Random House, 1969. 374 pp. LC 69-10787. $10.95.

A survey of how the Negro has participated or been used in the South; includes much detail about politics in specific cities. A very useful place to begin, and is recommended for libraries which do not have extensive collections on cities or Black politics.

957. Holt, Michael F. **Forging a Majority: The Formation of the Republican Party in Pittsburgh. 1848–1860.** New Haven, Conn.: Yale University Press, 1969. 408 pp. NUC 69-136443. $18.50.

While the origins of the national Republican Party have been outlined, no one has done a study similar to that attempted by Holt, one based on a microscopic view of one urban community. Holt's examination of Pittsburgh shows the decisions confronting politicians in cities and the tensions which helped contribute to the rise of an important political party.

958. Hunter, Floyd. **Community Power Structure: A Study of Decision Makers.** Chapel Hill, N.C.: University of North Carolina Press, 1968. 297 pp. NUC 70-89104. $7.50, pap. $2.25.

Noted for the most significant sociological statement of the thesis that a local elite exercises power in American communities. Hunter drew his conclusion from a study of Atlanta and claimed a small, socially interacting elite determined policy informally behind the scenes. This classic sociological study should be in every library.

959. Katz, Stanley N. **Newcastle's New York: Anglo-American Politics, 1732–1753.** Cambridge, Mass.: Harvard Unversity Press, 1968. LC 68-14261. $8.

Focuses on the political relations between the British Empire and one American colony, with frequent reference to New York City. For those libraries which have more extensive collections.

960. Ladd, Everett Carll, Jr. **Negro Political Leadership in the South.** Ithaca, N.Y.: Cornell University Press, 1966. 348 pp. LC 66-11048. $12.50. Atheneum, pap. $3.95.

Black political involvement in two North Carolina cities, Winston-Salem and Greenville. This reprint contains a new preface by Andrew Hacker and should be available for students of Black urban political activity in the South.

961. Lavine, David. **The Mayor and the Changing City.** American Birthright.
New York: Random House, 1966. 172 pp. LC 67-2269. $4.59.
Topic is New Haven. Its mayor in 1966, Richard D. Lee, gained a
reputation as a progressive mayor who urged extensive urban renewal for his
community. Aimed at young readers, specifically junior high school students.

962. Leinwand, Gerald, ed. **The City as a Community.** Problems of American
Society. New York: Washington Square Press, 1970. 192 pp. LC 73-12586.
Pocket Books, pap. $.95.
The curriculum committee of the Trenton, New Jersey, public schools provided
editorial assistance for the series, which contains both text and readings.
Recommended for general use.

963. Levermore, Charles Herbert. **The Republic of New Haven; A History of
Municipal Evolution.** Port Washington, N.Y.: Kennikat, 1966 (orginally published in 1886). 342 pp. LC 66-25926. $12.50.
Still valuable to present-day readers. Levermore studied the growth of municipal
government in New Haven using an evolutionary schema. Shows both insight
into the records and into the late 19th-century mind. Recommended for research purposes.

964. McCandless, Carl A. **Urban Government and Politics.** New York: McGraw-
Hill, 1970. 517 pp. LC 74-95816. $11.50.
Assumes that conflict is the keynote to city politics. The purpose of politics is
to provide a setting in which conflict can be resolved in a manner which will be
acceptable to both winners and losers. Should be available only in small libraries
which do not have extensive materials in the area.

965. Maier, Henry W. **Challenge to the Cities: An Approach to a Theory of
Urban Leadership.** New York: Random House, 1966. 210 pp. LC 66-19852.
pap. $2.95.
Maier, who was mayor of Milwaukee, outlines his program for successful government. His formula is to know the problems of the city, to research solutions,
and to understand the structure of government. Nontechnical, so high school
students can manage it.

966. Marando, Vincent L., with Dennis L. Thompson. **The Metropolitan
County in Arizona.** Tucson: University of Arizona Press, 1971. LC 70-152042.
pap. $1.50.
Marando looks at an attempt to eliminate competing governmental authorities
and to have county-wide government. It is recommended for those involved in
the study of alternative governmental systems in metropolitan areas.

967. Merriam, Charles Edward. **Chicago: A More Intimate View of Urban
Politics.** The Rise of Urban America. New York: Arno Press, 1970 (originally
published in 1929). 305 pp. LC 71-112579. $12.
Merriam was a pioneer American political scientist who also was involved in
Chicago politics in the early 20th century, serving as Alderman and standing as

Republican candidate for mayor in 1911. Merriam was a reformer but saw the struggle in Chicago politics as being between special interest groups. Merriam knew Big Bill Thompson, Clarence Darrow, and Insull; he included descriptions of these colorful characters in his book, which is recommended for libraries with sections on urban politics and urban history.

968. **Metropolitics.** Simile II, Didactic Systems, 1971. $25, $3 for sample set. *Metropolitics* is a simulation game which is designed for junior or senior high school students. It involves 18 to 35 players who divide into four teams. The emphasis is upon the possible forms of urban government rather than the political process, per se. Because of this concentration, the game is well suited to broadening the horizons of its players.

969. Morgan, David R., ed. **Urban Management.** New York: MSS Information Corp., 183 pp. LC 72-8662. $10, pap. $5.
The theory and practice of governing metropolitan communities. Technical and geared to those who are actively engaged in the field, this belongs in large libraries with significant collections in the complexities of city governance.

970. Mushkat, Jerome. **Tammany: The Evolution of a Political Machine, 1789 –1865.** Syracuse, N.Y.: Syracuse University Press, 1971. LC 78-150346. $15.
Most studies of New York City machine politics begin with Boss Tweed, mainly because of his undisputed color and because of the opposition he aroused. Mushkat starts earlier and shows how the roots of the political machine were already established at the beginnings of the Republic. Scholarly, but of benefit to urban historians and political scientists.

971. National Conference of Social Welfare. **Politics and the Ghetto.** Roland L. Warren, ed. New York: Atherton Press, 1969. 214 pp. LC 77-90771. $7.95.
Essays on political organizations and their relationship to ghettoes. These show how the concentrated population does offer political gain but also how it is susceptible to economic exploitation. While of interest primarily to those involved in urban political development, it also can be read with profit by those who are concerned about the elimination of urban problems.

972. **Neighborhood Control in the 1970's: Politics, Administration and Citizen Participation.** George Frederickson, ed. San Francisco: Chandler, 1973. 290 pp. LC 73-3044. $8.95.
Fifteen original essays taken from a conference on public administration and neighborhood control. The range of subjects is wide, from decentralization to model cities to political evaluation of educational policies. Varies in quality and interest but does show what issues exist under the rubric of neighborhood control. It is recommended for libraries with collections on urban policies and urban problems.

973. Nordlinger, Eric A. **Decentralizing the City: A Study of Boston's Little City Halls.** Cambridge, Mass.: MIT Press, 1973. 310 pp. LC 73-157031. $12.50.
Nordlinger's is an account of how an experiment in city government worked. The city of Boston set up 14 little city halls throughout the city in order to

achieve better relations with the citizens and to make city services more efficient. Although restricted in topic and from a scholarly press, it is not particularly difficult. Could be ordered for more general usage.

974. O'Connor, Edwin. **The Last Hurrah.** Boston: Little, Brown, 1956. 427 pp. LC 55-11224. $7.95. Bantam, pap. $1.25.

This famous novel about boss politics in Boston is a fascinating account of an Irish politician. Highly recommended for the general public.

975. Parsons, Stanley B. **The Populist Context: Rural vs. Urban Power in a Great Plains Frontier.** Westport, Conn.: Greenwood Press, 1973. 205 pp. LC 72-824. $11.

Quantitative study of the political influence of rural and urban voters in the West during the farmers' revolt. It is a technical and highly specialized study which has utility for urban historians as well as urban political scientists who are involved with factoring out the statistical behavior of voting populations.

976. Patterson, Ernest. **Black City Politics.** New York: Dodd, Mead, 1974. 310 pp. LC 73-15388. $5.95.

Patterson looks at city government from a Black perspective and decries the lack of input from Blacks in decision-making situations. Discusses the relationship of race to patronage, civil service, and other elements of city life.

977. Peel, Roy Victor. **The Political Clubs of New York City.** Port Washington, N.Y.: Kennikat, 1968 (originally published in 1935). LC 68-18356. $7.

The role political clubs played in municipal government. Peel was most interested in the contemporary clubs of his day so he offers a glance at the impact of the New Deal on local institutions. While because of its topic and age this reprint does not have wide appeal, it is of more than antiquarian interest.

978. Polsby, Nelson W. **Community Power and Political Theory.** New Haven, Conn.: Yale University Press, 1963. 144 pp. LC 63-7946. $7.50, pap. $2.45.

Polsby was a student of the political scientist Robert Dahl at Yale and wrote this book to further elucidate Dahl's argument for a pluralistic model of community power. He extended Dahl's thesis to a number of other communities and did prove it to his satisfaction. Good for a theory of how cities are run.

979. Riddle, Donald R., and Cleary, Robert E., eds. **Political Science in the Social Studies.** 36th Yearbook. National Council for the Social Studies, 1966. $5, pap. $4.

A valuable and necessary reference guide for the social studies teacher.

980. Robson, William A., and Regan, D. E., eds. **Great Cities of the World; Their Government, Politics and Planning,** 3rd ed. 2 vols. Beverly Hills, Cal.: Sage Publications, 1972. 114 pp. LC 75-167876. set $50.

This reference work includes data on the governmental structure of the cities examined, the political situation, the municipal services, the finance, the intergovernmental relations, the management, the state of planning, as well as projections for future growth and development. The editors are English and the cities are Amsterdam, Belgrade, Birmingham, Buenos Aires, Cairo, Calcutta, Chicago, Copenhagen, Delhi, Ibadan, Johannesburg, London, Los Angeles, Manila, Mexico City, Montreal, New York, Osaka, Paris, Pretoria, Rio de Janeiro, Rome, Stockholm, Sydney, Tokyo, Toronto, and Warsaw. Should be in all libraries, except the smallest.

981. Rogers, David. **The Management of Big Cities: Interest Groups and Social Change Strategies.** Beverly Hills, Cal.: Sage Publications, 1971. LC 77-15167. $8.95.

The ways in which three cities—New York, Philadelphia, and Cleveland—provide services to residents. Rogers shows how and why the intentions of city governments are frequently frustrated or changed in emphasis. Belongs in scholarly libraries.

982. Sorauf, Francis J. **Political Science: An Informal Overview.** Social Science Seminar Series. Columbus, Ohio: Merrill, 1965. 115 pp. LC 65-21163. $4.95, pap. $2.50.

This is an introductory book suitable primarily for novices in the field.

983. The States and the Urban Crisis. Alan K. Campbell, ed. Englewood Cliffs, N.J.: Prentice-Hall, 1970. 215 pp. LC 79-104842. $5.95, pap. $2.45.

Essays describing what state governments have and have not done and projecting what they should do in order to ease both the financial and governmental difficulties of cities. Of special interest to those with some acquaintance with the structure of American political institutions.

984. Taft, Charles Phelps. **City Management: The Cincinnati Experiment.** Port Washington, N.Y.: Kennikat, 1971 (originally published in 1933). LC 73-93074. $12.50.

Taft was chairman of the Men's Organization of the City Charter and has written a history of the reform movement in Cincinnati. An inside look at urban problems from the vantage point of a member of the establishment. This reprint has a new introduction by Taft.

985. Weinberg, Kenneth C. **Black Victory: Carl Stokes and the Winning of Cleveland.** New York: Quadrangle, 1968. LC 68-26451. $5.95.

This is an account of the political experience of the first Black mayor of Cleveland. Carl Stokes won because of skillful campaign techniques and because of the ability to attract white as well as Black voters. Not difficult; should prove of interest to readers concerned with Black urban politics.

986. White, Leonard Dupee. **The City Manager.** Westport, Conn.: Greenwood Press, 1969 (originally published in 1927). 355 pp. LC 68-57647. $15.50.

An example of a scholarly study of the form of urban government advocated by progressive reformers. The reprint shows how the institution has worked in the cities in which it has been adopted. Belongs in libraries with collections on urban government.

987. Williams, Joyce E. **Black Community Control: A Study of Transition in a Texas Ghetto.** New York: Praeger, 1973. 277 pp. LC 72-85984. $17.50.

Details the changing political situation in a Black ghetto in the Southwest and the attempts by Black citizens to gain more control over their lives. Useful for those libraries which are developing or have developed sections on ethnic or minority groups in the city.

988. Williams, Oliver P., and Adrian, Charles R. **Four Cities: A Study in Comparative Policy Making.** Philadelphia: University of Pennsylvania Press, 1963. 334 pp. LC 63-7853. $10.

Surveying the decision-making efforts of four communities, this book offers case studies of problems facing political leadership in cities.

989. Wilson, James Q. **Negro Politics: The Search for Leadership.** Glencoe, Ill.: Free Press, 1960. 342 pp. LC 60-10906. $6.50, pap. $2.95.

Classic study by a well-known political scientist of the problems of Blacks in achieving more political power. While finished prior to the upsurge in Black awareness in the 1960s, it still has much to recommend it, and is a basic book for collections on black and urban politics.

990. Wilson, James Q., ed. **City Politics and Public Policy.** New York: Wiley, 1968. 300 pp. LC 67-30636. pap. $4.95.

Essays demonstrating how the announced policies of communities operate in practice, given the political nature of their implementation. There are essays on such matters as the enforcement of traffic laws and treatment of law violators. Recommended for those libraries whose patrons desire to know how abstract concepts are clothed in hard reality.

991. Winter, William Orville. **The Urban Polity.** New York: Dodd, Mead, 1969. 516 pp. LC 69-18471. $9.95.

An account of the workings, often less than adequate, of city government and other decision-making entities. Popularly written, and should be acquired mainly for general circulation to lay readers.

992. Yates, Douglas. **Neighborhood Democracy: The Politics and Impacts of Decentralization.** Lexington, Mass.: Lexington Books, 1973. 202 pp. LC 73-7732. $12.

Yates's study combines theory with analysis of cases of decentralization. The book is short, making his discussion necessarily brief. Yates is a political scientist and his book is a scholarly one suitable to be used by those with an acquaintance with the language of behavioral scientists.

Urban Biographies

The writing of the history of individual cities predated the formal organization of the social sciences. The need to identify both common and unique elements in the history of a community seems to have been almost universal. Indeed, as city developers plotted the towns, journalists and amateur historians were chronicling their growth. Urban biographies preceded urban histories; the history of a particular town appeared before the history of American towns. But the advent of professional urban historians did not end the writing of urban biographies; indeed, urban historians often found the continuing investigation of specific communities to be of value in understanding the process of urbanization.

This section contains the histories of a number of towns and cities, some of them in the recent past and others in the more distant past. It includes material on colonial cities, on 19th-century cities, and on those whose growth in the 20th century was most spectacular. The focus in these biographies varies; at times it is on the elements which caused the town to grow while surrounding communities withered; at other times it is on the ethnic elements which compose the city and on their interrelationships. In some of the biographies, the singular events take priority; in others, the connection of the development of the city with national or international trends is the theme. In all cases, the core is the wide and varied experiences which made American cities possible.

993. Bridenbaugh, Carl. **Cities in Revolt: Urban Life in America, 1743-1776.** New York: Knopf, 1966. 433 pp. LC 55-7399. Capricorn, pap. $4.50.

The succeeding volume to *Cities in the Wilderness* discusses the role of the cities in the Revolution. It is the authoritative work on this theme. Primarily for reference.

994. Bridenbaugh, Carl. **Cities in the Wilderness: The First Century of Urban Life in America.** New York: Knopf, 1960. 500 pp. NUC 64-60275. $10.95. Capricorn, pap. $4.

Bridenbaugh has been a pioneer in the development of urban history, and this book helped to establish his reputation. It concentrates upon five cities— Boston, New York, Newport, Philadelphia, and Charleston—taking them from their inception to the Revolution.

995. Bridenbaugh, Carl. **Seat of Empire: The Political Role of Eighteenth-Century Williamsburg,** rev. ed. New York: Holt, 1958. 85 pp. LC 58-13522. $3.95, pap. $.95.

The discussion of the part played by Williamsburg in the Revolution can be assigned to readers who are interested in how the Revolution caught hold in the South.

996. Bridenbaugh, Carl, and Bridenbaugh, Jessica. **Rebels and Gentlemen: Philadelphia in the Age of Franklin.** New York: Oxford University Press, 1962. 383 pp. NUC 64-6742. pap. $2.95.

The most comprehensive look at urban life in the leading city of the colonies at the time of the Revolution. For better readers or for reference purposes.

997. Chapman, Edmund H. **Cleveland: Village to Metropolis; A Case Study of Problems of Urban Development in Nineteenth Century America.** Cleveland: Western Reserve Historical Society, 1965. 165 pp. LC 64-24777. $7.50.

Chapman shows how Cleveland expanded greatly in this era, partly from its natural location and partly from its connection with Rockefeller interests. For research purposes.

998. Chicago. International Film Bureau, 1971. 6 filmstrips. Color. 3 records or cassettes. Sale $60, sound on cassette $66.

Filmstrips on the history of Chicago, designed for intermediate and high school students. Audiotapes accompany the filmstrips. The titles are "The Chicago Portage" (45 fr., 10 min.), "Ft. Dearborn Massacre" (39 fr., 11 min.), "Chicago Becomes a Port City" (51 fr., 13 min.), "Chicago Builds and Chicago Burns" (52 fr., 12 min.), "Chicago Says, 'I Will'" (57 f., 12 min.), "Chicago, the Big City" (69 fr., 11½ min.). This series is a good one for showing the growth of the city and the way in which Chicago overcame the problems created by the fire.

999. Chicago Fire. CBS Television/Young America Films, 1956. (You Are There.) b/w. Sound. 28 min. Walter Cronkite, narrator. O.P.

The Chicago fire of October 8, 1871. Chicago emerged from the fire to become a great industrial city. While this film is more concerned with the causes and consequences of the disaster than with the development of Chicago, the patterns of growth can be seen. On an elementary level.

1000. Chicago: Midland Metropolis. Encyclopaedia Britannica Films, 1963. 16mm. Color and b/w. Sound. 22 min. Color $240, b/w $135.

Physical and social characteristics of Chicago serve as the focus for this film, which attempts to show why Chicago became a major urban center and what problems it encountered in urban development. For junior and senior high school students.

1001. Clark, John G. **New Orleans, 1718–1812: An Economic History.** Baton Rouge, La.: Louisiana State University Press, 1970. 395 pp. LC 77-119115. $10.

The history of New Orleans down to 1812 is primarily the story of slow growth under Spanish and French rule. Clark takes the history of New Orleans as reflective of lack of economic opportunity and of lack of goods to market. Useful in a section on urban biographies.

1002. Cole, Donald B. **Immigrant City: Lawrence, Massachusetts, 1845–1921.** Chapel Hill, N.C.: University of North Carolina Press, 1963. 248 pp. LC 63-3915. $7.50.

Lawrence, Massachusetts, a textile town that attracted many workers in the middle of the 19th century and which had more than its share of urban problems as a result. Useful for reference purposes.

1003. Condon, George E. **Cleveland, The Best-Kept Secret.** Garden City, N.Y.: Doubleday, 1967. 372 pp. LC 66-20930. $5.95.

A popular history with much information. Fits nicely into collections of urban biographies; it has more style than most.

1004. Condon, Thomas. **New York Beginnings: The Commercial Origins of New Netherlands.** New York: New York University Press, 1968. 204 pp. LC 68-28003. $8.

This is a geographically oriented book which covers the origin of New York City at New Netherlands and New Sweden. Can be used as an historical reference as well as a geographic one, and is recommended for those libraries which have a need for scholarly books of this type.

1005. Conzen, Michael P. **Frontier Farming in an Urban Shadow: The Influence of Madison's Proximity on the Agricultural Development of Blooming Grove, Wisconsin.** Madison, Wis.: University of Wisconsin Press, 1971. LC 73-158576. $10.

There are relatively few studies of the impact cities have had on the economic life of the surrounding farm communities. This is one of the few. It is a scholarly work and ought to be ordered by those libraries with collections on urban history and the factors influencing community growth.

1006. Denton, Daniel. **A Brief Description of New-York: Formerly Called New-Netherlands.** Ann Arbor, Mich.: University Microfilms, 1966. LC 66-25654. $3.55.

Denton visited New York City in 1670 and wrote a book based on this experience. He included in it a sketch of the physical characteristics of the city as well as of the agricultural region surrounding it and the Indians living nearby. A valuable source on the history of colonial New York City; should be in libraries with research demands.

1007. Dix, John Adams. **Sketch of the Resources of the City of New York: With a View of Its Municipal Government, Population, etc., From the Foundation of the City to the Date of the Latest Statistical Accounts.** Rise of Urban America. New York: Arno Press, 1970 (originally published in 1827). LC 79-112538. $6.

John Adams Dix concluded that New York City was destined to be the leading commercial city in the world. His prediction came from his historical analysis which was that, from its inception, the city had been dedicated to economic ends. This reprint discloses the attitude of city promoters of the time and deserves a place on shelves of libraries with collections in urban history.

1008. Earle, Alice Morse. **Colonial Days in Old New York.** Detroit: Singing Tree Press, 1968 (originally published in 1890). LC 68-21767. $8.50.

Social history of Dutch New Netherlands containing data on education, child-rearing, crime and punishment, religion, and recreation. Has many excerpts from records, diaries, and letters. Because of these selections, it is necessary for research libraries.

1009. Eighteenth-Century Life in Williamsburg, Virginia. McGraw-Hill Films, 1957. Color. 44 min. Rental from University of Illinois. $13.65.

The social stratification of Williamsburg as well as the architecture of the area appears in the film. It nicely catches the urban-rural flavor of Williamsburg. Suitable for primary through senior high school.

1010. Fishwick, Marshall W., and Rouse, Parke, Jr. **Jamestown: First English Colony.** New York: American Heritage, distributed by Harper & Row, 1965. LC 65-23440. $5.95.

This volume in the American Heritage Junior Library is amply illustrated and treats settlement in such a manner that the book can be used for junior high school readers.

1011. Fogelson, Robert M. **The Fragmented Metropolis: Los Angeles, 1850–1930.** Cambridge, Mass.: Harvard University Press, 1967. LC 67-20876. $11.95.

The best work on Los Angeles' development.

1012. Freedom Trail in Boston. WBZ-TV/International Film Bureau, 1965. 16mm. b/w. Sound. 27 min. Sale $165, rent $9.

Panoramic view of Boston, concentrating upon the elements which played a significant role during the Revolution. The student can see Boston Common, the Old North Church, Faneuil Hall, the Old State House, and other landmarks. Even the uninformed reader can discern the careful planning of Boston which took into account natural features.

1013. The Game of Empire. Education Development Center/Denoyer-Geppert, 1970. $76.

This game is designed for an understanding of mercantilism; the development of the port of Norfolk is illustrated through the mercantile concepts. For the junior high school student.

1014. Historic Plymouth. International Film Bureau, 1965. 16mm. Color. Sound. Sale $165, rent $9.

Reenacts the establishment of Plymouth and then visits present-day historic sites. Suitable for elementary through high school classes.

1015. Innes; John H. **New Amsterdam and Its People: Studies, Social and Topographical, of the Town Under the Dutch and Early English Rule.** 2 vols. Port Washington, N.Y.: Friedman, 1969 (originally published in 1902). LC 68-58927. each vol. $10.

Sidney T. Pomerantz has added a new introduction to this reprint of a landmark social history of the beginnings of New York City. The work still has merit for those interested in social mobility and the process of immigration, even though it was written before the advent of quantified research methods.

1016. James, D. Clayton. **Antebellum Natchez.** Baton Rouge, La.: Louisiana State University Press, 1968. LC 68-28496. $10.

Natchez was not a typical southern city nor even a typical Mississippi River town, but its changing character influenced by steamboat traffic does show much about the nature of American urban growth. Not for every reader, but it could be included in a section on urban biography with considerable profit.

1017. The Jamestown Colony, 1607–1620. Coronet Instructional Films, 1957. 16mm. Color and b/w. Sound. 16 min. Color sale $150, rent $7.50. b/w sale $82.50, rent $5.

The Jamestown festival of 1957 which celebrated the colony's 350th anniversary is captured on film. Jamestown was reconstructed for the festival, and the film explains the design of the village and the materials used, both of which reflected European rather than American experience.

1018. Kane, Lucile M. **The Waterfall That Built a City; The Falls of St. Anthony in Minneapolis.** St. Paul, Minn.: Minnesota Historical Society, 1966. 224 pp. LC 66-63543. $5.

The city referred to is Minneapolis and the argument advanced by Kane is that federal improvements to the Mississippi River contributed much to making Minneapolis what it is today. Interesting; goes beyond the usual urban biography.

1019. Katzman, David M. **Before the Ghetto: Black Detroit in the Nineteenth Century.** Urbana, Ill.: University of Illinois Press, 1973. 254 pp. LC 72-76861. $10.

Patterns of housing, employment, and mobility of Blacks in Detroit before the large influx in the 20th century. The story is an interesting one since Detroit served as a point of entry into Canada for runaway slaves. Recommended for library collections in urban history or in Black history.

1020. King, Grace Elizabeth. **New Orleans; The Place and the People.** Westport, Conn.: Negro Universities Press, 1968 (originally published in 1895). 404 pp. LC 68-55897. $17.00

An account of turn-of-the-century New Orleans and, as such, has value as an historical document. Recommended for libraries with urban biographies and urban history collections.

1021. Landis, Paul Henry. **Three Iron Mining Towns: A Study in Cultural Change.** New York: Arno Press, 1970 (originally published in 1938). LC 72-112555. $6.

Landis' study concerns three Minnesota towns in the Mesabi Range: Hibbing, Eveleth, and Virginia. These boom towns were altered considerably in 1912 when the residents undertook to improve their communities' municipal services largely by increasing taxes on the mining companies. The towns then had to endure the wrath of these mining companies. The story of three unusual towns whose development was unlike others.

1022. Leech, Margaret. **Reveille in Washington, 1860–1865.** Westport, Conn.: Greenwood Press, 1972 (originally published in 1941). LC 72-138121. $19.50.
A study made at the beginning of World War II, it is an account of the impact of the Civil War on the nation's capital; it is the result of much research, yet it reads easily and pleasantly. More suited to a general audience, although it also meets sophisticated needs.

1023. Lennon, Donald R., and Kellam, Ida Brooks, eds. **The Wilmington Town Book, 1743–1778.** Raleigh, N.C.: Division of Archives and History, North Carolina Department of Cultural Resources, 1973. LC 73-177609. $10.
Of interest to specialists in the beginnings of colonial towns in the American South. For libraries with research potential in the area.

1024. Lippincott, Horace Mather. **Philadelphia.** Port Washington, N.Y.: Friedman, 1968 (originally published in 1926). 259 pp. LC 78-124995. $10.
Lippincott wrote this history from an insider's point of view and with emphasis upon social and intellectual factors. The book is pleasant reading and reflects the attitudes of an earlier time. Ought to have a place with other city biographies even though it is 50 years old.

1025. Lockridge, Kenneth A. **A New England Town: The First Hundred Years; Dedham, Massachusetts, 1636–1736.** New York: Norton, 1970. 208 pp. LC 69-14703. pap. $2.65.
The history of Dedham, Massachusetts. Lockridge claims Dedham tried to emulate an English village and duplicated the old as much as possible. Another book with possibilities for research.

1026. Lord, Clifford L. **Teaching History with Community Resources.** New York: Teachers College Press, 1964. LC 64-15864. The pertinent volumes in this series are

> *Cincinnati.* Louis L. Tucker. 1968. pap. $1.50
> *Houston.* Joe B. Frantz. 1968. pap. $1.50
> *Los Angeles.* Andrew Rolle. 1965. pap. $1.50
> *New York City.* Bayrd Still. 1965. pap. $1.50
> *Raleigh-Durham-Chapel Hill.* William S. Powell. 1968. pap. $1.50
> *Boston.* Walter Muir Whitehill. 1969. pap. $1.50

Those in the series that are helpful on the West are

> *Arizona.* Madeline F. Pare. 1968. pap. $1.50
> *California.* Andrew Rolle. 1965. pap. $1.50
> *Colorado.* Carl Ubbelohde. 1965. pap. $1.50
> *Idaho.* Merle W. Wells. 1965. pap. $1.50
> *Utah.* Everett L. Cooley. 1968. pap. $1.50
> *Wyoming.* Lola M. Homsher. 1966. pap. $1.50
> *The Sacramento Valley.* Joseph McGowan. 1968. pap. $1.50

The pamphlets that are useful on the Midwest are

> *The Upper Mississippi Valley*. Walter W. Havighurst. 1966. pap.
> $1.50
>
> *The Ohio Valley*. R. E. Banta. 1967. pap. $1.50
>
> *The Wisconsin Valley*. August Derleth. 1968. pap. $1.50

There are six volumes in the series on immigrant groups which are recommended:

> *The Star of Hope: The Finns in America*. John L. Kolehmainen.
> 1968. $1.50
>
> *The Germans in America*. Carl Wittke. 1967. pap. $1.50
>
> *The Greeks in America*. Theodore Saloutos. 1967. pap. $1.50
>
> *The Irish in America*. Carl Wittke. 1968. pap. $1.50
>
> *The Mexicans in America*. Carey McWilliams. 1968. pap. $1.50
>
> *The Norwegians in America*. Elinor Haugen. 1967. pap. $1.50

1027. Los Angeles from the Air. Gary Goldsmith Films, 1960. 16mm. Color. Sound. 16 min.

Los Angeles from a helicopter with a fine view of the Civic Center and the Coliseum. The view also shows the impact of freeways on this scattered city. Can be used to illustrate architectural design and scale.

1028. Lotchin, Roger W. **San Francisco, 1846–1856: From Hamlet to City.** New York: Oxford University Press, 1974. 406 pp. LC 73-90351. $12.50.

Lotchin's study of ten years in San Francisco's history during the early period of American possession is broader than the title indicates. He tries to show how the changes in San Francisco parallel those which were occurring in other cities of the time. Though specialized, the book treats a period and area in urban history not often considered.

1029. McKelvey, Blake. **Rochester.** 3 vols. Cambridge, Mass.: Harvard University Press, 1954–1956. LC 49-10783, LC 56-11284, LC A45-4785. O.P.

Later volumes contain the story of the impact of Eastman Kodak on the city and can be used as a case study of industrial growth.

1030. McKelvey, Blake. **Rochester on the Genesee: The Growth of a City.** Syracuse, N.Y.: Syracuse University Press, 1973. 292 pp. LC 73-12094. $7.50.

McKelvey is the leading authority on Rochester as he is the official historian of the city. An interesting case study of the third largest city in New York State, a city which possesses similar characteristics of other American cities and unique ones of its own.

1031. Mayer, Harold M., and Wade, Richard C. **Chicago: Growth of a Metropolis.** Chicago: University of Chicago Press, 1969. 510 pp. LC 68-54054. $25, pap. $8.50.

A collaborative effort between a geographer and an historian to describe the development of a particular city in social and spatial terms.

1032. Mease, James. **The Picture of Philadelphia, Giving an Account of Its Origins, Increase and Improvements in Arts, Sciences, Manufacturers, Commerce and Revenue. With a Compendious View of Its Societies, Literary, Benevolent, Patriotic, and Religious. Its Police—the Public Buildings—the Prisons and Penitentiary Systems—Institutions, Monied and Civil—Museum.** New York: Arno Press, 1970 (originally published in 1811). LC 75-112561. $15.

Mease's view of Philadelphia in 1810 encompassed the economic, social, and political aspects of the city. His book has been the base of studies of Philadelphia's jails and the city's attitude on penal reforms. This reprint is recommended for those libraries with an interest in urban history and the development of social services.

1033. **New Orleans—Marketing Community.** Society for Visual Education, 1970. (Working in U.S. Communities.) 1 filmstrip (56 fr.). Sound. Color. 1 disc. 16 min. $8.

Although not indicated by the title, the film's approach is an historical one outlining the growth of New Orleans through changes in economic inputs. For junior high students.

1034. **New Salem Story—Lincoln Legend.** E. I. du Pont de Nemours/Teaching Film Custodians, 1963. (The Cavalcade of America.) 16mm. b/w. Sound. 30 min. Sale $125.

While the major interest in this film is Lincoln, the town of New Salem occupies much of the scene. Adapted from a 1953 Cavalcade of America series, the film can be shown in elementary grades as well as in high school.

1035. Nordstrom, Carl. **Frontier Elements in a Hudson River Village.** Port Washington, N.Y.: Kennikat, 1973. 199 pp. LC 72-91175. $9.95.

Nordstrom studies the town of Nyack, New York, using Turner's frontier thesis as an organizing concept. It is an effort which also touches on social history; the daily lives of the citizens of Nyack is examined. Has broad appeal.

1036. Peterson, Arthur E., and Edwards, George W. **New York as an Eighteenth Century Municipality.** Port Washington, N.Y.: Kennikat, 1967 (originally published in 1917). LC 67-16260. $25.

In this study of colonial New York, Peterson traced developments down to 1731 and Edwards took them from that time to 1776. The result was a two-volume work which has been reprinted as one. The study was extremely thorough, concentrating upon governmental organization, regulation, and the provision of municipal services. Because of its detailed analysis, it remains an extremely valuable starting point for those interested in colonial New York or in colonial cities in general.

1037. Pierce, Bessie L. **A History of Chicago.** 3 vols. New York: Knopf, 1937-1957. LC 37-8801. O.P.

The standard history. Students interested in the history of the establishment of Chicago should look here first.

1038. Pomerantz, Sidney I. **New York: An American City, 1783-1803: A Study of Urban Life,** 2nd ed. Port Washington, N.Y.: Friedman, 1965. 531 pp. LC 64-11843. $12.50.

A specialized study for research purposes.

1039. Powell, Sumner Chilton. **Puritan Village: The Formation of a New England Town.** Middletown, Conn.: Wesleyan University Press, 1963. 215 pp. LC 63-8862. pap. $2.95.

A painstaking work which traces the founding of Sudbury, Massachusetts. It contains a number of maps, charts, drawings, and photographs. Powell looks to the English background as the source of the ideas about the town, but he also notes the American circumstances which changed the plans. Full of detailed facts and microscopic research; only the most motivated reader will tackle it.

1040. Reinders, Robert C. **End of an Era: New Orleans, 1850-1860.** New Orleans: Pelican, 1964. 250 pp. LC 65-4950. $12.50.

The political currents in New Orleans just before the Civil War. Reinders uncovers the issues that most agitated the citizenry, the proposed solutions to urban dilemmas, and the beginnings of urban political organizations. Should be included in those libraries which have an interest in the early years of this city.

1041. Rogers, George C., Jr. **Charleston in the Age of the Pinckneys.** Norman, Okla.: University of Oklahoma Press, 1969. 187 pp. LC 68-31371. $3.95.

Rogers describes the growth of Charleston from the middle of the 18th to the middle of the 19th century, from a colonial town to a southern city. Recommended as a case study of antebellum southern urban growth.

1042. Rutman, Darrett. **Winthrop's Boston: Portrait of a Puritan Town, 1630-1649.** Chapel Hill, N.C.: University of North Carolina Press, 1965. LC 65-13667. $8.25. Norton, pap. $3.25.

A study of the forces that shaped Boston. Rutman, as one of the new social historians, sees a number of factors but discounts Puritan ideology. Like *Husbandmen of Plymouth*, this one is difficult but rewarding.

1043. **San Francisco—Story of a City.** Paul Hoeffler Productions/Walt Disney Productions, 1963. 16mm. Color. Sound. 21 min. Rent $7.50.

An excellent review of the history of San Francisco, including the days of sailing, the transcontinental railroads, and the lives of farmers, cattlemen, loggers, and merchants.

1044. Singleton, Esther. **Social New York Under the Georges: 1714-1776: Houses, Streets, and Country Homes, with chapters on Fashions, Furniture, China Plate and Manners.** 2 vols. in 1. Port Washington, N.Y.: Friedman, 1969 (originally published in 1902). LC 68-58928. $10.

A detailed look at the social customs of upperclass New Yorkers. It re-creates the daily life and habits of the individuals who made up this particular class. Contains much information on pre-Revolutionary America and is recommended for those libraries which have serious researchers using them.

1045. Still, Bayrd. **Milwaukee: The History of a City.** Madison, Wis.: State Historical Society of Wisconsin, 1965. 638 pp. LC 65-65450. $8.50.

How the unique skills of Germans in Milwaukee helped the beginnings of the brewing industry. For research projects.

1046. Tolles, Frederick B. **James Logan and the Culture of Provincial America.** Boston: Little, Brown, 1957. 228 pp. LC 57-6439. O.P.

Logan was secretary to the Proprietor of Pennsylvania; Tolles' account of his life casts much light upon the development of the colony and the city. Useful for reference.

1047. Tolles, Frederick B. **Meeting House and Counting House: The Quaker Merchants of Colonial Philadelphia, 1682-1763.** New York: Norton, 1963. 292 pp. LC 69-64881. pap. $2.95.

Philadelphia's growth depended largely upon the energy and enterprise of the Quakers in that city. Tolles' book shows why Philadelphia grew to become the second largest city in the British Empire by the time of the Revolution. Useful reference for teacher and student.

1048. Waldorf, John Taylor. **A Kid on the Comstock: Reminiscences of a Virginia City Childhood.** Dorothy Waldorf Bryant, ed. Palo Alto, Cal.: American West Publishing Co., 1970. LC 73-108628. $5.95.

Waldorf's account of growing up in a western mining town will appeal not only to urban historians, but to general readers who are sympathetic to different life-styles.

1049. Walsh, Richard. **Charlestown's Sons of Liberty: A Study of the Artisans, 1763-1789.** Columbia, S.C.: University of South Carolina Press, 1959. 166 pp. LC 59-15684. pap. $1.95.

Revolutionaries in the South were also found in cities, as Walsh's study of Charleston makes clear. While the major emphasis is upon the Sons of Liberty in Charleston, the book includes much helpful information on that southern city in the Revolutionary period. Recommended for those libraries where extensive collections of urban history can be made.

1050. Warden, G. B. **Boston, 1689-1776.** Boston: Little, Brown, 1970. 404 pp. LC 70-100577. $12.50.

Boston's development from the termination of the charter of Massachusetts Bay Company to the beginning of the Revolution. Excellent case study of the growth of a colonial city and can be handled by mature adults.

1051. Warner, Sam Bass, Jr. **The Private City: Philadelphia in Three Periods of Its Growth.** Philadelphia: University of Pennsylvania Press, 1968. LC 68-21557. $7.50, pap. $2.95.

A conceptual basis for examining the American city is gained through this example of Philadelphia. Warner studies Philadelphia in the years 1770-1780, 1830-1860, and 1920-1930. His conclusions are that the American failure to meet urban problems is historical and revolves around the failure of the idea of community to contain "privatism" and the search for wealth.

1052. Washington D.C.—Story of Our Capital. Coronet Instructional Films, 1956. 16mm. Color. Sound. IU-Color, rent $4.75; b/w. GS-678, rent $3.15.

The original plans of L'Enfant for Washington are the basis for this film, which traces the growth of the city from its beginnings. The work of Banneker can be discussed in conjunction with the visual aspect of Washington.

1053. Weitzel, Tony. **Chicago: I Will.** Cleveland: World, 1967. LC 67-22909.

A popular history of the Windy City. It makes no pretense of being scholarly but is a rather breezy look at the growth of this major midwestern city. Should circulate well to general readers.

1054. Wells, Robert W. **This Is Milwaukee.** Garden City, N.Y.: Doubleday, 1970. LC 75-127617. $6.95.

Journalistic account of Milwaukee's political and cultural development. Popularly written and aimed at the general reader.

1055. Wertenbaker, Thomas J. **Norfolk: Historic Southern Port,** rev. ed. Marvin W. Schlegel, ed. Durham, N.C.: Duke University Press, 1962. 417 pp. LC 62-10054. O.P.

A research resource for its treatment on the beginning of a city. Its acquisition is recommended.

Journals on Urban Themes

The journals listed are those which libraries should consider as basic to the study of the urban scene. Although this is not an exhaustive list, several journals are listed in a variety of subfields in urban studies. If a library wishes to emphasize a particular field, these journals should be the cornerstone of the collection.

AIA Journal (formerly **Journal of the American Institute of Architects**). 1900. m. $5 (qualified subscribers). Robert M. Koehler. American Institute of Architects, 1785 Massachusetts Ave. N.W., Washington, D.C. 20036. Illus. Circ: 30,000.

American City Magazine. 1909. m. $15. William S. Foster. Buttenheim Public Corporation, Berkshire Common, Pittsfield, Mass. 01201. Illus. Circ: 32,000.

American Institute of Planners Journal. 1935. bi-m. $10. David R. Godschalk. American Institute of Planners, 917 15 St. N.W., Washington, D.C. 20005. Illus. Circ: 12,000.

American Society of Civil Engineers, Urban Planning and Development Division, Journal. 1964. 1–3 issues per year. $6. William L. Grecco. American Society of Civil Engineers, 2500 S. State St., Ann Arbor, Mich. 48104. Illus.

Architectural Forum. 1892. 10 issues per year. $12 ($6 to students and faculty members of accredited schools of architecture). Peter Blake. Whitney Publications, Inc., 130 E. 59 St., New York, N.Y. 10022. Illus. Circ: 40,000.

Architectural Record. 1891. m. $20 ($7.50 to architects and engineers). Walter F. Wagner. McGraw-Hill, Inc., Box 430, Hightstown, N.J. 08520. Illus. Circ: 52,000.

Chicago History. 1970. 4 issues per year. $10. Isabel S. Grossner. Chicago Historical Society, North Ave. and Clark St., Chicago, Ill., 60614. Illus. Circ: 7,500.

City; Magazine of Urban Life and Environment. 1967. bi-m. $10. Donald Conty. National Urban Coalition, 2100 M St. N.W., Washington, D.C. 20037. Illus. Circ: 50,000.

Education and Urban Society. 1968. q. $15 (individuals, $10). Louis H. Masotti. Sage Publications, Inc., 275 Beverly Dr., Beverly Hills, Cal., 90212. Illus.

Ekistics: Reviews on the Problems and Science of Human Settlements. 1955. m. $12. J. Tyrwhitt and G. Bell. Athens Center of Ekistics of the Athens Technological Organization, Box 471, Athens, Greece. Illus. Circ: 4,000.

Enforcement Journal. 1962. bi-m. $12. Frank J. Shira. National Police Officers Association of America, 2801 E. Oakland Park Blvd., Fort Lauderdale, Fl. 33306. Illus. Circ: 17,000.

Environment and Planning: International Journal of Urban and Regional Research. 1969. q. $13.50 (institutions, $27). A. G. Wilson. Peon, Ltd., 207 Brondesbury Park, London NW 25 JN, England. Illus.

Growth and Change, A Journal of Regional Development. 1970. q. $7.50. David F. Ross. College of Business and Economics, University of Kentucky, Lexington, Ky. 40506. Illus., index. Circ: 1,200.

Housing and Urban Development Trends. 1968. q. free. SDC: HH 1.14; Charts. U.S. Dept. of Housing and Urban Development, Washington, D.C. 20410.

Journal of Criminal Law, Criminology, and Police Science. 1910. q. $15. Jon F. Steffesen. Williams and Wilkins Co., 428 N. Preston St., Baltimore, Md. 21202. Circ: 4,186.

Journal of Housing. 1944. 11 issues per year. $8. Dorothy Sazzolo. National Association of Housing and Redevelopment Officials, Watergate Building, 2600 Virginia Ave. N.W., Washington, D.C. 20037. Illus. Circ: 15,000.

Journal of Regional Science. 1958. 3 issues per year. $12. Walter Izard and Benjamin H. Stevens. Regional Science Research Institute, Box 8776, Philadelphia, Pa. 19101. Illus. Circ: 2,700.

Journal of Urban Analysis. 1972. q. (2 vol. per year). $35 (individuals, $25). Stanley Altman, Edward Beltramic, and Edward Blum. Gordon and Breach, One Park Ave., New York, N.Y. 10016. Illus, index, adv. Circ: 1,000.

Journal of Urban History. 1974. q. $20 institutions, $12 teachers and professors, $10 students. Raymond A. Mohl. Sage Publications, Inc., 275 S. Beverly Dr., Beverly Hills, Cal. 90212.

Land Economics: A Quarterly Journal Devoted to the Study of Economic and Social Institutions. 1925. q. $15. Mary Amend Lescohier. Social Science Building, University of Wisconsin, Madison, Wis. 53706. Illus. Circ: 3,600.

Metropolitan. 1935. bi-m. $5. Larry T. Moore. Bobit Publishing Co., 1155 Waukegan Rd., Glenview, Ill. 60025. Illus. Circ: 11,163.

National Civic Review (formerly **National Municipal Review**). 1911. m. (Sept.–July). $7.50. William N. Cossella, Jr. National Municipal League, 47 E. 68 St., New York, N.Y. 10021. Illus. Circ: 6,200.

Nation's Cities. 1963. m. $6.00. Patrick Nealy. National League of Cities, 1612 K St. N.W., Washington, D.C. 20006. Illus. Circ: 58,000.

New Atlantis, The: An International Journal of Urban and Regional Studies.
1969. s-a. $10. Paolo Ceccarelli. Marsilio Editori, Piazza de Gasperi
41,35100 Padova, Italy. Subsc. to Sage Publications, Inc., 275 S. Beverly
Dr., Beverly Hills, Cal. 90212. Illus.

Oppositions. 1973. q. $15. Institute for Architecture and Urban Studies, 8
W. 40 St., New York, N.Y. 10018. Illus.

Planning: A Newsletter of the American Society of Planning Officials. 1934.
m. (Feb.–Mar. combined). $15. Virginia Curtis. American Society of Plan-
ning Officials, 1313 E. 60 St., Chicago, Ill. 60637. Illus. Circ: 10,000.

Public Administration Review. 1940. bi-m. $25. Dwight Waldo. American
Society for Public Administration, 1225 Connecticut Ave. N. W., Washington,
D.C. 20036. Illus. Circ: 12,500.

Public Management. 1919. m. $6. David S. Arnold. International City Man-
agement Association, 1140 Connecticut Ave. N.W., Washington, D.C. 20036.
Illus. Circ: 16,000.

Regional Studies, Journal of the Regional Studies Association. 1967. q. $20.
Peter Hall. Pergamon Press, Inc., Maxwell House, Fairview Park, Elmsford,
N.Y. 10523. Illus.

Society (formerly **Trans-Action; Social Science and Modern Society**). 1963.
m. (combined issues July–Aug., Nov.–Dec.). $9.75. Irving L. Horowitz. Box
A, Rutgers—the State University, New Brunswick, N.J. 08903. Illus. Circ:
75,000.

Transportation Journal. 1961. q. Membership (nonmembers, $10). Charles
A. Taff. American Society of Traffic and Transportation, 547 W. Jackson
Blvd., Chicago, Ill. 60606. Illus. Circ: 3,500.

Urban Affairs Quarterly. 1965. q. $10 (institutions, $15). Peter Bouxsein.
Sage Publications, Inc., 275 S. Beverly Dr., Beverly Hills, Cal. 90212. Illus.
Circ: 2,500.

Urban Crisis Monitor. 1967. w. $4.35. Urban Research Corp., 5464 S. Shore
Dr., Chicago, Ill. 60615.

Urban Land; News and Trends in Land Development. 1942. m. (July–Aug.
combined). Membership $10. Robert E. Boley. Urban Land Institution,
1200 18 St. N.W., Washington, D.C. 20036. Illus. Circ: 5,200.

Urban Life and Culture. 1972. q. $20 (teachers $10, students $8). John Lof-
land. Sage Publications, Inc., 275 S. Beverly Dr., Beverly Hills, Cal. 90212.

Urban Review. 1966. q. $12. Arthur Tobier. APS Publications, 150 Fifth
Ave., New York, N.Y. 10011. Illus.

Urban and Social Change Review (formerly **Institute of Human Sciences Re-
view**). 1967. s-a (fall and spring). $4 (institutions, $6). David Horton Smith.
Institute of Human Sciences, Boston College, Chestnut Hill, Mass. 02167.
Illus. Circ: 4,500.

Urban Studies. 1964. 3 issues per year. $7.50. G. C. Cameron (American Advisory Ed.: Anthony H. Pascal). Longman Group Ltd., 5 Bentinck St., London W1M 5RN, England. Distributed by: Sage Publications, Inc., 275 S. Beverly Dr., Beverly Hills, Cal. 90212. Illus. Circ: 4,000.

Producer/Distributor Directory

Addresses are given for sellers of all the nonprint media items listed in the bibliography. A complete address list of U.S. book publishers is in each annual edition of *Books in Print* (Bowker), a standard reference found in libraries and bookstores.

This directory is current as of Fall 1975, but since there are constant changes in ownership and location of producers, as well as in distributorship of specific items, the user may wish to consult annual editions of *Audiovisual Market Place* (Bowker) if he or she has difficulty in obtaining a title.

ABT Associates
55 Wheeler St.
Cambridge, Mass. 02138

AV-ED Films
910 N. Citrus Ave.
Hollywood, Cal. 90038

American Association for the
  Advancement of Science
1515 Massachusetts Avenue N.W.
Washington, D.C. 20005

American Institute of Architects
New York Chapter
20 W. 40 St.
New York, N.Y. 10018

American Institute of Biological
  Science
1401 Wilson Blvd.
Arlington, Va. 22209

Paul S. Amidon Associates Inc.
1966 Benson Ave.
St. Paul, Minn. 55116

Artisan Productions
7707 W. Sunset Blvd.
Hollywood, Cal. 90028

Association of American Geographers
1716 16 St. N.W.
Washington, D.C. 20009

Audio Visual Narrative Arts Inc.
Box 398
Pleasantville, N.Y. 10570

BFA Educational Media
Div. of Columbia Broadcasting
  System Inc.
Box 1795, 2211 Michigan Ave.
Santa Monica, Cal. 90406

Bailey Films, *see* Paul Burnford-
  Bailey Films

Arthur Barr Productions Inc.
3490 E.   oothill Blvd.
Box 5667
Pasadena, Cal. 91107

Board of Global Ministries
78-20 Reading Rd.
Cincinnati, Ohio 45237

Paul Burnford-Bailey Films
6509 DeLongpre Ave.
Hollywood, Cal. 90028

CBC Learning Systems
Box 500
Station A
Toronto, Ont., Canada N5W1E6

CRM/McGraw-Hill Films
Del Mar, Cal. 92014

Caedmon Records Inc.
505 Eighth Ave.
New York, N.Y. 10018

Center for Cassette Studies Inc.
8110 Webb Ave.
North Hollywood, Cal. 91605

Chelsea House Publishers
70 W. 40 St.
New York, N.Y. 10018

Chicago, City of
Mayor's Office
121 N. LaSalle St.
Chicago, Ill. 60602

Chicago, City of
Urban Renewal Dept.
Graphics Div.
320 N. Clark St.
Chicago, Ill. 60610

Chicago City Missionary Society
2016 W. Evergreen
Chicago, Ill. 60602

Classroom Film Distributors Inc.
5610 Hollywood Blvd.
Los Angeles, Cal. 90028

Contemporary Films/McGraw-Hill
1221 Ave. of the Americas
New York, N.Y. 10020

Coronet Instructional Media
Div. of Esquire Inc.
65 E. South Water St.
Chicago, Ill. 60601

Davidson Films Inc.
3701 Buchanan St.
San Francisco, Cal. 94123

Denoyer-Geppert Audio-Visuals
5235 Ravenswood
Chicago, Ill. 60640

Didactics Corporation
700 Grove St.
Mansfield, Ohio 44095

Dimension Films
666 N. Robertson Blvd.
Los Angeles, Cal. 90069

Walt Disney Educational Media
Company
800 Sonora Ave.
Glendale, Cal. 91201

Doubleday Multimedia
Div. of Doubleday & Company
1371 Raynolds Ave.
Irvine, Cal. 92705

Dynamic Films Inc.
888 Seventh Ave.
New York, N.Y. 10019

Ebsco
First Ave. N. at 13 St.
Birmingham, Ala. 35203

Educational Audio Visual Inc.
Pleasantville, N.Y. 10570

Educational Dimensions Group
Box 126
Stamford, Conn. 06904

Ed-Venture Films
1122 Calada St.
Los Angeles, Cal. 90023

Encyclopaedia Britannica Publications Ltd.
Instructional Materials Div.
2 Bloor St. W.
Toronto, Ont., Canada M4W 3J1

Filmstrip House Inc.
6633 W. Howard St.
Niles, Ill. 60648

Stuart Finley Inc.
3428 Mansfield Rd.
Falls Church, Va. 22041

Ginn & Company
Subs. of Xerox Corporation
191 Spring St.
Lexington, Mass. 02173

Graphic Curriculum Inc.
Box 565 Lenox Hill Station
New York, N.Y. 10021

Guidance Associates Inc.
737 Fifth Ave.
New York, N.Y. 10022

Hammond Inc.
515 Valley St.
Maplewood, N.J. 07040

Harcourt Brace Jovanovich Films
Div. of Harcourt Brace Jovanovich
  Inc.
Polk & Geary Sts.
San Francisco, Cal. 91409

Hearst Metrotone News
235 E. 45 St.
New York, N.Y. 10017

Hester & Associates
11422 Harry Hines
Dallas, Texas 75220

Indiana University
Audio-Visual Center
Bloomington, Ind. 47401

Instructional Simulations Inc.
2147 University Ave.
St. Paul, Minn. 55104

Interact
12160 Woodside Ave.
Lakeside, Cal. 92040

International Communications Corporation Films
501 Fifth Ave.
New York, N.Y. 10017

International Film Bureau
332 S. Michigan Ave.
Chicago, Ill. 60604

Iowa State University
Media Resources Center
Ames, Iowa 50010

Johns Hopkins University Press
3400 N. Charles
Baltimore, Md. 21218

Lansford Publishing Co. Inc.
1088 Lincoln Ave., Box 8711
San Jose, Cal. 95155

Learning Corporation of America
1350 Ave. of the Americas
New York, N.Y. 10019

Line Films
Box 2328
Capistrano Beach, Cal. 92624

McGraw-Hill Films
Div. of McGraw-Hill Book Co.
1221 Ave. of the Americas
New York, N.Y. 10020

Harold Mayer Productions Inc.
155 W. 72 St.
New York, N.Y. 10023

Michigan State University
Instructional Media Center
East Lansing, Mich. 48824

Millikin Publishing Company
11 Research Blvd.
St. Louis, Mo. 63132

Multi Media Corporation
4030 Mount Carmel Tabasco Rd.
Cincinnati, Ohio 45244

Multimedia Publishing Corporation
100 S. Western Highway
Blauvelt, N.Y. 10913

National Audiovisual Center (GSA)
Washington, D.C. 20409

National Film Board of Canada
1251 Ave. of the Americas
New York, N.Y. 10020

Pacifica Tape Library
5316 Venice Blvd.,
Los Angeles, Cal. 90019

Pact of Wayne County Community College
163 Madison
Detroit, Mich. 48227

Popular Science Audio Visual Center
355 Lexington Ave.
New York, N.Y. 10017

Prentice-Hall Media Inc.
Sub. of Prentice-Hall Inc.
150 White Plains Rd.
Tarrytown, N.Y. 10591

Progressive Pictures
635 Mornhill Dr.
Oakland, Cal. 94611

Psychology Today Films
1 Park Ave.
New York, N.Y.

Rand McNally & Company
Box 7600
Chicago, Ill. 60680

S. L. Film Productions
Box 41108
Los Angeles, Cal. 90041

Warren Schloat, acquired by
Prentice-Hall Media Inc.

Science Research Associates Inc.
Sub. of IBM
259 Erie
Chicago, Ill. 60611

Scott Education, acquired by
Prentice-Hall Media Inc.

SIMILE
Western Behavioral Science
Institute
1150 Silverado
LaJolla, Cal. 92037

Social Studies School Service
10000 Culver Blvd.
Culver City, Cal. 90230

Society for Visual Education Inc.
Div. of The Singer Company
1345 Diversey Highway
Chicago, Ill. 60614

Sterling Educational Films
Div. of Walter Reade Organization
241 E. 34 St.
New York, N.Y. 10016

Studio 16 Educational Films
2135 Howell
San Francisco, Cal.

Teaching Film Custodians, *see*
Indiana University Audio-Visual
Center

Teaching Resources Films
An Educational Service of the
New York Times
2 Kisco Plaza
Mt. Kisco, N.Y. 10549

United Methodist Film Service
1525 McGavock St.
Nashville, Tenn. 37203

United World Films
425 N. Michigan
Chicago, Ill. 60611

University of California Extension Media Center
2223 Fulton St.
Berkeley, Cal. 94720

University of Illinois
Visual Aids Service
1325 S. Oak St.
Champaign, Ill. 61820

University of Illinois Press
Urbana, Ill. 61801

Urban Media Materials Inc.
212 Mineola Ave.
Roslyn Heights, N.Y. 11577

**Washington University Audio Visual
  Department**
Box 1061
Washington University, St. Louis,
  Mo. 63130

Wayne State University
5980 Caff Ave.
Detroit, Mich. 48202

Western Behavioral Science Institute
1150 Silverado
La Jolla, Cal. 92037

Western Publishing Company
850 Third Ave.
New York, N.Y. 10022

Westinghouse Learning Corporation
Sub. of Westinghouse Electric Corp.
100 Park Ave.
New York, N.Y. 10017

Zipporah Films Inc.
54 Lewis Wharf
Boston, Mass. 02110

Author Index

Listings below refer to entry numbers.

Title Index

Titles are grouped in two categories: Books and In-print Materials, and Other Media. Listings refer to entry numbers.

Books and In-print Materials

Other Media (discs, films, filmstrips, games, slides, transparencies)